CHARLES DICKENS AND
HIS PERFORMING SELVES

Charles Dickens and His Performing Selves

Dickens and the Public Readings

MALCOLM ANDREWS

OXFORD
UNIVERSITY PRESS

OXFORD

UNIVERSITY PRESS

Great Clarendon Street, Oxford OX2 6DP

Oxford University Press is a department of the University of Oxford.
It furthers the University's objective of excellence in research, scholarship,
and education by publishing worldwide in

Oxford New York

Auckland Cape Town Dar es Salaam Hong Kong Karachi
Kuala Lumpur Madrid Melbourne Mexico City Nairobi
New Delhi Shanghai Taipei Toronto

With offices in

Argentina Austria Brazil Chile Czech Republic France Greece
Guatemala Hungary Italy Japan Poland Portugal Singapore
South Korea Switzerland Thailand Turkey Ukraine Vietnam

Oxford is a registered trade mark of Oxford University Press
in the UK and in certain other countries

Published in the United States
by Oxford University Press Inc., New York

British Library Cataloguing in Publication Data

Data available

Library of Congress Cataloging in Publication Data

Data available

Typeset by Laserwords Private Limited, Chennai, India
Printed in Great Britain
on acid-free paper by
Biddles Ltd., King's Lynn, Norfolk

ISBN 978-0-19-927069-9

3 5 7 9 10 8 6 4 2

For Nigel, with love

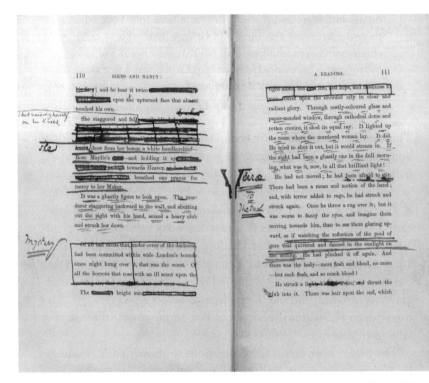

'Sikes and Nancy: A Reading': Dickens's Prompt-copy, pp. 110–11. Henry W. and Albert A. Berg Collection of English and American Literature, The New York Public Library, Astor, Lenox and Tilden Foundations.

Preface and Acknowledgements

When the readings by Charles Dickens shall have become matter of history and the waves of time have rolled over the present marvellous era, there will be hundreds who to their children and grandchildren shall tell that they heard and saw the man who has painted life as it is in England, and to a great extent universal life, with a master hand.

Sanders' News-Letter, Daily Advertiser, 26 August, 1858

Those grandchildren are long gone. As I near the end of writing this book, there are a few of Dickens's *great*-grandchildren—his closest living relatives—who still just recall the occasions 70 years ago when as children they gathered at Christmas to hear Dickens's son reading *A Christmas Carol*. Sir Henry Fielding Dickens was then (in the early 1930s) a frail, bird-like octogenarian: sixty years before, he had attended his father's very last Reading in London, on 15th March 1870. Grandfather Harry read with passion. Tears poured down the old man's cheeks as Bob Cratchit returned from visiting Tiny Tim's grave. When, near the end, the redeemed Scrooge in a frenzy of joy threw open the window onto a brilliant sunlit world, the reader's false teeth flew out.

The bridge back across the generations to those public Readings by Charles Dickens has all but gone. They are lost events. The sound of Dickens's voice never made it on to the phonograph (he died seven years before its invention). His silent voice survives in the novels and journalistic essays and we enjoy reading the same texts as Dickens's contemporaries did. Not so the Readings, and they constituted Dickens's third professional career, one to which he devoted as much passionate attention as he did to his fiction and journalism. All we have left is a few relics. We have his worn prompt-copies, but he never stuck to these in performance; and they are now resonantly silent, locked up in library bookcases. We still have his Reading desk, minus one or two components, with its faded red velvet covering. We have a few statuesque pictures of him at the Reading desk, posed for the camera. We have sheaves of eyewitness accounts from newspaper reviews, friends and family, many of them vividly detailed; and the more striking those details the more one realizes the scale of what is now irretrievable—the event itself. Here is how one person recalled the end of one of those Readings, over forty years after the event:

Gently, slowly the book was closed, and the solitary figure seemed to glide from the stage, yet the vast audience remained silent—for hours; it was only seconds, but the seconds seem hours. Then the people let themselves go; they had the weary man back, and they thundered their approval. He stood there slowly bowing, the tears of heartfelt emotion running down his pale cheeks.

If only we could summon the weary man back for an encore. This was audio-visual Dickens, in a series of performances of quite remarkable virtuosity as he crowded his red-draped, gas-lit Reading platform with his own noisy characters. It was like watching the man create his fictions—*become* his fictions—in a furnace of energy.

This book reaches back to those events, hoping to grasp some sense of their drama through excavations and one or two tentative dramatic reconstructions. In both these forms of retrieval I have drawn heavily on contemporary eyewitness accounts. I have tried to understand more clearly why Dickens was drawn to this new career late in life, what he and his audiences got from it, and how the Readings transmitted and transmuted the writings. Ruskin remarked that when Dickens wrote he often chose to 'speak in a circle of stage fire': that, literally, is how Dickens read aloud his writings, under the 'garish lights' (as he put it) of his gas-lamps, to two or three thousand listeners at a time.

I must acknowledge some formidable debts. The first and greatest is to Philip Collins, not only for what he has given all of us in published form in his work on the Readings, but also for the mass of his unpublished and private research papers—decades of work—which he handed to me one day in Leicester. It was an act of stupendous generosity. Several friends have read all or parts of this book: these include my wife, Kristin, whose interest and support throughout has been so encouraging. I am especially grateful to Jeremy Tambling and Michael Slater for their detailed comments and suggestions on the whole draft, and to the anonymous reader for Oxford University Press. The Charles Dickens Museum has been an invaluable resource for the illustrations and for much primary research material, and I have been greatly helped by Andrew Xavier, Florian Schweizer, and Sophie Slade there.

Parts of some of the chapters have been published elsewhere in a modified form as essays. A note on the suspected forgery of the New York portrait of Dickens by Mathew Brady (in Chapter 4) appeared in *History of Photography*, Vol. 28(4) (2004). The account of Dickens's platform 'set' (in Chapter 4) was published in *Dickens Quarterly*, 21(4) (2004). The discussion of impersonation and the influence of Charles Mathews in Chapter 3 became part of an essay on 'Performing Character' for the *Palgrave Advances in Charles Dickens Studies* (2005), edited by Robert Patten and John Bowen.

The method of referencing in this book is unconventional. In an effort to keep the litter of superscript reference numbers off the pages of text I have given the sources in the endnotes, identified by page number: each quotation is cued in by (normally) its opening phrase (in bold type), followed by the reference to its source. The other point to mention is that I have capitalized 'Reading' to distinguish the public recitation from the private act of 'reading'.

Contents

List of Illustrations

A Premiere:
New York, December 1867

On Saturday 7 December 1867, Charles Dickens and George Dolby boarded the Shore Line train at Boston for the nine-hour journey to New York. They reached the city at 6 that evening. Dickens was very tired. His persistent cold showed signs of worsening to influenza. He was 55. His face was deeply lined, the skin grainy but highly coloured, weather-beaten. He carried himself like a naval officer, upright and alert. 'A little, trim-looking gentleman', he seemed: his eyes were 'filled with an energy which seemed to be unconfined'. To another, Dickens's eye had a terrible restlessness, 'like a comet in a cage [. . .] he always seems as if he had something *on* his mind as well as *in* it.'

The two men established themselves in a suite of apartments in the Westminster Hotel, Irving Place. It was quiet and comfortable. The Westminster was smaller than many American hotels and designed more on 'the Eurōpiăn principle' (in Dickens's imitation of American pronunciation): 'an admirable mixture of a first-class French and English house'. Dickens particularly appreciated its French cuisine and provision of a French waiter specially detailed to serve them. All in all, 'one might be living in Paris'. His need for privacy was met by his being able to come and go by a discreet side entrance and private staircase that led directly to his bedroom; and a boy had been stationed outside the sitting-room door to keep intrusive admirers at bay. Dickens felt content with the seclusion, a necessary condition for his strenuous bouts of public performance. 'The platform absorbs my individuality, and I am very little troubled.'

After dinner that evening, the two men took a short wander through the gas-lit streets near their hotel. Dickens failed to recognize much of what he saw, so many had been the changes to the city since his first visit a quarter of a century earlier. 'New York is grown out of my knowledge', he reflected, 'and is enormous. Everything in it looks as if the order of nature were reversed, and everything grew newer every day, instead of older.'

On their return to the hotel, Dickens went to bed, leaving Dolby to cope with the mass of accumulated correspondence, including 100 or more letters from hungry autograph collectors. Dickens had made it a rule while in America never to open letters addressed to himself, except those from Europe or those from friends whose handwriting he recognized. Dolby was prepared to endure much in the service of the man who had become his hero, his appreciative 'Chief'. He was living through what, nearly twenty years later, he was to call 'the brightest chapter of my life'. The scale of popular enthusiasm both for Dickens and for the Readings was unprecedented and brought extraordinary pressures for Dolby, who was always in the front line. In Boston tickets for the first readings (2nd, 3rd, 5th and 6th December) had gone on sale on Monday morning, 18 November, the day after Dickens's landing at Halifax. People had begun queuing the night before. An hour before the ticket office opened at 9 o'clock the queue was half a mile long. In New York it was much the same. Queues for the tickets that were to go on sale at 9 a.m. the day of the Reading began late the previous evening. By five in the morning the queue had formed two lines of 800 each. By 8 a.m. there were 5,000 people. The queues stretched half to three-quarters of a mile, and even a place in those queues could fetch $20. Mattresses and blankets were brought by the waiting people in hopes of being able to get some sleep. Night temperatures were some way below freezing: singing, dancing, and occasional fighting temporarily helped the queue to forget the chill. Many of the earliest to arrive in the queues were the ticket speculators or people hired by the speculators. Being near the front of the line when the ticket office opened, they bought up blocks of the prime $2 seats, intending to sell them off for $15 or more. They were not wholly successful, and sometimes were forced to sell off the residue at the last minute for 50 cts. each. As a result on some occasions many seats remained unoccupied. All tickets were sold for the first New York Reading, amassing over $16,000 in receipts.

1. Buying tickets for the Dickens Readings at Steinway Hall, New York. *Harper's Weekly*, 28 December 1867.

After breakfast next morning, Sunday the 8th, Dickens and Dolby went to inspect the Steinway Hall, on 14th Street, where Dickens was to give his readings, starting Monday evening (Fig. 1). Dickens used to refer to this kind of reconnaissance as 'taking the bearings' of the place, and he did it at every new venue. At first the hall profoundly depressed him. It was huge, capable of seating 2,500 people: 'My hardest hall', he called it later. He felt that it would be impossible to produce any effect in it. Furthermore, there were two large balcony recesses at the far end, which he was sure would be bad for sound. They set about testing the acoustics, according to their familiar routine. Dickens stood on stage while Dolby prowled around the auditorium. They carried on a conversation in a low tone all the time, identifying areas where sound went dead. Dickens was much cheered to find the acoustics generally excellent, though in the event not all the audience shared this judgement, and the recesses had to be screened off.

That afternoon they spent quietly walking the city streets and riding in Central Park, the cold weather prompting Dickens to muffle himself right up. At least he avoided recognition: 'If you were to behold me driving out', he wrote to his daughter, 'furred up to the moustache, with furs on the coach-boy and on the driver, and with an immense white, red, and yellow striped rug for a covering, you would suppose me to be of Hungarian or Polish nationality.' On Monday evening, about six o'clock, Dickens's valet, Scott, took his evening clothes down to the Steinway Hall. Half an hour later Dickens arrived, to prepare for his first New York Reading: the Trial scene from *Pickwick* and 'A Christmas Carol' (he usually opened new venues with this pair). He spent a quarter of an hour at his Reading desk in the empty hall, tuning up, as it were, and then went to his dressing room.

As Dickens disappears into his room, we will join the audience assembling at the front of the Hall, as if it were to be our first experience of a Dickens Reading, reconstructed from accumulated eyewitness accounts of that and similar occasions.

The evening is bright, with the moon veiled in a soft, grey snow-cloud. The crowd outside the Hall is not large. The 'Speculators' aren't causing much trouble, because all the tickets have long been sold. Just a few noisy touts are in high energy during these last minutes before the show starts, desperate to sell off their grossly overpriced passes, and calling, 'Five dollars downstairs and four dollars up stairs.' One $2 ticket just went for $12. We hear later of tickets passing hands for $26. The police *are quiet and efficient. Carriage after carriage draws up and lets out its passengers. The nervous excitement is contagious. It's as if we're about to get our first sight of some famous work of art, or the Niagara Falls.*

Pushing past these crowds and into the familiar Steinway foyer, we make our way up the stairs, and it seems to take longer than any of us ever remember. Finally we're in the auditorium: a tremendous gathering, buzzing, swaying, chattering, calling. It looks an immensely distinguished audience too. We discover later from press reports that there are lawyers, doctors, bankers, merchant-princes; poets, artists, theatre managers, and famous actors; and journalists by the score. As we settle into our seats, we become aware again of the preciousness of the event: the questions buzzing around were not so much 'Hello—how are you?', but 'Where did you get your ticket?' We overhear extraordinary stories of adventures in order to secure tickets. Later in the week we learn of one group who attended Thursday night's Reading. To their great surprise they met some friends from Brooklyn, who had somehow managed to brave a ferocious snow storm to get across there. 'Why', said one of the group to the new arrivals, 'we wouldn't have come over from Brooklyn on such a night as this to hear the Apostle Paul.' 'No, nor would we, but we came to hear Dickens.'

Bit by bit, after much surging and seething, the human sea settles into calm. We now see the Reading platform. The set-up is interesting. There's a large maroon screen—a kind of backcloth. In front of that and about 12 feet off the ground is a horizontal row of gas-jets with a tin reflector. This is supported by two lateral rods each carrying a small gas-jet. In the centre of this softly lit, warm-coloured frame is a little red-covered Reading desk: it seems to glow under the subdued lights. Someone walks on to the stage—a sudden hush: this can't be Dickens? No. He crosses the stage, turns up a gas-jet burner or two, stays a few seconds to check it all, and leaves. The red frame glows more brightly.

All of a sudden a door opens and an elderly bearded man walks briskly and soundlessly, with a kind of gliding movement across the stage. He strides straight across, book in hand, head partly down as if wanting to avoid too much applause. Then he reaches the desk and stops, and faces us. Charles Dickens. He's in evening dress, with a bright buttonhole, a purple waistcoat, and a glittering watch-chain. He stands behind the desk and looks out at the audience. He seems distinctly calm and self-possessed. There's a round of applause, fairly sober but prolonged. He stands calmly, bowing easily once or twice. The applause lasts for nearly half a minute. He's about medium height, perhaps a little shorter, but he carries himself in a very upright manner. He has a rosy face, a broad brow, steel-grey hair thin on top, with two tufts just above the ears brushed forward, like the beard—in fact all brushed rather fiercely forward, looking as if there were a gale behind him. Lively eyes—they flash like diamonds as they move rapidly across the vast audience, taking them all in. Yes, a lot of glittering eye movement there, above the juicy nose and the bushy moustache and beard. He's finely dressed, a little showy with the big watch-chain and those gold shirt-studs glinting in the flare of the gas-lamps. How ought 'Charles Dickens' to look? Perhaps a massive genius ought to look . . . well . . . massive, to have more sheer physical presence than the man here on the platform?

While the applause goes on, he continues to glance, unhurriedly, around the hall as if, reciprocally, he is quickly taking stock of us. We can't believe he's actually here—Dickens, here, just yards away! That glance—rapid but intense—is extraordinary. Up to now the encounter has been rather formal—our applause and his acknowledgement. But that steady, raking glance at us changes things. If ever a look spoke it was just in that movement of the eyes: it felt as if he were making friends with us all. His eyes seem to have the power of meeting those of every separate person in the audience, and all the while a slight smile plays around his lips.

But his rolling eyes are now also asking us to let him begin his reading. As soon as the applause dies down, he speaks:

'Ladies and Gentlemen . . .'

He waits a second or two for silence—

'. . . I am to have the pleasure of reading to you first to-night, "A Christmas Carol" in four staves. Stave One'—

Dead quiet now in the vast hall.

'*MARLEY WAS DEAD: TO BEGIN WITH . . .*'

The greatest storyteller alive is here, before us, telling his greatest story.

At the end of the first paragraph, there are whispers that Dickens doesn't seem to have a very powerful voice—'A bit husky and monotonous.' We have to agree. There's also the slightest hint of a lisp. And why does he always use that rising inflection at the end of each sentence? His manner is very engaging. There's nothing formal in the reading, no particular strain or effort. It's exactly as if he were telling the story for the first time, freshly, just for us. The left hand holds the book, the right hand moves continually, slightly indicating the action described. There's really nothing to distinguish the performance from a parlour reading.

But now he comes to introduce us to Scrooge, and instantly things change. Reading becomes acting, and a magnetic current runs between reader and listeners. He suddenly becomes Scrooge, and it's as if he, Dickens, has disappeared. What we see is Scrooge, and what we hear is Scrooge: the old features, the pointed nose, the shrewd grating voice. He draws his face down into his collar, like a great turtle drawing in his head, puts on a surly look and speaks in a gruff voice. Now comes Scrooge's nephew, then little lisping Bob Cratchit (we didn't know he lisped: the story didn't tell us). Each character comes alive and is utterly distinct, both from the other characters and from Dickens the reader: a blind man could see them all distinctly. He does it not just through different voices but with different facial settings—a comical twist of the mouth to the right, a savage twist to the left, eyes rolling, eyebrows jigging up and down. He rubs and pats his hands, flourishes all his fingers, shakes them, points them. At the Cratchit dinner he stirs the gravy, mashes the potatoes, dusts the plates, tastes the punch and smacks his lips and sniffs the pudding; the very smell of the feast seems to steal around us. He can use his hands freely because he seems hardly at all to need to hold his book. He must know it off by heart. He just dives in and out of each of these characters—twenty-three different characters, each with an individual tone!

Dickens actually puzzles you with his complete abstraction from himself while he spends time dazzling you with so many different personalities.

But on some occasions—usually when he says something that makes the audience laugh heartily—he lets down the curtain from his face and smiles. And the smile turns to laughter as he laughs along with his audience. At those moments we come closest to him. The smile is quite wonderful: quick, curious, and beautiful. That smile is the secret of the man's whole nature.

We're soon lost in the story—or is it in the storyteller?

1

A Community of Readers

Now, the question I want your opinion on, is this:—Assuming these hopes [of becoming a professional Reader] to be well-grounded, would such an use of the personal (I may almost say affectionate) relations which subsist between me and the public, and make my standing with them very peculiar, at all affect my position with them as a writer? Would it be likely to have any influence on my next book? If it had any influence at all, would it be likely to be of a weakening or a strengthening kind?

To F. M. Evans, 16 March 1858: *Letters* VIII, 533

In 1841 Dickens declared to his readers, 'to commune with you, in any form, is to me a labour of love'. He was confessing to what became a life-long professional commitment and a species of private addiction. Communication with his public in any form, but particularly as a writer and Reader, was his route to community of feeling, the sense of a shared life. Notice that Dickens writes 'commune', not just 'communicate'. As journalist, magazine 'conductor', actor, serial novelist, speech-maker, Dickens maintained an extraordinarily energetic level of communion with that public in a wide variety of ways. The Readings took him one step closer to a personal intimacy with those who had come to know and to depend on him for over twenty years.

As suggested by the letter quoted above, to his publisher Frederick Evans, written on the eve of his turning professional as a Reader, Dickens was acutely sensitive to the impact the public Readings might have on that relationship. A few days later, he outlined his reasons to Forster for wishing to turn professional, and he stressed that very relationship in the same terms: 'Will you then try to think of this reading project [. . .] with a view to its effect on that peculiar relation (personally affectionate, and like no other man's) which subsists between me and the public?' This was his chance personally to meet that vast readership, to see and hear how they responded to what he had written, to guide their responses in another kind of transmission of his imaginary world, and to be himself moved and inspired to further creative improvisation. As he observed in prefacing his first paid Reading, 'I have long held the opinion, and have long acted on the opinion, that in these times whatever brings a public man and his public face to face, on terms of mutual confidence and respect, is a good thing.' This was communion of the most direct kind possible between a storyteller and his readers.

That 'personally affectionate' relationship—'like no other man's'—had been carefully cultivated years before Dickens met his public face to face. Because the peculiar character and success of the Readings was born from and nourished by the 'communion' so lovingly fostered by Dickens, because it was the foundation for that extraordinary rapport with his audiences, I want to examine the nature of that particular relationship as it evolved over the two decades before Dickens took to the platform as a supplementary career. We will then examine the problems he faced as he prepared to take a step that might have jeopardized those 'personal relations' he had developed with his readers, who were soon to become his listeners.

SERIALIZATION AND THE BONDED READER

At the end of his Final Farewell Reading, at St James's Hall, London, on 15th March 1870, Dickens gave a short valedictory speech. The conclusion was as follows:

Ladies and gentlemen, in but two short weeks from this time I hope that you may enter, in your own homes, on a new series of readings, at which my assistance will be indispensable; but from these garish lights I vanish now for evermore, with a heartfelt, grateful, respectful, and affectionate farewell.

The Readings had evolved from the peculiar relationship Dickens had developed with his readers as a serial novelist. Appropriately, now that the Readings had come to an end, the Reader–listener relationship could dissolve back into the old, familiar novelist–reader companionship. He looks forward to assisting them, in their own homes, on a 'new series of readings'. He will continue to be 'indispensable' to them. Face-to-face contact is what Dickens was really saying farewell to here, and it was a terrible wrench for him to give up these occasions. He comforted himself and his listeners by assuring them that he was only exchanging the Readings for another kind of regular rendezvous: his vicarious visits to the homes of his readers as the monthly instalments of his new novel *The Mystery of Edwin Drood* began its publication two weeks later.

Serialization had been the foundation of the special relationship Dickens developed with his readers. This is where we need to start. In considering the effects of serialization on the reception of Dickens's fiction, I mean to concentrate not on the mechanics and statistics of the business, but on the more affective aspects. What relation had fiction to the experience of everyday life in the circumstances of part-issue of a story over a year and a half? What was the nature of the bond that this form of serialization established between Dickens and his readers? How do such considerations relate to the Readings?

Linda Hughes and Michael Lund, in *The Victorian Serial* (1991), characterize serialization as 'a literary form attuned to fundamental tendencies in the age at large', and they suggest a number of ways in which the significance of the serialized novel may be related to cultural developments in Victorian England:

The assumption of continuing growth and the confidence that an investment (whether of time or money) in the present would reap greater rewards in the future were shared features of middle-class capitalism and of serial reading [. . .]. Evangelical and Utilitarian ethics [. . .] insisted on steady application over great reaches of time to achieve distant rewards [as an analogy to perseverance with a serialized novel][...]. Victorian concepts of time underwent great changes: time both shrank into tightly focussed compartments (railway and factory time), and expanded (geological and evolutionary time).

The first of these points might be supplemented by Roger Hagendorn's observation that serialization is well adapted to a society that 'perpetually defers desire in order to promote continued consumption', and thus 'emerges as an ideal form of narrative presentation under capitalism'. The last of these three points bears on the scale of the seeming contraction and expansion of a novel when it is experienced at first piecemeal over nineteen months and then as a single volume over a few weeks. All of these points suggest how hospitable the culture was at that period to the development of this form of publication—or indeed how it produced this form of publication. But it was manipulated in different ways and with varying degrees of ingenuity.

Hughes and Lund also propose, persuasively, a number of ways in which, for the individual reader, serial fiction can become productively confused with reality, and it is this that I want to concentrate on. The serial reader of Dickens does not commute as consciously and deliberately as the book reader might between imaginary and real worlds:

Reading did not occur in an enclosed realm of contemplation possible with a single-volume text; rather, Victorian literature, because of its parts structure, was engaged much more within the busy context of everyday life. It was not possible to enter into an imaginary world and remain there until the story's end; instead readers repeatedly were forced to set aside a continuing story and resume everyday life. In that space between readings, their world continued to direct a barrage of new information and intense experience at readers; and that context complicated and enriched the imagined world when the literary work was resumed.

Experience of the real world was more immediately cross-fertilized with and inflected by experience of the fiction (and vice versa) as the monthly instalments came and went, and this was because that fiction came in a shape less formally discrete than a book. It was more of a public event, or series of public events: well advertised, the instalment arrived for everyone at the same time each month or week. The reading routine was woven into the standard calendar of one's life over an extended period. It struck its roots in the reader and grew slowly but steadily.

The rapid, vivacious exchange between real life and fiction is not, of course, new with nineteenth-century serialization. The cultural historian Robert Darnton has persuasively argued that 'reading and living, construing texts and making sense of life, were much more closely related in the early modern period than they are today'. It may thus be that Victorian serialization gave that traditionally symbiotic relationship one final, hefty blood-infusion before living one's life and living one's novels began to go their more separate ways. Serialized fiction, then, integrated its imaginary world little by little into the real world, partly because the serial reader was less conscious of reading 'a book'. The serial reader was also, in one sense, more passive than the book reader, since the pacing of his or her reading was largely determined by the author and the publisher. The reader was subject to the simple publishing fact of timed, piecemeal issue of a story, as well as prey to the author's conscious structural exploitation of the individual instalment, the points at which the narrative was suspended, and the relation of the part to the larger fictional unit. As a reader of serial fiction you cannot control or force the pace. You wait for its world to return to you, as it does at regular intervals, whereas a book's unfolding sequence waits for you to give it your attention. Serialized fiction also insinuates itself readily into the experience of everyday life because the reader may well be less judgemental about it than about a book, tending to receive it as one might receive the unassuming periodical miscellany in which it is often housed. Furthermore it seems, as it runs its piecemeal course, about as provisional and inconclusive as any short stretch of one's own life might be. This relative suspension of the kind of judgement one might make of a book, a finished text, extended to the process of formal reviewing in the magazines of the day, as one critic has observed: 'it tended to deflect critical response, since serial publication made eventual appearance in book form anticlimactic, diminishing the impact of critical confrontation.'

The serial novel gathered substance, form, and weight as a cumulative sequence of ephemera. Imperceptibly, incrementally, the flimsy pamphlets evolved into something else—a book. Serialized fiction was drip-feed imaginative nourishment—no danger of indigestion in bingeing on other worlds. Fiction's being thus a part of the body and identity of miscellaneous ephemera gave it peculiarly expressive powers, as Christopher Kent has remarked: 'The intrinsically fragmented mode of the periodical press, with its variety, flexibility, and open-endedness, made it a particularly appropriate vehicle for the Victorian novel's attempt to capture the complexity and contingency of modern life.' Let us try to focus a bit more narrowly the effects of serialization's engineered continuity between the fictional and real worlds.

The opening sequences of a Dickens novel could mean a stretch of two or three monthly instalments: twelve chapters could take a quarter of a year to read. Dickens's openings sometimes confront us with the experience of dense miscellaneity, like the ephemeral material carried in contemporary magazines. As the chapters and the months go by, what have seemed at first fragmentary and heterogeneous components begin to connect. This teasing suspension of clear orientation and pattern was a deliberate opening strategy, as Dickens explained to Forster in planning *Little Dorrit*: 'to shew people coming together, in a chance way, as fellow-travellers, and being in the same place, ignorant of one another, as happens in life; and to connect them afterwards, and to make the waiting for that connection a part of the interest'. To assemble a cast of characters who do not know one another, in a 'chance way', helps the serial reader feel that the random social dynamics of life in this imaginary world are identical with those in the real world—'as happens in life', Dickens observes. Thus the different rhythms of reading, author-imposed rather than reader-determined, have consequences for the way in which one negotiates one's way into the fictional world.

Growing acquaintance with the fictional characters developed at much the same pace as the reader's growing acquaintance with new people in his or her own personal life: it imitated the hesitant feeling of one's way towards new friendship. Fictional characters generated in this way became real presences in one's personal life: people gossiped about them in ways indistinguishable from their discussions about new acquaintances in the real world. As the *National Magazine* remarked in 1837, 'The characters and scenes of this writer [Dickens] have become, to an extent undreamed of in all previous cases, part of our actual life.' Laman Blanchard, writing in *Ainsworth's Magazine* in 1844 made the point even more forcefully. Dickens's monthly instalments caused 'a most ridiculous confusion in the brain' to the extent that it 'no longer separates the fictitious from the real':

The literary and the social have become the same. The imagination seizes on some of the favourite characters, and regards them with the same force and entireness of identity with which it recognizes the persons we met at Bloomsbury, or in Buckinghamshire, last spring or autumn.

This smudging of the dividing line between art and life helped to promote a sense of the life-likeness of the fictional world. Hughes and Lund described the rhythms of assimilation: 'Reading one instalment, then pausing in that story, the Victorian audience turned to their own world with much the same set of critical faculties they had used to understand the literature.'

Contemporary opinion about serialization, and specifically about the disconcertingly close interweaving of its imaginary world with the everyday world of its Victorian readers, was very mixed. Those who were anyway hostile to novels as liable to promote unruly fantasies and desires saw in serialized fiction an even more sinister threat. One example of a utilitarian and somewhat puritanical attitude of this kind is this attack on serialization from *The North British Review*:

It is not a mere healthy recreation like a match at cricket, a lively conversation, or a game at backgammon. It throws us into a state of unreal excitement, a trance, a dream, which we should be allowed to dream out, and then be sent back to the atmosphere of reality again, cured by our brief surfeit of the desire to indulge again soon in the same delirium of feverish interest. But now our dreams are mingled with our daily business [. . .] the new number of Dickens, or Lever, or Warren [. . .] absorb[s] the energy which, after the daily task, might be usefully employed in the search after wholesome knowledge.

Fiction in instalments is here seen as contaminating rather than refreshing the ordinary business of the reader's life, because it 'mingles with our daily business' so insidiously. Here is how Dickens views the broader issue of the relation of his fiction to the day-to-day lives of his readers: 'We had sometimes reason to hope that our imaginary worlds afforded an occasional refuge to men busily engaged in the toils of life, from which they came forth none the worse to a renewal of its strivings.'

All this meant that Dickens could use serialization as a means of intervening regularly in the lives of his readers, thereby creating in them a degree of reliance on himself ('my assistance will be indispensable' in the *private* readings of *Edwin Drood*) that matched his reliance on their affection and attention. The relationship grew richly complex in its mutual personal dependency. It was exactly from this fertile ground that the phenomenal success of the Readings (Dickens's personal appearance before his readership) sprang and flourished, and it was back to this ground that Dickens could retire after the Readings ended.

In its obituary tribute to Dickens, *The Illustrated London News* made several observations on the experience of reading Dickens's early serialized fiction:

His method of composing and publishing his tales in monthly parts, or sometimes in weekly parts, aided the experience of this immediate personal companionship between the writer and the reader. It was just as if we received a letter or a visit, at regular intervals, from a kindly observant gossip, who was in the habit of watching the domestic life of the Nicklebys or the Chuzzlewits, and who would let us know from time to time how they were going on. There was no assumption in general, of having a complete and finished history to deliver; he came at fixed periods merely to report what he had perceived since his last budget was opened for us. The course of his narrative seemed to run on, somehow, almost simultaneously with the real progress of events, only keeping a little behind, so that he might have time to write down whatever happened, and to tell us.

Although Dickens's later novels could not be described as having quite this casual, gossipy effect on the reader, he had clearly already established his narrative persona as a certain kind of garrulous, entertaining confidant, and he wanted to sustain that. In reinforcing this impression of being a regularly visiting, chatty companion, Dickens did indeed in some novels more or less synchronize the seasonal progress in the unfolding story with the actual seasonal changes over the months of issuing the novel. These two considerations—the synchronizing of imaginary and real time, and the narrator-as-visiting-gossip—break down the sense of the generic conventions associated with reading a novel: as *The Illustrated London News* remarked, with a Dickens serial 'there was no assumption [...] of having a complete and finished history to deliver'. The forward momentum in reading a novel was compromised by this sense of a discrete regular 'visit', with news bulletins: it was more a sense of catching up with events.

Dickens had an acute sense of this degree of involvement of his imaginary world with the real lives of his readers, and he was to manipulate this very consciously in the Readings. He was impressed, for example, by an enthusiastic private encomium on his fiction from Arthur Helps, Clerk to the Privy Council, and replied in these terms: 'Very few things touch me so nearly as the knowledge that my fancies have become a part of lives like yours.' The stock acknowledgement—'I'm glad you like my book'—is here elaborated into something much more intensely specific. Dickens is deeply excited by the testimony that people incorporate his creations into their private lives. It is like being welcomed into their homes—a particular source of gratification, perhaps, for someone with persistent memories of having been a neglected waif. In his Preface (1839) to the final double-number of *Nicholas Nickleby* Dickens elaborated on the kind of relationship he was trying to develop with his readers. He quotes at some length an extract from Henry Mackenzie's *The Lounger*, a series of weekly essays (1785–7). In this piece Mackenzie compares 'the author of a periodical performance' with the writer who does not publish his work until he has had plenty of time to refine the text, who 'must have withdrawn many an idea which in the warmth of composition he had conceived, and altered many an expression which in the hurry of writing he had set down.' The periodical writer is in a very different position:

[He] commits to his readers the feelings of the day, in the language which those feelings have prompted. As he has delivered himself with the freedom of intimacy and the cordiality of friendship, he will naturally look for the indulgence which those relations may claim; and when he bids his readers adieu, will hope, as well as feel, the regrets of an acquaintance, and the tenderness of a friend.

These sentiments, characteristic of the author of *A Man of Feeling*, are then strongly endorsed by Dickens as he brings N*ickleby* to its close:

With such feelings and such hopes the periodical essayist, the Author of these pages, now lays them before his readers in a completed form, flattering himself [. . .] that on the first of next month they may miss his company at the accustomed time as something which used to be expected with pleasure; and think of the papers which on that day of so many past months they have read, as the correspondence of one who wished their happiness, and contributed to their amusement.

The emphasis is not so much on the experience of finishing a novel as on the loss of a close companionship sustained by regular correspondence (albeit one-way correspondence). In endorsing Mackenzie's views Dickens also aspires to an intimacy between writer and reader, and a sense that the serial writer has a special licence to be more open with his feelings. The stress on the immediacy of the transmission of feelings, unrefined, spontaneous, and on the reciprocation of those feelings anticipates the special dynamic of the Readings.

The serial is also a contract of continuity. Dickens pledged to provide serial instalments of his fiction more or less indefinitely. Thus one novel might end as its successor has already begun. This overlapping happened in the early years of his novel writing. It has partly the effect of blurring novel endings and beginnings, as the monthly provision extended into a sustained exercise in instalment fiction over four or five years. Simply to be providing monthly portions of fiction came to seem just as important as shaping a discrete novel. Jennifer Hayward has drawn attention to the formulation of Dickens's extraordinarily tautologous pledge to his readers at the conclusion of number 10 of *Pickwick Papers*—'we shall keep perpetually going on beginning again, regularly':

The complex temporal involutions of this sentence parallel serialization's complex author/audience relations [. . .] 'going on' enforcing continuity, 'beginning again' the eternal rebirth of the serial, and their doubling signaling the inexhaustibility of the text, its celebration of excess. Finally, 'regularly' [. . .] the most essential signifier in the statement, since it offers a crucial reassurance.

Dickens's statement is a covenant. It is also a symptom of a growing addiction on the part of the author and a hope that the addiction will become a two-way condition.

The serial issue of novels created communities of readers as well as complex and intimate forms of communion between author and public. Reading aloud to the family or to a group who might have banded together to subscribe to the new monthly instalment meant that the experience of fiction was a gregarious occasion just as much as it was for others a private solitary entertainment. The various practices of communal reading aloud and their relation to Dickens's public Readings are discussed in the next chapter, as are some of the implications of challenging the still commonplace assumption that reading was a predominantly private experience for the Victorians. The point to make here, in the larger context of the Readings, is that Dickens had *listening* audiences for his work years before he himself appeared on the platform to read aloud: he had from the start a vast readership who first *heard* rather than *read* those stories as they unfolded month by month. He himself arrived on the public platform as yet another reciter of his works, as far as huge numbers of his readers were concerned: but of course he was also *the* Reader.

Collective listening to the instalment parts was one way of consolidating this community of readers. Another was the extent to which interest roused in the story's events and characters fed into the conversation of readers (as mentioned earlier) and thereby brought isolated readers together. 'In the case of *Middlemarch*', wrote R. H. Hutton, 'those will understand it best and value it most who have made acquaintance slowly during the past year with all its characters, and discussed them eagerly with their friends, in all the various stages of their growth and fortune'. Speculation about the characters' futures had a special piquancy when only one person in the whole country—the author—knew for sure what the next stages of development were to be. Everyone else shared exactly the same limits to their knowledge, as each instalment slowly shunted the action forward a little way and then paused. In effect the serial author orchestrated synchronized communal reading for tens of thousands of people—a further anticipation of Dickens's Reading performances. For example, over the weekend of 30–31 January 1841 perhaps half a million people in Britain were reading or hearing the new weekly instalment (Number 44) of *Master Humphrey's Clock*, the death of Little Nell. This amounted to a national event, corroborating Benedict Anderson's claims for the power of the periodical press and serialized fiction in constituting 'imagined community' (though he mistakenly believed Dickens serialized his novels in 'popular newspapers'). A sense of the full scale and impact of the communal experience of a first-run Dickens novel might best be understood by those who follow television soap operas. In calculating the narrative currents and turns of his serialized story, Dickens could manipulate the emotional mood of a large part of the nation, just as he was to do more immediately and intimately in the public Readings. 'What a thing it is to have Power', he mused, in reporting to his wife on a private Reading of *The Chimes*.

Serial fiction also reinforced the sense of a community of readers by positing a range of contemporary social issues, debating and dramatizing them, and thereby inviting the readers during the slowly developing run of the novel to involve themselves in the debate. It was a way of culturally enfranchising large swathes of the people of England. In this respect it matched the declared aims of *All The Year Round*, which was designed 'to assist in the Discussion of the Social Questions of the Day'. Trollope sardonically conceded, in *The Warden*, that the real power to engage public opinion and promote social reform now lay with the novelist, and in particular 'Mr Popular Sentiment' (i.e., Dickens):

We get on now with a lighter step, and quicker [than the traditional investigative machinery of social reform]: ridicule is found to be more convincing than argument, imaginary agonies touch more than true sorrows, and monthly novels convince, when learned quartos fail to do so. If the world is to be set right, the work will be done by shilling numbers.

Dickens's mature social-problem novels were designed as powerful stimulants, not just in what they said but in the way in which the cajoling, teasing, fire-breathing, hustling presence of the author obtruded itself. Dickens declared in a speech in 1855, 'I believe that, in order to preserve it [Parliament] in a state of real usefulness and independence, the people must be ever watchful and ever jealous of it; and it must have its memory jogged; it must be kept awake; when it happens to have taken too much Ministerial narcotic, it must be trotted about, and must be hustled and pinched in a friendly way, as is the usage in such cases.' The activity prescribed is exactly the mode of Dickens's hyperactive prose, especially when addressing social and political failings in the fiction. In fact, the mode is pretty habitual and pervasive: Dickens seemed permanently anxious never *ever* to let his reader slide into a doze.

It was not only a matter of the communal raising of issues, but also of impressing solutions. Dickens's lifelong theme as a writer was connection, the reuniting, as in a family, of a fragmenting society, and the mitigation of the harsher effects of social and economic divisions. The Readings sustained this commitment in their own way, as Helen Small has observed: 'Dickens's readings were not, as might have been expected, aimed purely or even primarily at the middle classes. They were conceived and promoted as occasions which would bring together readers from widely differing social backgrounds as one reading public.' That is the point: 'one reading public'. The practice of serialized fiction, with its high circulation across all divisions of society, its protracted forms of collective communication, on a reliable, regular basis, and its group-reading reception, constituted an enactment of those very themes of communication and inclusiveness.

Many years ago John Sutherland asked the question how Dickens managed so consistently to triumph in the form of the independent, twenty-part, shilling-a-month serial format when his rivals failed fairly consistently (however much their fiction might have flourished within the serial magazine format). Has the question ever been satisfactorily answered? In winding up these speculations about the special relationship between Dickens and his readers, developed over the years since *Pickwick* and extended in the Readings, I want briefly to say something about two factors that would have contributed to his singular success in engaging so many readers so consistently: these have to do with his assertive presence in his writings, as he projects his impresario role, and the distinctive voice that sounds from the pages, even in silent reading. Both these have obvious bearings on the nature of the Readings, as we shall see later.

First we might just note, in relation to Sutherland's question, that Dickens himself had qualms about the dangers of his success as a serial novelist. In 1841 he wrote of how he thought he had 'spoilt the novel sale—in the cases of Bulwer, Marryat, and the best people—by my great success', and how his imitators were 'deluging the town with every description of trash and rot'. He had been producing instalments of fiction month by month almost continuously for three and a half years, since April 1836, until *Nicholas Nickleby* came to an end in September 1839. Six months later he began producing weekly instalments of fiction, which ran uninterrupted for another year and a half (*The Old Curiosity Shop* and *Barnaby Rudge* in *Master Humphrey's Clock*). He therefore decided (in 1841), in order to avoid making himself 'too cheap', to stop writing for a year and then issue a novel in the standard three-volume form. In other words he decided to relinquish serialization. A week later he changed his mind: the year's pause was confirmed but the new work would appear 'in monthly parts *instead* of a Novel'. It is interesting that he put it this way, as if there were something generically different in what he was doing as a serial writer of novels from what the novelist did. But why did he change his mind? For one thing, the year away from writing would not have worked if he had had to supply a completed novel by the end of it; so to begin a serialized novel at the end of that free year would give him more of a break from composition. For another thing, the economics of the monthly format were more advantageous to the publishers (as long as their author was Dickens). But undoubtedly another factor was the recovery of that sustained relationship with his public that serialization promoted and that he would forfeit in observing a year's silence and then issuing a complete three-volume novel.

Within days of this decision to revert to the old monthly format he was drafting an announcement to his readers that *Master Humphrey's Clock* was to close, and it was in this announcement that he wrote of its being a 'labour of love' to commune with his readers. He and they had 'travelled together through [. . .] Eighty-seven Weekly Numbers'. This idea of travelling companionship struck the keynote of his sentiments in the announcement. The concept of fellow-travelling over a protracted period, where that specific period of travelling companionship is determined by the author, simply could not apply in the case of a single-volume novel. Steven Connor has remarked on Dickens's 'sense of intimacy with his readers [that] almost approached collaboration', and Dickens regarded his serial fiction as a kind of creative companionship. He once described the attraction of throwing himself into a dramatic role (in this instance the character of Richard Wardour in *The Frozen Deep*): 'the interest of such a character to me is that it enables me, as it were, *to write a book in company* instead of in my own solitary room, and to feel its effect coming freshly back upon me from the reader'. In effect,

ever since the start of *Pickwick,* Dickens had been writing his books
'*in company*', promoting that special intimacy with his public in a
form that, month by month, enabled him to 'feel its effect coming
freshly back' on him from his readers. The barrier between writing
and public Reading promised to disappear in one plan Dickens had,
for the launch of his professional Readings in 1858. His vicarious
presence in his readers' experience of his stories was to be replaced by
his actual presence: a Christmas Story by Charles Dickens would be
premiered at a public Reading. During his planned tour of London
and the provinces, so he proposed, he would be returning around
Christmas 'to read a new Christmas Story written for the purpose'.
Oral transmission, after all, was one of the most ancient forms of
publication of fiction.

It was that sense of sharing the public response as the novel was
building that Dickens was to reinforce in the Readings. As he told the
audience at his very first public Reading, at Birmingham, one of the
great incentives for him in taking on this enterprise was 'the wish to
have the great pleasure of meeting you face to face at this Christmas
time, and *accompany you myself* through one of my little Christmas
books' (my italics). The language is just the same as that used to
describe his sense of having travelled together with his readers through
the weekly numbers of *Master Humphrey's Clock.* The Birmingham
Reading was 'A Christmas Carol'. Just a few pages into that story
Scrooge's nephew insists that Christmas was the time to think of
other people 'as if they really were fellow-passengers to the grave,
and not another race of creatures bound on other journeys'. Dickens
altered 'passengers' to 'travellers' in the Reading version of the 'Carol'.
It is an interesting change: 'passengers' denotes the passive occupants
of a vehicle wholly controlled by its driver, whereas 'fellow-travellers'
suggests a shared exploration of journeying. Fellowship, friendship,
travelling companionship, these are for Dickens a key part of the
experience of composition: 'my countrymen', he wrote in drafting
that statement about the course of the *Clock,* 'have given my writings,
as they were myself, a corner in their hearts and homes, and a place
among their house-hold gods.' Most novelists want celebrity and the

widest possible readership. Dickens seems exceptional in wanting not only celebrity but friendship, personal affection, a permanent place in people's lives, and a corner in their homes. Serialization gave him the chance to develop this relationship, and the Readings gave him the chance to confirm it. Serialization bonded writer and reader over a long period. Bradley Deane has underlined the practical advantages, whereby 'writers could gauge the popularity of story lines and characters as they wrote, while readers, for their part, could influence the direction of the novel's plot, registering the degree of their approbation either collectively, through consumption, or individually, through letters to the writer.' This began from the start of Dickens's career as a novelist. Every month of *Pickwick* he was bombarded with suggestions for its development, and had to issue a notice in Part XV to warn correspondents away. Deane goes on to argue that Dickens, far from defending serialization against its critics ('probably the lowest artistic form yet invented', according to the *Prospective Review* in 1851), shared their concerns, but to compensate for its desultory mode of proceeding 'proposed an image of himself as the greater unity of his text', promoting a special personalized relationship with his readers throughout the run of the novel. This happened in *Pickwick*, to counterbalance that moment in the popular print revolution when mass production and circulation of texts seemed to alienate the author from the reader in a form of new industrial relations. Just over twenty years later, Dickens made a very similar move. He came out from behind his texts altogether and established his presence as a public storyteller unmediated by any publishing industry.

Dickens worked hard on what he called this 'labour of love', not just by public assertions of the kind announced in *Master Humphrey's Clock*, but by developing a very strong personality as a narrator. The reader is continually aware of his orchestrating presence as well as his boisterous narrative voice, and these two together strongly reinforce the intimate personal bond with his readers on which the success of his serialized fiction was founded and on which the public Readings were to capitalize. Let us consider first the issue of presence.

I have already mentioned his establishing his narrative persona as a certain kind of garrulous, entertaining confidant, but he does more than this, in his sustained effort to intensify the bond with his public. He asserts his presence within the text with a degree of energy and flamboyance unmatched by his rivals. Dickens thought of his readership as an audience from the start: they were attending a performance by a gifted soloist, one who was both conductor and instrumentalist, every time they opened their monthly or weekly instalment of one of his stories. Halfway through the writing of *Pickwick Papers* he described himself as 'Mr Pickwick's Stage Manager'. The difference between what one usually thinks of as a stage manager, unobtrusively organizing the show from backstage, and the way Dickens assumed the role in his novels is that Dickens was a very prominent and audible managerial figure. He may have worked hard behind the scenes, but he worked just as hard in front of them. It was a role he assumed with relish, in real life: he was an amateur stage manager and director of formidable energy, creativity, and efficiency. He took as much trouble in directing the many amateur productions in which he was involved as he did in orchestrating his written fiction, in terms of attention to details of setting, props (how much time does Dickens the novelist lavish on his props!), and ensuring that the 'show' reflected his interpretation of character and action; and we shall see (in Chapter 4) just how painstaking he was in designing his Reading 'set' and the infrastructure for the tours. He was an autocratic presence, involving himself in every aspect of amateur theatricals. In the last year of his life he confided what he called his 'day-dream' to a friend:

To settle down for the remainder of my life within easy distance of a great theatre, in the direction of which I should hold supreme authority. It should be a house, of course, having a skilled and noble company, and one in every way magnificently appointed. The pieces acted should be dealt with according to my pleasure, and touched up here and there in obedience to my own judgment; the players as well as the plays being absolutely under my command.

It was a dream of extending the controls he self-evidently enjoyed as a novelist to the practical world of theatre production. His roles as novelist and stage manager are closely related. Dickens's energetic participation in theatrical enterprises has a long history, of which the following is just a brief summary.

At school in London, at Wellington House Academy, he was an enthusiastic initiator of various theatrical events—'always a leader at these plays', recalled one of his schoolfellows. He took part in some productions in Canada, during his first visit to America in 1842. Indeed he seems to have masterminded the show:

I had regular plots of the scenery made out, and lists of the properties wanted; and had them nailed up by the prompter's chair. Every letter that was to be delivered, was written; every piece of money that had to be given, provided; and not a single thing lost sight of. I prompted, myself, when I was not on; when I was, I made the regular prompter of the theatre my deputy; and I never saw anything so perfectly touch and go, as the first two pieces.

Back in England he involved himself in a number of theatrical events in association with various philanthropic causes. He mounted a production of Ben Jonson's *Every Man in His Humour* on behalf of Leigh Hunt in 1847. The production was repeated the following year at the Haymarket Theatre in London to promote the endowment of a curatorship of Shakespeare's house at Stratford; and it was repeated yet again in 1850 at Lord Lytton's home at Knebworth, where it was accompanied by the performance of Mrs Inchbald's farce, *Animal Magnetism*. Dickens directed and acted on each occasion. In 1851 Dickens toured with the amateur production of Lytton's play *Not So Bad as We Seem* and the short farce co-written with Mark Lemon, *Mr. Nightingale's Diary*. Dickens starred in both, and directed both, and according to R. H. Horne, appeared during this period to be 'almost ubiquitous and sleepless'.

Wilkie Collins's play, *The Lighthouse*, was directed by Dickens in 1855, and he also took one of the principal roles in it. Collins's

The Frozen Deep (with some contributions from Dickens) was performed in January 1857, first in Dickens's house, then before the Royal Family in London, and then at Manchester. Again, it was directed by Dickens and he also took the leading role. At that point, after a decade of intermittent 'managing' and performing in amateur theatre productions, Dickens's involvement in ensemble acting and play directing came to an end. Eight months later, in the Spring of 1858, he launched his new career as a solo public Reader. The Readings were a natural, logical, and inevitable replacement for the amateur theatricals, just as they were a natural extension of the relationship he had cultivated with his readers. How right he was when he confided to Forster, 'I have often thought, that I should certainly have been as successful on the boards as I have been between them.'

Dickens's daydream of managing a great theatre stressed the absolute control he would have over all aspects of the theatre's activities. The dream of complete control over the representation of imaginary worlds is a very Dickensian fantasy. The public Readings, as he devised the whole enterprise, fulfilled this dream by ensuring that he would have at his command a large cast of characters but no acting personnel to shepherd and bring up to scratch. As Carlyle told him, 'Charley, you carry a whole company of actors under your own hat.' He would be in absolute control of the script, at liberty to improvise wherever he felt so inclined. He meticulously designed the set and props for his Readings; he determined the choice of repertoire, the venues, and the dates and times of performances. In effect, in this form of delivery of his work, he was author, publisher, and adaptor: he had absolute power over the transmission of his own material. That felt presence of the master-manager of his writings had always been there in the novels and Christmas Books and journalism. In Stave Two of *A Christmas Carol*, the narrator describes Scrooge's proximity to the Ghost of Christmas Past, 'as close to it as I am now to you, and I am standing in the spirit at your elbow.' That is where the reader so often senses Dickens, and it is where he liked to think of himself as narrator, guiding the action, prompting the responses in close companionship with the reader. When, in 1849, he was contemplating starting a new journal, he hit on the idea of featuring a 'semi-omniscient' figure to be called 'The Shadow', to 'represent common-sense and humanity' and it would be 'everyone's inseparable companion'. This figure, just like the 'Carol''s narrator, would be 'at everybody's elbow'. Much the same idea characterized Dickens's later 'Uncommercial Traveller', as the publisher Arthur Waugh noted, in reflecting on the last decade of Dickens's life:

[The 'Uncommercial' project] showed once more its author's insatiable passion for keeping up a close personal hold upon his public, chatting, as it were, with his readers over the fire, and giving them, with every fresh conversation, more and more opportunities for intimate and confidential understanding of himself [. . .]. The wandering freedom of the traveller's life enchanted him. He liked to fancy himself 'upon the road', treating his readers with the genial and confidential garrulity which ought to be part of every traveller's stock-in-trade. The readings were only another, and a much more exhausting, outlet for the same ambition. Movement, change, and sympathy had become absolutely necessary to his nature.

This puts very well the case for the Readings as continuity rather than innovation in Dickens's career.

Let us now consider that 'voice', the almost audible extension of Dickens's extraordinary presence in his writings. His presence on the Reading platform in this hybrid combination of acting and reciting gave literal physical immediacy to that 'voice' and that 'presence' that, as the invisible author, he had already made such a hallmark in his novels.

The distinguished novelist and critic Vladimir Nabakov once suggested that Dickens's voice was actually the principal attraction in all his work; the *voice* and not the substance of the novels themselves: 'We just surrender ourselves to Dickens's voice—that is all [. . .] the enchanter interests me more than the yarn spinner or the teacher [. . .] this attitude seems to me to be the only way of keeping Dickens alive, above the reformer, above the penny novelette, above the sentimental trash, above the theatrical nonsense.' We may talk about the lack of unity, the structural incoherence in a Dickens novel—or at any rate in early Dickens. But how much does it matter? Isn't most of it anyway a conduit for Dickens's voice and high-spirited managerial improvisation? Indeed, doesn't the whole unruly ensemble—the clumsy structure, creaking machinery, abrupt changes of direction, thronging miscellany of characters—amount to an ideal means of throwing into even sharper relief the dominant unifying voice of the creator, as Bradley Deane suggested? This 'voice', the manifestation of this obtrusively powerful personality who is generating and organizing the text, comes across as disconcertingly amplified. Robert Garis, whose study *The Dickens Theatre* was one of the first and best to explore this phenomenon, has written, 'The loudness of Dickens's voice and of its expressive devices is virtually a physical, even an acoustic, phenomenon: it produces a condition in which the explicit intention of the insistent voice all but totally fills our consciousness.' That effect of vocal resonance was a part of his inimitable style. Dickens's readers were, from the start, his 'auditors'. They virtually *heard* him as they turned the pages of his stories month by month: then later, in 1858, as Dickens embarked on his professional Readings tours, that voice could be heard resounding through the halls of provincial cities up and down the country. What Garis describes as 'virtually' an acoustic experience for the novel reader ceased to be 'virtual' in 1858.

The assertive voice and the sense of a powerful managerial presence in orchestrating the fiction must account for much of the success of Dickens as a serial novelist: both were, of course, central to the success of the Readings. So was his proven devotion to his readers. The love that went into the labour of serialized fiction was reciprocated, at least in terms of his readership's growing dependency on Dickens. This was confirmed in the view of the obituarist writing in *The Illustrated London News* in 1870:

The obvious effect [of the serialization of Dickens's novels] was to inspire all his constant readers—say, a million or two—with a sense of habitual dependence on their contemporary, the man Charles Dickens, for a continued supply of the entertainment which he alone could furnish. He was personally indispensable to them [...]. If each of his stories had appeared complete in three octavo volumes, with the lapse of a couple of years between one work and another, the feeling of continual dependence on the living author would have been less prevalent among us.

Dickens's concern to be 'personally indispensable' to his readers fuelled all his writing, not just his fiction. It became an explicit part of his mission as a journalist. Here he is delivering the same sentiments in his 'Preliminary Word' at the launch of *Household Words* in 1850:

We aspire to live in the Household affections, and to be numbered among the Household thoughts, of our readers. We hope to be the comrade and friend of many thousands of people, of both sexes, and of all ages and conditions, on whose faces we may never look.

This aspiration to be 'comrade and friend' with all his readers was evidently fulfilled, and across the full social range, as two very different people testified. Charles Eliot Norton, the Harvard Professor of Fine Arts, wrote in 1868:

No one thinks first of Mr Dickens as a writer. He is at once, through his books, a friend. He belongs among the inmates of every pleasant-tempered and large-hearted person. He is not so much the guest as the inmate of our homes.

Dickens in this case was indeed a good personal friend. However, in another case, the sense of friendship was unrelated to personal acquaintance. Dickens's son related the following story: 'A friend of mine told me just after my father died he happened to be in a tobacconist's shop, when a labouring man walked in, ordered his screw of tobacco, and throwing his money on the counter, said, "we have lost our best friend".' These testimonies to the importance of personal friendship abound, and it is clear that this friendship had been established long before Dickens became a public Reader. He launched that career on a full tide of good will, as he explained in defending his initiative to Forster and others. During his first provincial tour as a professional in 1858 he wrote to Angela Burdett

Coutts, revelling in the way people everywhere expressed 'a personal affection for me and the interest of tender friends in me'. He added that it was especially gratifying 'at this time [...] in this Autumn of all others', presumably referring to the bitter break-up of his marriage and the formal separation that summer. The Readings satisfied the state of violent restlessness that accompanied the miseries and recriminations of this whole episode. More importantly, the affectionate reception from his public was an emotional reassurance at a time of emotional loss. This was another reason for his wanting at this time to become a professional Reader. A further reason, and an important one for Dickens, was the prospect of increased earnings to help with his new home at Gad's Hill, the exactions of a large family, and the obligations to support his now estranged wife. A lot hung on the popular success of the Readings.

The transition from a novelist who enjoyed an extraordinary bond with his readership to a public Reader was highly controversial. We should now examine how far Dickens's relationship with his community of readers changed once he became a professional performer of his own writings. That was the anxiety expressed in his 1858 letter to his publisher, Evans, quoted at the start of this chapter: would it affect the 'personal relations' with them? The problems were twofold: he risked being seen as associated too closely with *demi-mondaine* public theatre and all the prejudices against it; and he was making an ungentlemanly commitment to performing for money.

ANTI-THEATRICALITY AND READING FOR MONEY

Dickens launched his professional career as a Reader when the long-rooted prejudices against the theatre were still very deep. The idea of giving public Readings for money had been in his mind at least twelve years before he went professional in 1858. In 1846, after giving a private reading of one of the *Dombey* monthly parts then in publication, he wrote to Forster with some recognition of the risks to his reputation:

I was thinking the other day that in these days of lecturings and readings, a great deal of money might possibly be made (if it were not infra dig) by one's having Readings of one's own books. It would be an *odd* thing. I think it would take immensely. What do you say?

Those prejudices and the more general anxiety about a gentleman's reading in public for money are rehearsed in the arguments urged by Forster to dissuade Dickens from taking this step: 'It was a substitution of lower for higher aims; a change to commonplace from more elevated pursuits; and it had so much the character of a public exhibition for money as to raise, in the question of respect for his calling as a writer, a question also of respect for himself as a gentleman.' It was also dangerously close to a career in the theatre. However distinguished one might be as a professional actor, it seemed that for the Victorians the distinction was always carried at a lower social level than that enjoyed by one's peers in other professions. One of the most eminent actors of the day, William Macready, a good friend of Dickens's, recorded in his diary how late he came to the realization of these prejudices against his profession:

My experience has taught me that whilst the law, the church, the army and navy give a man the rank of gentleman, on the stage that designation must be obtained in society (though the law and the Court decline to recognize it) by the individual bearing [. . .]. I was not aware, in taking it, that this step in life was a descent from the equality in which I had felt myself to stand with those [. . .] whom our education had made my companions.

It was not until the census of 1861 that actors were first classed as professional men, along with authors, artists, and musicians.

The nineteenth-century prejudices against the theatre had to do both with the theatre's perceived bohemianism and with something more elusive, the perception of a dangerous mutability inherent in the acting profession itself—the very public display of role-playing. Jonas Baring, in his study *The Anti-Theatrical Prejudice*, identifies these qualities—mimicry, spectacle, and ostentation—as the targets for puritanical distrust. As Alison Byerly puts it, in an absorbing article on the scholastic and domestic connotations of reading aloud, 'The Victorian fascination with the theatre was matched by a profound uneasiness about an art form whose purpose was, in a sense, deception, and whose medium was the human body.' She argues that public Reading performances 'were able to escape the taint of theatricality for three reasons: because of their origin as a form of private recreation, because of their association with the educational reform movement, and because of their reliance upon the power of the individual voice to confer authenticity where a cast of characters would suggest artifice'. We shall be exploring the origins of public Readings and their educational associations in the next chapter. Here we are concerned with the moral 'taint of theatricality'.

The socially competitive middle classes and those whose moral attitudes had been strongly influenced by the puritanism of the Evangelical revival were keen to distance themselves from the world of the theatre and its associated laxity of moral conduct, both before and behind the proscenium arch. One contributor to the 1832 Parliamentary Select Committee, 'on Dramatic Literature', expressed the middle-class squeamishness about theatre-going very clearly: 'I think it a decided objection to any man carrying his wife or sister to the theatre, when he is compelled to take them through a crowd of women of notoriously bad character.' On the death in 1835 of the great comic actor and impersonator, Charles Mathews, several respectful newspaper and journal obituaries, wishing to enhance their accolades, made a special point of reassuring readers that the actor's gentlemanly status had never been contaminated by the theatrical milieu in which he had passed his life. These remarks would very likely have caught the attention of Dickens, a fervent admirer of Mathews and himself on the threshold of celebrity, a young man very conscious of social status. The obituary reassurances, however, did not quite match Mathews's own experience: he had been ignominiously refused membership of the Beefsteak Club, because of his profession (though David Garrick had been a member), and so was acutely conscious of the stigma attaching to his career. He was one of those who gave evidence before the 1832 Select Committee. In the course of the questioning, he reflected on some of the changes in public attitudes towards the theatre that he had witnessed in his own lifetime:

MATHEWS: Formerly it was the fashion to go to the theatre; but now a lady cannot show her face at table next day, and say she has been at the theatre. If they are asked whether they have been at Covent Garden or Drury Lane [the only two 'legitimate' theatres, under contemporary licensing laws], they say: 'Oh dear no, I never go there—it is too low'.

COMMITTEE CHAIR: When was it the fashion not to go to the theatre?

MATHEWS: I think it has increased very much. I think I can remember when it was not the fashion to the extent it is now. I remember the time when it was no shame to go to see the legitimate drama; but it is now.

Four years later, these anxieties about the lowly social status of the theatre and the acting profession were comically figured in *Pickwick Papers*. Alfred Jingle, who has successfully deceived the Pickwickians as to his identity for several chapters in the opening numbers of the novel, is challenged to a duel by the outraged army officer, Dr Slammer, who takes him to be a respectable associate of the Pickwick Club. When Slammer hears of Jingle's true identity as a strolling actor, he abruptly withdraws his challenge since the engagement would be beneath his dignity as an officer and a gentleman. The social stigma on actors attached also to theatrical activities even where there were no professional actors involved. The episode of the theatricals in *Mansfield Park* (1814), when the participants knew they were risking reproach for such an activity, is one of the best-known instances of the fear of moral contamination when the world of the theatre invades the domestic sphere, though that does not seem to have troubled Dickens's home theatricals. Hostility towards the theatre in the early nineteenth century was intensified by contemporary Evangelical propaganda. The *Christian Observer*, one of the most influential Evangelical journals (numbering Hannah More, Thomas Babington, and William Wilberforce among its founders), pronounced in 1824 that 'A truly virtuous theatre is a solecism'. For

those, especially the young, with a susceptible imagination even to
read Shakespeare could provoke 'a dangerous elevation of the fancy';
and as for novels, 'By feeding continually the craving imagination,
novels become [...] a private dissipation.'

In a robust attempt to challenge such puritan orthodoxy, Hazlitt
published a paper, 'On Actors and Acting', in the *Examiner* (5 January
1817)—'to shew how little we agree with the common declamations
against the immoral tendency of the stage'. He argued that the
stage was a medium for wholly beneficial forms of entertainment
and instruction, for teaching us about ourselves, our society, and
our history. In the course of his essay Hazlitt suggests the extent to
which his fellow-humans owe their forms of expressive behaviour to
professional actors:

As *they* imitate us, we, in our turn, imitate them. How many fine gentlemen
do we owe to the stage? How many romantic lovers are mere Romeos in
masquerade? [...] They teach us when to laugh and when to weep, when
to love and when to hate, upon principle and with a good grace!

This leads us to consider the second suggested source of anxiety
or hostility towards the theatre, the implications of mutability in
the art of role-playing. Deborah Vlock, in *Dickens, Novel Reading,
and the Victorian Popular Theatre*, has argued that the Victorian
bourgeoisie were at the same time hostile towards and yet attracted
by the theatre. Whether they approved of theatre or not, modes
of theatricality pervaded their lives in formative ways and saturated
their culture: it is the paradox of 'an essentially theatrical culture
promoting antitheatrical ideology'. Hazlitt's comments about mutual imitation and role-playing in real life bear directly on this
contention. A society that is as preoccupied with its own identity
as were the Victorian middle classes, and one that is doing some
fairly earnest role-playing in its ordinary social life, is likely to have
ambivalent feelings towards the theatrical spectacle of role-playing.
We shall return to this in a later chapter, when considering the appeal
of theatrical impersonations.

Nina Auerbach, in her book *Private Theatricals*, confronts this ambivalence in her suggestion that the Victorians perceived theatricality as both recreation and threat. In this perception 'theatricality' is directly opposed to 'sincerity':

Reverent Victorians shunned theatricality as the ultimate, deceitful mobility. It connotes not only lies, but a fluidity of character that decomposes the uniform integrity of the self. [It encourages the] idea that character might be inherently unstable [. . .]. The theatre, that alluring pariah within Victorian culture, came to stand for all the dangerous potential of theatricality to invade the authenticity of the best self.

The theatre is the place where this instability, this fluidity, this kaleidoscopic mobility is not only licensed but positively celebrated. Viewed in this light, as a violation of approved norms of behaviour, the theatre resembles Bakhtin's concept of the 'carnivalesque':

As opposed to the official feast, one might say that carnival celebrates temporary liberation from the prevailing truth of the established order; it marks the suspension of all hierarchical rank, privileges, norms and prohibitions. Carnival was the true feast of time, the feast of becoming, change and renewal. It was hostile to all that was immortalized and complete.

Think how often Dickens introduces such iconoclastic presences into his novels, groups or individuals who, in Bakhtin's words, are 'opposed to all that is finished and polished, to all pomposity, to every ready-made solution in the sphere of thought and world outlook'. As already noted, Dickens's first fictional villain was the actor Jingle, a nimble practised rogue who duped the unworldly, staid, middle-class Pickwickians by a variety of impostures deliberately targeted at the pretensions of the individual Pickwickians—the 'poetic Snodgrass', the 'sporting Winkle', and Tupman the lover. Jingle performs each role, upstaging and outmanoeuvring the clubmen with his dizzying histrionic energy. It is one of *Pickwick*'s many substrata of irony that this group of solemn stock character-types, who owe so much of their constitution to the theatre, come face to face in

Jingle with the raw essence of protean theatricality. This invader from the world of theatre into the domestic sphere is the true spirit of the 'feast of becoming, change and renewal', a Lord of Misrule, 'opposed to all that is finished and polished': and he is cast as the villain. Here, on the chronological threshold of the Victorian age, there could hardly be a more paradigmatic confrontation between a role-conscious bourgeoisie and the world of the theatre.

The ambivalence about social mobility—the welcome, though disturbingly disorienting, opportunity for bettering oneself, changing one's social status—is related to feelings about the mutability of the self. Auerbach described theatricality as 'the ultimate deceitful mobility', perceived by the Victorians as a positive threat. This line of thinking has been developed in Joseph Litvak's study *Caught in the Act*. For Litvack sees in theatricality 'a set of shifting, contradictory energies' where the self is treated as 'not just a text but a contingent cluster of theatrical roles'. This is licensed, professionalized duplicity; actors, in Hazlitt's words, were 'the only honest hypocrites'.

Theatricality permeated ideas about the proprieties of social conduct, in perceptions and judgements about how people ordinarily express their feelings. English middle-class reserve by the middle of the century had become particularly pronounced. Emotional flamboyance was often demonized as a typically French or Mediterranean characteristic, or as the despised residue of Romantic 'sensibility'. It was seen as a symptom of unstable cultures where political and social disturbance was endemic: those who could not exercise control over their demeanour as individuals could not be expected to sustain a disciplined political constitution. What constituted 'theatricality' was therefore, in England, doubly anathematized, by association with the conduct of the *demi-monde* and with Continental habits of behaviour: in this climate Dickens's platform ambitions were distinctly risky. He himself confronted the implications of the terms 'theatrical', 'dramatic', and 'natural' in relation to French and English national characteristics when he reflected on a painting exhibition in Paris in 1856 and on some of the responses of his compatriots to the pictures displayed:

One of our most remarkable Insularities is a tendency to be firmly persuaded that what is not English is not natural. In the Fine Arts department of the French Exhibition, recently closed, we repeatedly heard, even from the more educated and reflective of our countrymen, that certain pictures which appeared to possess great merit—of which not the lowest was, that they possessed the merit of a vigorous and bold Idea—were all very well, but were 'theatrical'. Conceiving the difference between a dramatic picture and a theatrical picture, to be, that in the former case a story is strikingly told, without apparent consciousness of a spectator, and that in the latter case the groups are obtrusively conscious of a spectator, and are obviously dressed up, and doing (or not doing) certain things with an eye to the spectator, and not for the sake of the story; we sought in vain for this defect. Taking further pains then, to find out what was meant by the term theatrical, we found that the actions and gestures of the figures were not English. That is to say,—the figures expressing themselves in the vivacious manner natural in a greater or less degree to the whole great continent of Europe, were overcharged and out of truth, because they did not express themselves in the manner of our little Island.

The code of behaviour that required the middle-class Englishman to bear himself with 'external formality and constraint' (as Dickens characterizes the type) impressed itself partly by disparaging cultures where such manifestations of self-control were not observed. Continental forms of behaviour were stigmatized by association with the theatre. It was fine for 'vivacious' forms of self-expression to be seen on stage, but the standard currency of theatre in this respect was overdemonstrative artifice, the stylized manners of melodrama, and emphatically not to be confused with real life. Emotional restraint is thus naturalized as the behavioural norm in civilized life. Under such conditions of enforcedly muted self-expression (as Dickens perceived the case to be) the English were increasingly sensitized to those more unself-conscious expressions of intense feeling stimulated by events or situations. They (and Dickens means the middle classes primarily) avoided demonstrative displays of feeling, and tended to be censorious when they met them. When somebody in tears apologizes for 'making a scene' of himself, the phrase invoked is charged with the weight of all these anti-theatrical prejudices.

Dickens, however, is also making a finer distinction, between 'theatrical' and 'dramatic', and the distinction is not at all a matter of degree. 'Theatrical' conduct is conscious display, superficial spectacle. 'Dramatic' conduct is the natural, spontaneous expression of feeling unrelated to any consciousness of being observed. The two terms were sometimes used to identify what was distinctive about Dickens's own writings, as in these remarks by a reviewer of one of his Readings: 'He paints the outside man, not his inner nature. He is theatrical, not dramatic, in the sense in which Shakespeare is dramatic.'

The charges laid against theatre, therefore, demonize it and pro-letarianize it. It is culturally sited beyond the pale of middle-class respectability. It comes to be construed as a subculture dedicated to bohemianism, vagabondage, sexual promiscuity, overcharged expressions of passion, flamboyant artifice, intense role-playing. Dickens was always strongly attracted to most of these. However much he defended his Readings project to Forster on the grounds of its strengthening his relationship with his readership without forfeiting dignity, it was precisely the opportunity both to remain the distinguished author who had the affection of his community of readers ('Mr. Dickens' himself on the platform in evening dress) and at the same time to suspend that dignified identity in a series of full-blooded impersonations, in a display of mimetic promiscuity. The Readings up and down the country were quasi-theatrical binges legitimating his trespasses from drawing-room entertainment into a world of passionate extraversion, multivocal role-playing and vagabondage that had always excited him. It was a format in which he could reconcile domestic imperatives with forays into an imaginary *demi-monde*: these were worlds that had seemed mutually exclusive except perhaps in his home theatricals. He certainly expressed his sense, from time to time, that they were irreconcilable worlds, especially when a bout of these amateur theatricals had come to an end. Two days after his troupe had finished their tour with Boucicault's farce *Used Up*, in the summer of 1848, Dickens reported that he was 'very miserable. I loathe domestic hearths. I yearn to be a Vagabond.' Ten years later, when his own domestic hearth was in meltdown, and when he had become infatuated with Ellen Ternan, he looked forward to the prospect of exacting Reading tours as a distraction: 'I have a turning notion that the mere physical effort and change of the Readings would be good, as another means of bearing it.' It is analogous to his solitary nocturnal excursions into down-and-out east London, where he could become fleetingly an habitué of a milieu beyond the pale of Forster's world. He described such roaming as his 'amateur experience of Houselessness', to which he was so inclined that he thought he must be 'the descendant, at no great distance, of some irreclaimable tramp'. These were forays among people and into places that had for him, from earliest days, 'the attraction of repulsion'.

The Reading tours as an enterprise were thick with paradoxes: they represented a kind of vagabond flight from the domestic hearth, and yet they were occasions when Dickens tried to reconstitute domestic hearth in his emphasis on the audience's feeling itself to be a friendly community around a fireside. John Glavin has argued that for Dickens 'the lecture platform became the hearth-manqué': the Readings 'nostalgically appear to return to the world of communitarian readings but actually parody that experience, turning it into a commercial-profit-making enterprise where the passive audience can only be read to, and never read with.' There is a refreshing sceptical shrewdness here, but Glavin underestimates the extent to which the vitality of the Readings relied on the strength of rapport between Dickens and his audience. Really passive audiences froze him. Responsive, 'active' audiences galvanized him, and generated a current of sympathy that made these events, in their own way, miraculously communitarian.

These then were some of the ideas that lay behind the strong objections, from friends and family, to Dickens's decision to become a professional public Reader. The most vehement opponent was probably his closest friend, Forster. Here is how Forster, in the biography, put the case for the opposition: 'It might be a wild exaggeration to fear that he was in danger of being led to adopt the stage as a calling, but he was certainly about to place himself within reach of not a few of its drawbacks and disadvantages.' Dickens was patient and determined in meeting and overcoming Forster's objections, as he prepared his own mind for the new enterprise. The advice he wanted from his publisher, Evans, related to the likely impact of the Readings both on relations with his public and on the sales of his books: 'If it had any influence at all, would it be likely to be of a weakening or a strengthening kind?'

DEBUTS

What, in the event, *was* the public perception as Dickens made his debuts around the country as a professional performer? Did he strain that special relationship with the community of his devoted readers? *The Times* in its report on Dickens's 15 April 1858 charity Reading in London (on behalf of the Hospital for Sick Children) welcomed the news that the 'benevolent "reader" is at last about to employ his elocutionary talents for his own advantage'. Newspaper reviews of the First Series of Readings (August 1858–October 1859) give us an idea of how people felt about seeing Dickens come to them in person in order to give paid platform performances of his work. Some were positively hostile. In October 1858 the *Derby Mercury* attacked Dickens for making 'merchandise of himself', by associating himself with the likes of showmen such as T. P. Barnum and Albert Smith: 'Mr. Dickens has seriously damaged the future of his reputation and influence', and lowered 'the position of literary men in the social scale'. Others, well aware of the risk Dickens had taken, felt the general benefit to the public outweighed the possible lapse in propriety: 'however people may cavil at his taste in thus reading his own works, the sight of so successful a writer is a treat of so rich a character that we are inclined to accept the good without a murmur.' Here are some thoughtful and reasoned comments on the matter from a review in a Plymouth newspaper near the start of this Series:

It has been objected that there is something derogatory in a gentleman of Mr. Dickens' position in the field of literature, seeking to make money in a way which, until Mr. Thackeray set him the example, was certainly unusual. We cannot, however, see any reason why an author should be debarred from so ready a means of realizing substantial pecuniary results, if it so pleases him. It is a question which he has singly to settle with himself; if he is conscious that with this literary unreserve mingles no love of vulgar notoriety, he need not hesitate to add to the store in his purse, whilst he can, at the same time, contribute to the rational enjoyment of thousands of his countrymen and women. Many a good lesson has been taught in the silent perusal of his works, and that lesson is not likely to be less effectual when it is conveyed through the medium of the living voice of the author himself.

The writer does not commit himself or herself to any moral principles concerning paid public performances and social respectability, though acknowledges that others have made it an issue in this first year of Dickens's new career. It is left to the discretion of the literary 'gentleman' himself to decide whether he feels any impropriety in such an activity. As far as this reviewer is concerned there need be nothing wrong in it. On the contrary, the 'good lesson' to be derived from Dickens's writings remains a 'good lesson' whether it is read silently or recited aloud by its author. If Dickens's writings are a force for good, then one might reasonably argue that the more they are propagated, in whatever form (within the author's control), the better. The first word in that phrase 'rational enjoyment' protects the critic from seeming unduly permissive in what is evidently a controversial issue. The transition from private reading ('silent perusal') to public recital was not a problem in the view of this writer. However, the author's transition from study to platform was more risky. Again in 1858, another writer, James Friswell (one of Dickens's first biographers) expressed his reservations about Dickens's enterprise: 'Mr. Dickens, always fond of imagining a close, a very close, perhaps a too close, connexion between himself and his public, has, as we have seen, lifted the green curtain which generally hangs before an author's desk.' His hesitant criticism is levelled both at the move to public performance and at Dickens's lifelong preoccupation with seeing his readership as a kind of close companionship. Although he

may disapprove of both, Friswell at least recognizes the continuity
and consistency of Dickens's peculiar relationship with his readers.

As to Dickens's bringing himself personally before a large public
by means of the Readings, the *Liverpool Daily Post*, again near the
start of this tour, made the point, at some length, that Dickens was
already a very public person in England:

Mr. Dickens has not hidden himself. In theatres, at 'soirees,' at meetings,
he is well known by 'sight' through the country [. . .]. The risk Mr. Dickens
ran was loss of caste—the loss implied in the phrase 'too cheap.'

However, continues the article, Dickens is by no means an indis-
criminate wooer of popularity. He will not, for example, accept
aristocratic patronage: 'The lion will not be fed or petted by great
ladies who would deck their saloon with a man of genius simply as
an attraction.' Dickens's public appearances as a speech-maker or
as an amateur actor are not instances of an inferior talent imposing
itself vulgarly on as wide an audience as possible: Dickens after all
was 'the best after-dinner speaker of his day', and 'so admirable an
actor that no "professional" regards him as an amateur'. In other
words, his talents earned him the right to public exposure, and he
went before his public only in those contexts where the exercising of
such talents was appropriate. So far, so good.

These present 'readings', however, are a considerable enlargement of the
experiment. The author here ceases to write, but begins to read—as a
method of making money for himself. The book that he sells for a shilling
[per monthly instalment] he reads for five shillings a head. This is a novelty
in literature and in the annals of 'entertainments' [. . .]. In our epoch, it
is at first sight an egotistical and conceited proceeding for a gentleman
to declaim his own copy to an audience. To bring out his own jokes, by
dramatic jerks of the voice; to elaborate his own sentiments, by touching
deflections; to look dark and profound at the terrible passages, to shed or
make believe to shed, tears at the sad bits; and, then, with a knowing look at
the reserved seats, to wait for the expected titter—all this has its equivocal
aspect, as affecting the dignity of a man of whose self-respect and of whose
title to our respect none of us doubt.

Since the writer raises specific questions about ticket prices and earnings, let us just be clear about that before returning to the reviewer's criticisms. The 'five shillings a head' mentioned here is unfair. Four or five shillings was usually the top price only, for reserved seats in the stalls. Unreserved seats in moderately good positions were two shillings or half-a-crown. The prices for these two categories fluctuated. Not so the cheapest seats. Unreserved one-shilling tickets—the same price as for a monthly number of a Dickens novel—were always available elsewhere in the hall. Dickens consistently made a point of keeping aside cheaper seats for the poorer members of the audience. Even so, a shilling was not that cheap. A London labourer in the 1860s earned about a £1 a week (= 20 shillings). A London artisan earned nearly twice that amount.

Dickens certainly made money in these inaugural Readings, as he was to throughout his career as a Reader. For his 25 provincial Readings in August 1858 he cleared a thousand guineas after paying off many of the travel expenses. His annual income from his writings (excluding his two journals) over the last 25 years of his life averaged just over £2,900. By 1867 he could top that sum by giving just 50 two-hour Readings—say, a couple of months' intensive touring. In his four-and-a-half-month American tour, where he gave about 75 Readings, he netted nearly £19,000. His total earnings from the Readings amounted to about £45,000 (his total estate at his death was valued at £93,000).

Dickens's uncontained relish for the daily and weekly profits from the Readings was communicated in letters to family and close friends, and many of those remarks have only recently come to light. The family evidently felt it an unseemly enthusiasm. When Mamie Dickens and Georgina Hogarth published a three-volume selection from Dickens's letters in the 1880s they discreetly suppressed those passages where he gloated in detail on his sensational earnings. These censorings remained silently incorporated in the Nonesuch edition of Dickens's letters (1938), and were eventually revealed in the twelve-volume Pilgrim edition of the letters. Dickens justified his enthusiasm for the financial rewards likely to come from the

American tour by referring to his family commitments. He said that although his 'worldly circumstances were very good', he was saddled with 'his wife's income to pay [Catherine's yearly allowance was £600]—a very expensive position to hold—and my boys with a curse of limpness about them.' He insisted that he didn't 'want money' (meaning he didn't lack money), but still, 'at 55 or 56, the likelihood of making a very great addition to one's capital in half a year, is an immense consideration.'

The Liverpool reviewer quoted above, however, seems not to be too troubled about Dickens's Reading for profit. After all, to pay money for having a novel read to you by its author rather than for reading it yourself seems to come to much the same thing, a simple commercial transaction. He is prepared to concede the value of the Readings as measured by the popular reception: 'There was nothing wrong, by itself, in his reading to a room-full what he had written for the whole public; and if the room-full most assuredly liked the reading, what more had to be said?' The more pressing issues of taste and propriety in this reviewer's opinion had to do both with the 'theatrical' (rather than 'dramatic') behaviour on the platform and with the direct manipulation of the audience by the author, his more naked soliciting of their emotional responses by 'dramatic jerks of the voice', 'touching deflections', and tears.

There are two points to be made in response to this criticism of Dickens's platform style (criticism not generally echoed in reviews of the Readings): both of them concern the relationship between Dickens's style as a novelist and that as a Reader. In the first place, the heavy histrionic underscoring of mood, whether facetious or pathetic, to which the reviewer objects is in effect an extension or amplification of Dickens's characteristic rhetorical practice in the novels themselves: it is not peculiar to the way he projected his work in the Readings. The archness, the heavy sentimentalism, the sharp tonal switches, the rib-digging enjoyment of his own humour—these are all familiar Dickensian trademarks in the fiction. It would be strange if they did not translate into the platform performance of the same material. The second point somewhat undercuts the first. As we shall see in a later chapter, what struck many people about Dickens's Reading style in the 1860s was the relatively low-key naturalism of the narrative sections, the lack of staginess in his performance style. It is difficult to know whether the Liverpool reviewer was particularly fastidious on such points of acting style, or whether Dickens did indeed ham it up more during these first tours than in the later Readings. Anti-theatrical prejudices were much allayed, in general, by the realization that Dickens refined his histrionic style to the point where he could hardly be accused of being 'theatrical'. He wanted to come across as a gentleman in evening dress reading to a group of friends, thereby preserving as much of the drawing-room manner as was consistent with his being on a public stage before an audience of a thousand or two. The social composition of those audiences thus became an important indicator of the success of these aims, as well as confirmation that Dickens's venture had not jeopardized his standing with the community of his readers. Newspaper reports of provincial Readings often made a point of categorizing the kind of audience attending these occasions, as if to test the non-theatrical credentials of such events: 'The audience was highly respectable, and consisted in part of persons who would have considered the performance [of 'Christmas Carol', at Preston, in December 1861] an improper one if Mr. Dickens had worn a fancy dress and had been supported by others similarly attired "in another place" — to quote parliamentary language.' At a Reading in Wolverhampton in 1858 the reviewer was pleased 'to observe many clergymen among the audience', though that should not have been surprising: 'Mr. Dickens has ever used his powers for good purposes [and he is] one of the great moral teachers of the day.' However, some felt that since Dickens had been able to draw such audiences he ought to be all the more sensitive about the kind of material he performed—witness this review of a Reading (in Cork in 1858) of 'Mrs. Gamp': 'To conceive a highly respectable assembly being entertained for the greater part of an evening by Mr. DICKENS giving a miserable imitation of two old women using *low English slang* was really disgusting at this enlightened period.'

It has already been mentioned that Dickens was making his inaugural Readings tour in the summer of 1858, in the shadow of his broken marriage and its attendant publicity. By and large, the provincial newspapers were generous in their muted comments on this, though the coincidence of these two major developments in Dickens's life must have caused embarrassment. For example, the Huddersfield newspapers for 4 September announced Dickens's imminent arrival in town to give his Reading at the same time as printing his letter about his estrangement from his wife.

If the novels of Dickens were held to be a force for good—for promoting benevolent feelings and social reform—then the Readings would surely reinforce that. As a reviewer of Dickens's 1858 Reading of the 'Carol' at Leeds observed, 'Mr. Dickens is performing a good service by his readings, diffusing sentiments of kindliness and benevolence amongst all classes, whilst he affords entertainment in a most unexceptionable manner.'

It is possible that in addition to all the other reasons adduced by Forster and others to discourage Dickens from going professional, there was the question of the Readings derogating from the artistic status of the writer. According to one historian of professional theatre in this period, there was 'a widespread assumption that the actor was inferior to the writer, just as the singer or musician was inferior to the composer [. . .] based upon the belief that the actor or musician was not of himself capable of artistic originality.' This, of course, could hardly be held against Dickens the Reader.

Forster's biography of Dickens appeared some fifteen years after he had argued with Dickens over the propriety of his taking to the platform as a professional Reader. In the early 1870s Forster related that episode without any sense that he had changed his views over the intervening years. At almost exactly the same date, 1872, Charles Kent published his book, *Charles Dickens as a Reader*, celebrating the triumph of the Readings as a consolidation of the relationship Dickens had with his readers, and as contributing to an enlargement of that community. When he came to describe the time of Dickens's decision to read for money, he mentioned, contemptuously, 'certain fantastic notions as to its derogating, in some inconceivable way, from the dignity of authorship'. What must Forster have thought when reading that, especially since Kent's book was dedicated to him?

The Readings indeed confirmed that sense of a community of interests and mutual friendship between Dickens and his public. By the end of the 1860s this was publicly acknowledged: 'Not only in this country, but in America, he has strengthened the relations which exist between himself and his readers [. . .] and by the magic of his eloquence and the influence of his art, created fresh bonds of sympathy which will prove as lasting as their existence.' For his Dublin audience in 1869, according to a reporter who was there, 'His reading was not looked upon as a performance, but as a friendly meeting longed for by people to whom he has been kind.' These feelings were warmly reciprocated by Dickens. What he said to his last audience in America, at the Farewell Reading in New York on 20 April 1868, he might have said to any of his audiences, anywhere, or indeed to his vast readership: 'I shall never recall you as a mere public audience, but rather as a host of personal friends.'

2

Reading, Reciting, Acting

Mr. Dickens [. . .] then proceeded to read, or it might be said to recite, the well-known story—to recite it, for it was only at long intervals that even a casual glance at the book he held was at all necessary.

Belfast News-Letter, 28 August 1858

[A Dickens Reading] is not quite acting, and yet it is a great deal more than reading, as the 'recitation' of every public reader tends more or less to become.

Bath Chronicle, 14 February 1867

What is at issue in distinguishing between the experience of reading a novel silently to oneself and the experience of having it read aloud, between the solitary consumption of fiction and the recitation to someone else or to larger groups, between reading from a script and reciting from memory? Where can the line be drawn between acting and dramatic public recitation?

Like many people, the newspaper reviewers quoted above were puzzled as to how to classify the Readings. Dickens himself comically recognized the problems inherent in calling his performances 'Readings': '[People] don't quite understand beforehand what it is, I think, and expect a man to be sitting down in some corner, droning away like a mild bagpipe.' But Dickens read 'as if he were not reading, but telling his story plainly, and without apparent effort, to a circle of friends'. His performances crossed back and forth over the borderlines between reading, recitation, spontaneous storytelling, and acting. Before we look more closely at the mode of his particular performance, I want to consider some of the historical examples of reading in public in the Victorian period. By identifying the variety of contemporary reading practices then current, we may mark out the generic range against which Dickens's project was to be assessed and categorized.

COMMUNAL READING PRACTICES

How did Dickens's vast illiterate readership experience his novels? For thousands of people, what one might call 'their Dickens' came to them mediated through someone else's voice. Effectively it was less 'their' Dickens than the Dickens of their obliging interpreter. They listened to another voice inflecting the voice of Dickens that came off the page. The pages of text in the monthly instalment became a performance script. Those unable to read knew Dickens's texts only as a series of oral performances, whether in the form of a solo recitation or condensed into a stage adaptation. For them the publication of a Dickens story really happened when first it was read out loud: the production of the material printed instalment or volume—the solid commodity—was only a first stage, not the final stage, in the full multi-media publication process of Dickens's fiction; and people of different classes and backgrounds encountered it at different points in that extended process. There were several institutions catering for this more diverse and protracted form of publication. We will take three: Penny Readings, subscription reading groups, and family reading circles.

Penny Readings began in the 1850s, inspired by Samuel Taylor's public readings of William Howard Russell's Crimean War dispatches for *The Times* in the market square of Hanley in Staffordshire. This developed into his 'Literary and Musical Entertainments for the People' in 1856, at the town hall, for which a penny was charged. Between October 1857 and April 1858 nine Staffordshire towns were offering Penny Readings, with a total admission of 60,000—70,000.

Dickens's decision in 1858 to go professional caught the swelling tide of enthusiasm for public Reading entertainments.

Penny Readings for the poor were held in village and town halls and schoolrooms, as well as in Literary and Mechanics' Institutes. The Penny Reading, which became particularly popular in the 1860s (the decade of Dickens's greatest successes as a public Reader), might consist of an evening of songs, instrumental solos, and recitations. Performers were usually amateur enthusiasts. The low price of admission and a policy (in most instances) of 'No Reserved Seats' made these entertainments very attractive for the large local working-class population. Dickens joined with Scott, Tennyson, Hood, and Byron in being among the most popular authors for inclusion in Penny Reading repertoires. Joseph Chamberlain used to read the episode of Sam Weller's Valentine for Penny Reading evenings.

Special anthologies for Penny Readings were published in this decade, as well as advice on establishing and conducting them. The most substantial publication was edited by Joseph Carpenter, *Penny Readings in Prose and Verse*, a serial publication. Ten volumes of these *Penny Readings* accumulated over the years 1865–7. *Christmas Penny Readings*, a collection of 'Original Sketches', was published by George Fenn in 1867. Thomas Hood the Younger produced *Cassell's Penny Readings* between 1866 and 1868, with illustrations by, amongst others, H. K. Browne; and Hood also published *Tom Hood's Comic Readings, in Prose and Verse* in 1869 as a 'Companion' to Carpenter's *Penny Readings*. 'H.G.' offered *A Few Words on Penny Readings: with hints for their formation and management* in 1864. Once again we note that Dickens certainly chose the right decade in which to pitch his own Readings.

The explosion of popularity of the Penny Readings in the 1860s is hard to account for. *The Times* observed in 1868:

Readers are abundant; there is not a literary institution that does not in the course of a year publish a programme of entertainment in which some plays or poems to be 'read' by some person of celebrity, general or local, do not hold a prominent place, and for the innocent amusement of the poor 'penny readings' in the parish schoolroom are now commonly encouraged by every clergyman who takes a practical interest in his flock.

The mention of literary institutions is a clue to the ancestry of public Readings. Courses and lectures given in Mechanics' Institutes up and down the country proliferated in the early nineteenth century. As one historian of the practice of platform Readings put it:

As the century wore on, those who came to the platform to educate no longer dominated the scene. Sometimes entertainers read from the works of popular authors; eventually they were replaced by authors who first served on committees to plan the various programs. Occasionally, these authors delivered lectures. Finally, however, they began to read from their own poetry and fiction.

Another historian, H. P. Smith, noting the project's connection with adult education, associated it also with a revolt against the cult of 'useful knowledge'. Dickens's first public Reading, in December 1853, was to raise funds for the newly established Birmingham and Midland Institute, and in his speech on the occasion he spoke of the prospect of its being 'a great Educational Institution . . . educational of the feelings as well as of the reason'. His Reading of the 'Carol' was designed precisely to entertain and to educate the feelings of his listeners. This declaration was made just months before he began to work on *Hard Times*. He was always hostile to the 'hard facts' educational ideology where it had come to dominate such institutions and to make them sometimes ashamed of mounting programmes of pure entertainment. This was amusingly sketched in his Uncommercial Traveller essay, 'Dullborough Town' (1860), when he visited Dullborough's desolate Mechanics' Institution. In looking at the lists of lectures advertised for the Institution (on gas, the Solar System, the geological periods, the steam engine, etc), 'I fancied I detected a shyness in admitting that human nature when at leisure has any desire whatever to be relieved and diverted.' In the Library records of book borrowers he finds 'a painfully apologetic return of 62 offenders who had read Travels, Popular Biography, and mere Fiction descriptive of the aspirations of the hearts and souls of mere human creatures like themselves'. Dickens's Readings, so often performed in these kinds of institutions, aimed to 'educate the feelings'. At least one observer of Dickens's Readings (in *The Critic* in September 1858) recognized the powerful influence for good that Dickens could exercise through his Readings, both in educating the 'emotional sympathies' and in touching all classes of society:

Mr. Dickens scarce knows the force of the engine which he holds in his hands—has scarcely mastered the scope and destination of his great design. He is now delighting elegant wearers of opera-cloaks and carriers of bouquets, dangling loungers who come to satisfy an idle curiosity, and stout well-to-do middle-class citizens, who have been blessed with the taught ability to read and write. Descend a little lower in the social scale, and we come upon a land containing thousands—nay, millions—who are only to be reached through their eyes and ears; to whom a printed book is a black, blurred, mysterious mass, notwithstanding many Acts of Parliament, educational commissions, and school-houses remarkable for their imposing style of architecture. Yet these people are men and women with hearts and souls—people willing to be taught, if they can be taught easily [. . .] ready to pay for being taught—people who know little, and never will know much, of moral principles, and who can only be reached and improved through their emotional sympathies.

The year after Dickens's 1853 visit, Macready gave a Reading at the Birmingham and Midland Institute, also as a fund-raising event, and Bulwer Lytton was also invited to perform (though declined). As long as Readings retained their 'platform' format, and were performed in town halls and Mechanics' Institutes, rather than amplifying into 'theatre' entertainment, they remained vestigially associated with an educational context. It took Dickens to insist on the value of such events as *emotionally* educative.

H. P. Smith also noted Joseph Carpenter's statement on the title page of his *Penny Readings*: 'for the use of members of literary and scientific institutions, recreation societies, mutual improvement associations, mechanics' institutes, young men's societies, working men's clubs and all kindred societies'. One of the forms of 'mutual improvement' offered by Penny Readings would have been a training in elocution for the working man. The 'H.G.' mentioned earlier claimed that 'the formation of a working men's elocution class will be found indispensable to the sustaining of readings for the people'.

In its October 1868 review (cited earlier) of the launch of Dickens's Farewell Series, *The Times* offered a brief history of 'readings': throughout the review 'readings' was always in quotation marks, as if to suggest that the term had not quite yet been naturalized into the language, and by extension that the genre had not been fully accommodated culturally. *The Times* referred to Charles Kemble's public Reading of *Cymbeline* (in 1844) as the first significant instance of what it felt had since become an epidemic, across all classes of society.

Whatever the educational and entertainment value of these events, the Penny Readings had certain disadvantages when compared with the smaller reading groups. They tended to restrict the range of both the readership and the Dickens repertoire. Where the readership was concerned, the halls could be intimidatingly rowdy for women. Women also found it hard to leave the family home and young children for an evening, and perhaps harder still to find the money to pay for their entry, especially if their husbands and sons had already committed family pennies to the event. Sometimes special efforts might be made to ensure that women had an equal opportunity to attend these entertainments. Thus Charles Kingsley (according to his wife's later recollections), when he organized a series of Penny Readings in the 1860s, 'arranged that, while the men and boys paid their pennies, the widows and poor over-burdened mothers should have free admittance'. Where the Dickens repertoire was concerned, the Penny Readings tended to select particular sections of particular novels for performance, and persevered with the popular items. Thus, unlike the smaller reading groups, which might make their way slowly through a whole novel, the Penny Reading was often neither a forum particularly welcoming for all the different age and gender groups, nor one for following a particular novel through its serialization.

This last point raises an interesting aspect of the consumption of the part-issue novels. Just as the reviews of a Dickens novel, while it was being serialized, excerpted generous passages for display and thereby began the process of promoting favourite scenes and characters, so the Penny Readings abstracted what were generally thought to be the highlights—character portraits and episodes that would work particularly well in performance, regardless of the larger narrative context for those scenes. It was one of several processes in the formation of a popular Dickens canon. Other processes included the re-shaping of the novels and Christmas books as they were scripted for contemporary stage adaptations, and the market for free-standing engravings and paintings of favourite episodes and characters. One can see that the fiction, continually circulating in a variety of fragmentary forms, media, and modes throughout Dickens's life, was being modified and refocused in response to popular prejudices. From the time the instalments of his novels first reached the bookstalls, Dickens was being rapidly and continuously anthologized. The *Pickwick* Trial, for example, and the Cratchit family Christmas were favourite candidates for such popular canonization: the Trial had already featured on many a Penny Reading programme some time before Dickens added it to his repertoire in 1858. (By 1869, commented one reviewer of Dickens's own performance of 'Bardell and Pickwick', 'it had been done almost to the death.') All those finished, prefaced, well-bound novels had to compete culturally with their own anthological offspring.

Another form of communal reading took place in subscription reading groups. These were ad hoc establishments, meeting usually in private homes or shops. In one example, Shelton Mackenzie, one of Dickens's first biographers, reported his finding in a locksmith's shop a group of twenty men and women who had clubbed together to pay twopence to rent out a monthly part of a Dickens novel from a circulating library (they were unable to afford the shilling retail cost of the part) so that one of them could read it aloud. In another example, John Forster tells of the elderly charwoman who was unable to read but who was keeping up with *Dombey and Son* as it appeared in its monthly instalments: 'it turned out that she lodged at a snuff-shop kept by a person named Douglas, where there were several other lodgers; and that on the first Monday of every month there was a Tea, and the landlord read the month's number of *Dombey*, those only of the lodgers who subscribed to the tea partaking of that luxury, but all having the benefit of the reading.'

There were hundreds of such small, informal circles around the country, enabling the poor to listen to what they might not be able to read for themselves. This was not just a matter of organized neighbourhood circles: it happened within the home, within the smaller family unit, and certainly by the last third of the century was widespread. Between 1870 and 1918, according to one survey, half of all working-class interviewees indicated that reading aloud was practised in the house where they were raised. Sometimes such public Readings of Dickens for the poor were spontaneously launched. In December 1843 Frederick Evans, at that time one of the partners in the printing firm used by Dickens, sent a copy of the newly published *Christmas Carol* to his mother in Bristol. She showed it to a friend, James Staples, who was staying with her over Christmas. It was read by all in the house with great enthusiasm. 'What a pity so great a pleasure should be confined to so small a circle', reflected Staples. He resolved to read it in public to 'a class amongst whom such literature never circulated'. So he did, to a large audience of the poor in the neighbourhood, at Bristol's Domestic Mission Institution. The reading was such a success that he had to repeat it. A few months later he wrote to Dickens to tell him of the event. Dickens replied:

it would have given me heartfelt satisfaction to have been in your place when you read my little Carol to the Poor in your neighbourhood. I have great faith in the poor; to the best of my ability I always endeavour to present them in a favourable light to the rich; and I shall never cease, I hope, until I die, to advocate their being made as happy and as wise as the circumstances of their condition, in its utmost improvement, will admit of their becoming. I mention this to assure you of two things. Firstly, that I try to deserve their attention; and secondly, that any such marks of their approval and confidence as you relate to me are most acceptable to my feelings, and go at once to my heart.

Years later, after Dickens's death, Staples sent Dickens's letter together with an explanatory letter of his own, to Forster, for the biography. He remarked to Forster, 'I imagine I was among the first, if not the first, to read the Carol in public. Penny readings had not become an institution in those days.'

The oral transmission of a Dickens novel was not at all restricted to the poorer classes of society. Among the literate population, and among those who could afford quite easily to buy the monthly parts, it was often the practice to have family readings of the instalments as they came out, and these might sometimes be quite elaborate recitations. The playwright Herman Merivale told of one such family routine:

My grandfather's whole family of sons and daughters (a very large one), used to cluster round him to hear number after number read out to them. He always studied them himself for an hour or two, in order to be able to read them aloud with decent gravity, and his apoplectic struggles and occasional shouts made them feel bad—longing for their turn.

All in all, it may well be that there were more people who first *heard* or *watched* their Dickens than who *read* it themselves. As Philip Collins has remarked of this period, 'many people met contemporary literature as a group or communal, rather than an individual, experience'. This community emphasis has an important bearing on the status of Dickens's public Readings. When he took to the public platform with his books, he could both rely on a ready-made audience for Reading performances and draw on traditions of communal reading aloud.

Reading aloud from a printed script in drawing room, shop, village hall, or Mechanics' Institute was not the only way in which Dickens's fiction was, as it were, projected as a communal experience.

Deborah Vlock has eloquently argued a case for seeing as illusory and obstructive those conventional generic distinctions between theatre and the novel ('public' and 'private' arenas for cultural consumption):

The tropes of the theatre gave voice to other forms of artistic and popular expression; people read novels, newspapers, social criticism—indeed, just about everything worth reading—through the lens of popular performance. In other words, the 'drama' was not supplanted by the novel in the nineteenth century but merged with it, enabling the novel to exist[. . .]. What this means is that the Victorian novel did not really resemble the discrete package Miller [a reference to D. A. Miller's *The Novel and the Police*] imagines as privately and personally consumed, but was loose and fluid—particularly when published serially, as so many novels, including Dickens' were—and attentive to the theatrical developments which were at once its source and its competition.

Reading privately is never quite isolated from the communal reception of a novel. As reader-reception theorists have long insisted, private reading is always inflected by the reader's sense of a shared culture (this includes, but is broader than, Vlock's notion of everything being read 'through the lens of popular performance'). The writer in turn is drawing from that shared culture and playing to it. Dickens, more than most, as a narrator projects his consciousness that he is addressing a mass readership. This experience is sharpened by the sense induced by serial publication that thousands of people are coming to the same point in the unfolding story at the same time. So, as we saw in the last chapter, in that sense too, of shared synchronized reading, people met Victorian literature as a group or communal experience.

PUBLIC RECITALISTS

In *Our Mutual Friend*, Sloppy, to the great entertainment of Betty Higden, reads aloud the newspaper Police Reports. He adopts different voices in rendering the exchanges between magistrates, plaintiff, and defendants. These Reports formally lent themselves to dramatic recitation. They were partially cast in dialogue form, like a play-script. Here is an example, from 'Police Report Extraordinary' (reporting from Mansion House), in *The Morning Chronicle* of 13 December 1834:

Lord Winchester [presiding magistrate]: Ah, poor Mr.Barlow! I am afraid you are not up to the tricks of the swell mob. Why, if Ikey had kept possession of Mr.Bull's shop another fortnight, he and his brother thieves would have reduced him to beggary, and got possession of his property. And Ikey would, perhaps, have made himself head-clerk in your room, Mr.Barlow.

William Barlow: Oh Lord! Oh Lord! Oh Lord!

Lord Winchester: Well, Ikey Duke, what have you got to say in your defence?

Ikey Duke: Vy, your Vortship, this here gemman's clerk haggrawates his hoffenses by hinsinuating that it wore my fault that I comed into the shop. But the fact is, your Vortship, as how I wore freely hired by he for to sarve as head-shopman.

Shorthand enabled the penny-a-line reporters to amplify local details of recorded speech in this way. The Report is drawn and coloured for recitation in a variety of voices. It is a piece of drama, encouraging even the silent reader to *hear* the proceedings at Mansion House. In the adjacent column of the same issue of the *Chronicle* is a feature entitled 'Street Sketches.—*No.V*'. Its subtitle is 'Brokers and Marine Store Shops': its author, the young Dickens, signs himself 'BOZ'. The generically anomalous Police Report, designed for voices, half-theatre and half-reportage, consorts with Dickens's generically anomalous 'Sketches', which are also half-reportage and half-imaginative forays, fiction mixed with documentary, alive with the din of street voices, the precise accents of early nineteenth-century London. This kind of writing by Dickens and his fellow journalists was designed to appeal to the ear of the reader, whether or not it was actually recited aloud by gifted readers like Sloppy. The reader could *listen* to London in browsing through the columns of these journals. They were scripted temptations to performance, even for those sitting alone in their armchairs. This is implicit in the points made by Deborah Vlock on the fluidity of the Victorian novel, its ready permeability, in the reading experience, by 'the theatrical developments which were at once its source and its competition'. Thus, as she contends, 'a Dickens novel is not exclusively (and privately) literary, but expresses itself in three dimensions, so to speak: visually and vocally as well as narratively'.

The point of all this is to indicate the blurred dividing line between private reading and public recitation. That blurring is evident in the historical record of Victorian popular cultural practices (Penny Readings, subscription groups, family reading groups), and we do well to bear in mind that generic distinctions between the various ways in which novels came to their readers were much looser. When Dickens arrived on the public Reading scene the issues became even more complex: a private man reading in public; an author devising a new way to publish his own works; a gentleman exhibiting his talents for money in public; a natural actor occasionally bursting through the constrictions of a sedate drawing-room form of entertainment. But he was exceptional in so many respects: 'Hear Dickens, and die,' *The Scotsman* proclaimed in 1868:

You will never live to hear anything of its kind so good. There has been nothing so perfect, in their way, as those readings ever offered to an English audience. Great actors and actresses—Mrs. Siddons herself among them—have read Shakespeare to us; smaller actors, like the Mathews, elder and younger, John Parry, and others, have given 'entertainments' of a half-literary, half-histrionic order; eminent authors, like Coleridge, and Hazlitt, and Sydney Smith, and Thackeray, have read lectures—and many living authors lecture still—but all those appearances, or performances, or whatever else they may be called, are very different from Mr. Dickens' appearances and performances as a reader.

Dickens was one of many performing soloists at the Reading desk, but, as this review observes, his particular kind of Reading was *sui generis*, a highly individual instance of an increasingly popular and diverse form of entertainment. The most succinct and stimulating account of public Reading practices in the Victorian period is Philip Collins's 1972 article, 'Reading Aloud: A Victorian Metier'. Much of the following section draws gratefully on that article.

Reading aloud at home or at the houses of friends was much practised, as we have seen. Dickens himself began as a domestic reader of this kind, excited to have the chance to read aloud his recent Christmas Book or the latest instalment of *Dombey* to family and friends. Domestic readers to their small intimate groups would often have a strong sense of performance, even within such a private context, and would make an effort to project the text with some panache. Collins gives a number of eyewitness accounts of Tennyson's powerful, rhythmical readings, which might sometimes last for a couple of hours. William Morris also used to regale his patient friends with long recitations from his sagas. But the move from such domestic recitals to the public platform was a huge and dangerous one to make.

On the public stage, famous actors and actresses offered Readings: among them Mrs Siddons, Charles Kemble and his daughter Fanny, and Henry Irving. The repertoire for such performers was usually drawn from Shakespeare, though Irving's pièce de résistance was held to be his thrilling recitation of Thomas Hood's 'The Dream of Eugene Aram'. These, however, were public figures from the world of theatre. It was a different matter for those distinguished writers who took to the platform to offer lectures or Readings or some combination of the two. When Dickens gave his first public Reading, for charity, in December 1853, *The Times* remarked that it was an unprecedented thing in those days to hear authors reading their own works in public. However, just over four years later *The Illustrated London News*, welcoming Dickens to the professional Reading circuit, remarked that 'All our literati seem inclined to become "oral instructors"'.

While Dickens's performances were exceptional, the tradition of public Readings of literature was fairly well established, as one historian of the genre, Theresa Murphy, has demonstrated in an essay on what was termed 'Interpretation', in the third quarter of the nineteenth century. The sheer number of published manuals on the art of public speaking and literary recitation in America and Britain in this period was, according to Murphy, extraordinary; and it is clear from her study that while Dickens's genius as a performer was, of course, unique, 'it is also true that he reflected the taste, the teaching, and the technique of his contemporaries'.

There was a wide range of solo recitalist practices. I will give as an example one of the more bizarre performances of this kind. *The Times* of 15 March 1870 carried a little box advertisement for 'MR CHARLES DICKENS'S FAREWELL READING, in St. James's-hall'. It was the very last Reading he gave. Immediately below that there was another small advertisement for an event the following night: 'MR. J. M. BELLEW'S HAMLET, St. George's-hall, Langham-Place'. Bellew's *Hamlet* was one of the most extravagant Reading performances ever staged. Philip Collins describes the event:

On the stage, a company of actors are performing *Hamlet*; scenery 'novel and complete', according to the advertisements; costumes, as a reviewer noted, 'startlingly new but archaeologically correct'. But the most startling thing about the performance is that, although the actors' lips are moving, no sound emerges. Instead, down in the orchestra pit, gesticulating in unison or competition with the actors on the stage, is a soloist who speaks all the words.

The soloist was John Chippendale Montesquieu Bellew, a flamboyant clergyman turned professional Reader (not a radical metamorphosis). 'Poetry on Wheels' he called himself. He should have been the model for Mr Wopsle, the orotund church clerk in *Great Expectations* who converts to 'Mr. Waldengarver' for an acting career in London. Bellew had devised an entertainment that stopped just short of full theatre. He was an energetic recitalist of poetry and prose as well as drama, and could offer, among other attractions, a full-length *Macbeth* Reading, with an orchestral accompaniment (but without miming actors), and, in the year of Dickens's death, selections from *The Mystery of Edwin Drood*. Bellew seemed to some professional actors to set a benchmark as a public Reader, and especially in the handling of narrative was sometimes regarded as Dickens's superior. In its meditation on whether Dickens's performance could legitimately be termed a 'Reading' (see the epigraph to this chapter) the *Bath Chronicle* invoked the example of Bellew: 'Mr. Bellew for instance is a fine reader or reciter, whose delivery of many passages of poetry or prose it is difficult to distinguish from acting.' Actors could become public Readers: Readers could aspire to acting. Actors, Readers, and writers began to throng the platform to offer these 'half-literary, half-histrionic' entertainments from the mid-century onwards.

Does it matter whether the entertainment was classified as a 'Reading' or a 'recitation', or a kind of 'acting'? It did matter, for several reasons, and the careful negotiation between the different modes of transmission implied in these terms was important in determining the nature and success of Dickens's public Readings. As *The Times* had remarked in 1868, there were Readers of all kinds, in abundance, in this period. The popularity of this type of entertainment brought about a surge of professional Readers and lecturers, appealing to a relatively new audience constituency. The Penny Readings had now and again invited celebrities to perform, but we are concerned here with the larger-scale commercial enterprises in the big cities. In October 1862 *The Saturday Review* took stock of this phenomenon in a substantial article, 'Readings'. It had distinctly mixed feelings about what was happening. In general it welcomed the professional actor to the Reading circuit and deplored the untrained amateur who chose to foist his underdeveloped gifts on the public—'the intrinsic repulsiveness of readings by obscure persons'. Much of the article is an attempt to account for the contemporary popularity of Readings, and this it does by identifying a new kind of audience—or perhaps an old audience that had temporarily gone into self-inflicted isolation from most theatrical entertainments. There was a large and influential class of people (themselves influenced by Evangelical puritanism and notions of genteel respectability) for whom, as we saw in the last chapter, the theatre was an utterly unwholesome place to visit. A dramatic Reading, however, was an entertainment, whether in hall or theatre, that could be considered respectable: 'there are people who will hear actors read and will not see them act [...] grounded in their belief that acting is wicked, while reading is harmless.' A Reading is a 'doleful thing enough', *The Review* continued, but at least it ensured that those puritanical people who abstained from theatre-going could go to hear recitations of Shakespeare and other writers, and thus not develop 'utter ignorance of the greatest British classics'.

The *Saturday Review* was sharply critical of what it felt to be the hypocrisy of this 'semi-puritanical code', but it had identified a key feature of the new popularity of this form of entertainment. Its diagnosis is supported by George R. Sims, author of one of the greatest Victorian popular ballads, 'It is Christmas Day in the Workhouse':

In my youth and young manhood [1860s and '70s] there was a very considerable portion of the public who would not enter a theatre. The old prejudice against it still survived, and was by no means confined to the Nonconformist Conscience. And so there was always a plentiful supply of entertainment *arranged in such a way as to ease the scruples of the conscientious objector.* [my italics]

The *Athenaeum*, reviewing Bellew's *Hamlet*, confirms this explanation for the popularity of Readings as quasi-theatrical events that were morally safe: 'Moralists know well, however, the fascination exercised upon the mind by whatever is prohibited, and the class to which the theatre is tabooed forms the principal support of the semi-dramatic performances now in vogue.' The reviewer makes the additional point that Bellew's Readings 'have intellectual subtlety, which places them in complete contrast with the dramatic exposi- tions of living actors, and commends them to the attentive notice of Shakspearean [sic] students'. So, not only do Bellew's Readings allow a morally fastidious audience to (almost) see a play, they also afford a subtler interpretation of Shakespeare than could be offered by professional actors. Readings therefore were 'a sort of compromise, and many people who conscientiously think it wrong to go to a theatre have no scruples about attending readings'. They constituted a genre of dramatic entertainment within which the milieu of the domestic drawing room or the academic lecture room could be preserved while allowing some licence to introduce histrionic high colouring to the occasion. In thus allowing a large new audience to ease their consciences about theatre-going, Readings developed into a novel, hybrid type of entertainment of extraordinary popularity. 'It was not a reading—it was really a play without scenery,' remarked a Preston reviewer of Dickens's performance; but it was a 'play' quite permissible to attend. A key feature in this was the ambience developed by the recitalist.

Dickens was not the first, by any means, to try to recreate a drawing-room occasion on a public stage. Charles Mathews was one of the great prototypes in this respect, as we shall see in the next chapter. One of Mathews's successors in such solo 'table entertainments' was the Irish novelist and song-writer Samuel Lover. Lover was credited with having given a particular homely elegance to such entertainments, when he made his *debut* as performer of his own literary and musical compositions at the Princess's Concert Rooms in March 1844, on which occasion he was accompanied by two young women who took the singing roles. Note the emphasis on the domestic setting in this description by Samuel Lover's biographer:

The stage was fitted up like a drawing-room, for the reception of an evening party, with its chandeliers, fancy tables, sofas, piano, &c., and Lover and his fair companions seemed to be addressing, throughout their labours, rather a group of friends under his own roof than the money-paying public. This excellent idea, which was so natural in his circumstances, and which has so often been repeated with unimpaired effect, originated, as far as my memory extends, with himself.

A drawing-room ambience with a Reader in evening dress did, of course, mean that flamboyant histrionics could be seen as jarringly inappropriate. In mid-February 1869, a sharp-tongued columnist in *Illustrated Times*, 'The Theatrical Lounger', gave his views of some professional Readers:

I have always thought it a daring and cold-blooded act to come before an audience in the tail-coat and white tie of the period and mount a kind of secular pulpit in order to read the works of favourite authors[. . .]. Of late years I believe these readers have taken to playing antics in their pulpits [clearly a dig at Bellew]. They rave and rant; they mince and wince; they tuck up their shirt-sleeves, and run their fingers through their hair in frenzied fashion[. . .]. The simple gentleman in the white tie is a sufficiently painful spectacle, but the dress-coated gentleman who plays these monkey tricks seems to me a fit subject for a lunatic asylum.

The 'Lounger' does not mention Dickens, who was on that date on his way back from giving Readings in Ireland, but he excepts from his general condemnation a new arrival on the London Readings scene, P. B. Phillips. Phillips had read, among other items, a sketch drawn from *All The Year Round* and 'Chadband' from *Bleak House*. According to the *Athenaeum*'s own 'Lounger', Phillips read without any gestures whatsoever, thereby marking himself off from the usual practice of professional Readers (and probably thereby earning the approval of both Loungers). In a later chapter, on 'Performance', we shall be considering some of the contemporary guidelines about appropriate gestures for Readers or actors. The general rule was that the Reader should simply read clearly, and provide an intelligent, well-modulated, and self-effacing transmission of the text. Wilkie Collins, an indifferent Reader himself, wisely took the advice not to attempt any histrionics during his public performances:

I have never, in presenting myself to your notice, had the object in view of acting, or even attempting to act, as in my opinion the duties of the reader and the duties of the actor are widely at difference. My position as a reader is, as I understand it, this: I am in a very large parlour surrounded, I hope I may say, by friends, and it is my duty to keep myself in the background and to let my story find its way to your favour with whatever merits of its own it may be so fortunate as to possess.

He also said, in forthright manner, with a glance back at Dickens's practices, 'I don't flourish a paperknife, and stamp about the platform, and thump the reading desk.'

DICKENS THE READER

Let us now go back to distinctions drawn at the opening of this chapter: public, viva-voce storytelling and private, silent reading. The first is communal, the second is solitary. The first is an occasion for creating community, the second can be a respite from community. In a public Reading of his own work, the author organizes his dispersed readership (including the hundreds of his erstwhile silent readers) into a temporarily close community, and he himself becomes part of that community. That was where Dickens the novelist always wanted to be. His readership warmed to the rapprochement, and Dickens revelled in this new experience of companionship, as we saw in the previous chapter. As one newspaper put it, after enjoying a Reading of the 'Carol': 'the difference between his Christmas Carol as we read it by our firesides and his delivery of it from the platform last night, reminded us of the difference between a letter and a personal interview'.

The impact on a Reading of the close personal presence of the author was hard to define, and many eyewitnesses, as in the case just quoted, meditated on that particular experience. Let us test the stretch of this analogy—the letter and the personal interview. A letter sent into a private home is a reminder of a missing presence, a substitute for that presence. One could think of the serialized novels, with their instalments regularly finding their way into people's homes, as Dickens's way of keeping in touch each month or week with his vast numbers of correspondents. The model here is a kind of Corresponding Society of the type constituted in Chapter 1 of *Pickwick Papers*. Mr. Pickwick and his three fellow-clubmen are requested 'to forward [to their Club], from time to time, authenticated accounts of their journeys and investigations, of their observations of character and manners, and of the whole of their adventures, together with all tales and papers to which local scenery or associations may give rise'. The monthly or weekly instalments of Dickens's fiction established a de facto Corresponding Society between him and his regular readership over many years. In its obituary notice for Dickens in 1870, quoted in the previous chapter, *The Illustrated London News* used something like this analogy in describing the effect of his serialized fiction: 'It was just as if we received a letter or visit, at regular intervals, from a kindly observant gossip, who was in the habit of watching the domestic life of the Nicklebys or the Chuzzlewits, and who would let us know from time to time how they were going on.' Dickens's readers became used to this kind of quasi-epistolary relationship with their novelist, though it was essentially a one-way correspondence.

The Readings changed that relationship, or at least supplemented it. Correspondence developed into a series of 'personal interviews'. That sense of regular communication from a missing presence was now supplanted by isolated moments of actual companionship, or of encounters as near to companionship as was consistent with being in the same room as Charles Dickens: there he was, up on his platform, reaching out to envelop you once again in his imaginary world and this time wanting to accompany you in person.

This wish to convert his readership into companionship, or perhaps one might say to realize in a series of live encounters the always latent companionship he had sensed with his readers, by exchanging the 'letter' for the 'personal interview', was one of the main motives behind the Readings enterprise. Dickens would sometimes preface his 'Carol' Reading by stressing the pleasure for him of being now in a position to 'accompany' his audience through the story. He wanted the Birmingham and Midland Institute audience to know that he desired 'To accompany you myself through one of my little Christmas books.' Before reading to the Bradford Educational Temperance Institute the following year, he declared, 'Nothing can be so delightful to me on such occasions as the assurance that my hearers accompany me with something of the pleasure and interest I shall have in conducting them.' He is not lecturing; he is not reciting a new text from a lofty podium: he is joining their company and 'conducting' them on a narrative journey along a familiar path. In introducing his Reading of 'The Story of Little Dombey' to a

Brighton audience in 1858, he expressed the hope 'that his audience would speedily forget the cold light of day and lose themselves with him amidst those childish footsteps'. '*With* him'—that is the essential point. In the event, that narrative path was both familiar and yet newly paved in surprising ways for the audience, as indeed it turned out to be for Dickens himself as he joined their company. He laughed alongside his listeners, often surprising himself in so doing: he seemed almost as fresh to the familiar text each night as was his audience. These circumstances make his Readings different from what is implied in the term 'Reading' or 'recital'. 'Reader' is a term that designates both the person orally transmitting a story and the person receiving it. 'A Reading' was, for Dickens, ideally a joint enterprise, constituted by the close and audibly interactive companionship of recitalist and listeners. To reinforce this bond he explicitly urged his audiences to make their emotional responses clear and open as he read:

If you feel disposed as we go along to give expression to any emotion, whether grave or gay, you will do so with perfect freedom from restraint, and without the least apprehension of disturbing me.

The kind of Reading encouraged by Dickens was one that disrupted the formal relationships of public performance where the audience is conventionally composed of quiet, passive consumers, almost as quiet and passive as the private reader. As Susan Ferguson has remarked, Dickens's Readings overrode the conventional divide between reader and listener in several ways.

[The Readings] continued a process begun in the published works of transforming the professional and financial relationship of reader and author as buyer and seller and the hierarchical difference of author as teacher and reader as student into a type of relationship that elides such differences: friendship.

The audience completed the Reading not just by being there, as sedentary ticket-holders, nor by their end-of-performance applause, but by their audibly responsive companionship. This particular

Reader wanted to break down the audience's reserve. As he told his Bradford audience in 1854, at one of the earliest public Readings, 'I cannot desire anything so much as the establishment amongst us, from the very beginning, of a perfectly unfettered, cordial, friendly sentiment.' His speeches inviting unrestrained responses were more than just polite gestures of permission ('without the least apprehension of disturbing me'). He trusted 'they would laugh if they thought proper, or cry if they thought proper, as nothing could give him greater pleasure than to see them do so unconstrainedly'. It was more than just pleasure: it developed into a dependency. He told one acquaintance that during his London Readings he had sometimes been scarcely able to continue his reading, 'for the "genteel" frigidity of his audience'. What he most wanted was the spontaneous appreciation evident in unchecked tears or laughter, 'the absence of which almost "froze the words in his mouth" '. There was a mutual dependency: the audience conditioned the Reader, almost as much as Dickens swayed his audience.

The kind and degree of responsiveness Dickens wanted was not always forthcoming, for several reasons. One reviewer thought that he made his appeal for frank and audible reactions 'in rather a condescending way', and that his general appearance and demeanour tended to discourage such emotional informality:

He is in grande tenue: a white 'choker', that is not to be trifled with; [. . .] the oligarchically cut dress-coat; with a flower in the button, altogether checking free and easy laughing.

Against that judgement, there is plenty of evidence that, whether or not he explicitly encouraged that kind of relaxed responsiveness (and such introductory addresses were omitted in later years), Dickens's own manner engaged the audience's greater intimacy. One reviewer during his American tour compared him with the well-known actor and elocutionist George Vandenhoff: 'We do not think his rendition as artistic as that of Mr. Vandenhoff, but it is more genuine. The author laughs with the hearer all the time.' Dickens was, in fact, asking for something that went against the grain of English audiences of a certain kind: 'A mixed audience', according to a Peterborough newspaper review, 'invariably appears to be ashamed of susceptibility to the tender emotion.' At an Ipswich Reading of the sentimental 'Dr Marigold' Dickens was near to being disturbed not by the unguarded sobbing of some of the audience but by the outbreaks of coughing from those who were trying to smother their emotions. *The Worcester Herald*, after reporting Dickens's standard overture inviting uninhibited responses from the audience, commented brusquely, 'They very sensibly, in our opinion, enjoyed themselves in silence.' This did not help Dickens's enjoyment.

In addition to undermining the buyer–seller, reader–listener distinctions, Dickens's Readings also challenged the distinctions between public and domestic. A Dickens Reading was peculiarly poised between public entertainment and private rendezvous. The venue was always a public place, often cavernous and draughty, but in principle, and evidently sometimes in practice, the event itself brought the listeners some way back to the cosiness of their own private hearth. This was largely due to the ways in which Dickens introduced and pitched the Reading, 'like the quiet narration of a story by one's fireside—colloquial, easy, cultivated', according to one witness. 'He reads as if he were not reading, but telling his story plainly, and without apparent effort, to a circle of friends,' reported a Belfast newspaper. That is how Dickens wanted it to be, the magical conversion of a public into a domestic space. At Birmingham he calculated volume, projection, and register very carefully in order to achieve this: 'and—I believe—made the most distant person hear, as well as if I had been reading in my own room[. . .]. Soon[. . .] we were all going on together[. . .] as if we had been sitting round the fire.' Figuratively speaking, given fair draught insulation by having a substantial and warmly disposed audience, Dickens could single-handedly raise the ambient temperature. Rather like old Fezziwig's conversion of his workaday office-warehouse into a bright, warm ballroom, Dickens's Readings could transform a chill, echoing municipal hall into a homely, intimate hearth. 'I must go to

Bradford in Yorkshire, to read once more to a little fireside party of 4000,' he wrote jauntily to a friend.

It was both Dickens's reputation as well as his personality on the platform that helped to shape that bond. As his American friend James Fields remarked years after Dickens's death, 'Every one seemed drawn to that great sympathetic nature, and as if they longed in some peculiar way to give him their confidence!' That is one aspect of the distinctive nature of a Dickens Reading, as opposed to most other forms of public recitation in that period. The close companionship was energetically fostered by Dickens, and it converted a public recitation into an occasion for imaginary adventure and emotional bonding.

THE 'LIMITS OF READING'

Dickens read at Belfast in March 1867, and the reviewer for the *Northern Whig* congratulated him on striking just the right balance between acting and reading:

Mr. Dickens carefully avoids making his dramatic faculty too prominent in his reading. He does not, except on very rare occasions, act thoroughly *out*; he suggests, and suggests very forcibly[. . .]. He calls the imagination of his audience into play: they are to fill up what he leaves incomplete. This is just what the very best reading—that is, reading, and not acting—ought to be.

Dickens's impersonations of the characters in his story gave them vocal and gestural distinctiveness, but were evidently (for this reviewer) just sufficiently underplayed to stimulate imaginative completion by the listeners. Had Dickens acted them 'thoroughly *out*', he would have appropriated them mimetically to the point where the audience's interpretative appetite would have been blunted. What he was offering was 'a dramatic monologue without scenery', according to the *Preston Guardian*. The example of Dickens's Readings and the plethora of public recitals of one kind or another in the

1860s provoked quite a lot of discussion about what, ideally, a Reading should be, and at what point it shaded off into acting. We touched on this a little earlier. The distinctions made in the *Northern Whig*'s remarks provide a good starting point for reflecting on the implications of this concern with defining the genre.

Reading a novel to oneself makes demands on the imagination to supplement the novelist's world with extraneous information, 'to fill up what he leaves incomplete', as suggested earlier. This is particularly the case with visual and auditory information, elements supplied to a much greater extent by the public Reader through gesture, facial expressions, and vocal versatility. The private reader's imaginative resources, stimulated into activity by the novel, come from his or her storehouse of memory, that huge studio back-lot stacked with fragmentary sets, props, and costumes, dating from all past experiences. Private reading involves spasmodic, involuntary raids on that wardrobe and scenery store. We dress the novel's action, not in any particularly conscious or systematic way. The 'completing' of what the author 'suggests' is a process of amalgamation: a fictional description of a place, say, supplemented with remembered actual locations. Memories colonize the text, and the novel's world is concretized as a hybrid of the empirically real and the fictional, a construct of the author's and the reader's imaginations. This process of building a half-familiar, virtual world on the foundation of the text takes place in a silent private reading, when the reader determines the pace and rhythm of the reading, and lives with and in the story for a period of flexible length. In a public Reading by the author there is less freedom for such imaginative activity: one must concede that a particular character was originally meant to sound like *this*, or grimace like *that*. The story is told at someone else's pace and leaves less room for private imaginative and associative growths to luxuriate. However, just as Dickens invited his listeners, by precept and example, to participate openly with their laughter and tears, so, according to many reports, he encouraged their more active imaginative engagement by suggesting ('very forcibly'), rather than histrionically defining (acting 'thoroughly *out*'), his characters.

He thus allowed just enough space to stay open, so as to invite a more collaborative experience. This brings a public Reading closer to the experience of private reading and proportionately more distant from an acting performance; and therefore, for the *Whig* reviewer, it constitutes 'the very best reading'.

The Graphic, in reflecting on Dickens's Farewell Readings early in 1870, took stock of the range of views held on the limits of public Reading, and proposed degrees of permissible dramatic embellishment:

Some hold that it should be a mere colourless medium—or rather, like the various shades of the one colour in an engraving—without any attempt at ringing the various hues of acting. Others claim a wider domain, and hold that genius and versatility will at least *indicate* every hue and tone in dramatic character. The drama itself is born of mind; is independent of the paint, patches, wigs, clothes, popularly supposed to convey character. That this may be so is granted; but it will be urged that reading is a distinct province still—an even, level, unexcited current, tempered and regulated. Yet let this rule be strictly enforced, when you come to some passionate burst, this frail barrier must be broken through, or the effect will be tame. Even among what are called 'correct' readers there are degrees; and public readers especially find themselves obliged to resort to stimulating bursts, or their audiences nod. It is, indeed, mere refining; and those who have not dramatic gifts wisely extol the more regulated style.

This tension between demonstrative acting and level, 'colourless' reading is never resolved, and public Readers were aware of the fine balance they were negotiating—especially over the period of those ingrained puritanical concerns about the theatre and the acting profession. Different practitioners represented different ends of the scale, as we have seen: the reticent P. B. Phillips and the flamboyant Revd. Bellew, for example. Single practitioners could also, within a single performance, run the full length of the histrionic gamut, from sedate monophonic Reading to virtuoso polyphonics. Dickens, according to some, began as predominantly a recitalist in the plainer mode, but developed into a dramatic Reader. The following notice, from a Torquay newspaper, was written near the end of Dickens's

Reading career, and two weeks after he had introduced 'Sikes and Nancy' into his repertoire:

> That it is the player's rather than the author's art which elicits much of the approbation of the audience [. . .] is we think evident from the manner in which the applause is bestowed. It follows the points made by the reader, far more than the most skilfully arranged phrases or the most carefully expressed sentiments of the writer. We suspect Mr. Dickens thinks so too, for since his earlier readings these entertainments have gradually taken more and more the form of dramatic recitations.

Why is there this concern about how fully, within a Reading, one should shift into impersonations of the characters being presented? What lies behind the emphasis on 'indicating' or 'suggesting' character, as opposed to acting it out? One issue involved here is the often invoked opposition between two distinct Reading milieux: the genteel drawing room and the bohemian theatre. At the start of his professional Reading career Dickens seems to have struck a judicious balance between 'what would be pleasing in a private circle and what would be requisite on the stage':

> Any attempt to display great dramatic power in the presence of a dozen persons only, would be simply ridiculous; and every experienced play-goer knows that an excellent reader may prove to be an inferior actor. Mr. Dickens, having to read, not to act, before large audiences, so tones his manner that, whilst every varying change of character or incident is so strikingly marked as to arrest and fix the attention of his hearers, there does not appear to be the slightest tinge of exaggeration.

Here is one thoughtful meditation, from the New York paper *Nation* on where Readings properly belong:

> Most people, we dare say, will go to hear the readings [i.e. Dickens's Readings, in America] with a vague expectation that they are to be pleased as an actor pleases them, or rather they go with suggested reminiscences of great actors in their minds, and with little knowledge of what it is in which 'reading' properly so-called, consists. But there is no more of the theatre in the reader than there is in the accessories of which we have spoken

[Dickens's platform set], and how slight and simple those accessories are we have seen. The true theory of the performance is not that it is acting in which the actor, as much as possible, forgets himself into the very likeness of what he personates, but is rather that a gentleman dramatically tells a story among friends, indicating rather than perfectly assuming the characters of the personages brought before us; never wholly, indeed, never nearly, losing sight of his hearers and himself; never wholly, never, at any rate, for very long, getting away from the gentlemanly drawing-room, with its limiting conventionalities, into the wider and freer atmosphere of the stage. Readings are simply story-telling or declamation or the recitation of poetry with exceptionally good elocution and with occasional feats of imitation of a kind more or less subdued.

The point to highlight here is the distinction between recitation and acting, which Dickens's arrival on the Reading circuit made a subject of some controversy. *The Times*, welcoming his new series of Readings in January 1867, acclaimed Dickens's performance as 'worthy of a minute study, as showing the perfection to which the art of reading has been brought, and how closely it is beginning to perform the functions supposed to belong to histrionic talent only.' In *The Times*'s judgement Dickens 'not only delivers his dialogue dramatically, but to a certain extent he may be said to act his narrative passages'; and it was a matter of judging that 'certain extent' with precision. Reading properly belonged in the drawing room, with its 'limiting conventionalities', where, in the words of the *Nation*'s reviewer, 'a gentleman dramatically tells a story among friends'. The theatre, however, was the public world, where identities underwent transformations: 'the actor forgets himself into the very likeness of what he personates'. Characterization ought to be indicative only and should stop some way short of 'assuming' separate roles. 'Indicating' also respects the capacity of the listener's imagination to complete the character, in the ways we have already outlined. The public Reader has a responsibility to exercise control, both in terms of not indulging in exaggerated mimicry and in never 'forgetting' himself in projecting the story. This is the essential role of the controlling narrator, whose authoritative, orchestrating presence must be evident throughout the recitation and should never be subsumed into one of his characters.

That was the theory. Dickens's Readings, however, were, as already noted, *sui generis*. The Readings were Dickens's attempt to bridge those culturally determined separate spheres, the theatre and the drawing room, the public and the private. Just as he literally converted one of his own domestic rooms at Tavistock House into a theatre, so in the Readings he converted an essentially drawing-room entertainment into a species of public dramatic performance that made him the rival of any contemporary professional actor. He dissolved distinctions between public and private by inviting the public expression of private feelings in his audience. He dissolved them also in the manner he related to the material text. Any reader normally looks at the book he or she is reading; the private reader can hardly do without it. The public Reader, to preserve the sense of 'reading', needs visibly to engage with a book, needs to be seen lifting the story off the page and projecting it to the listeners. But 'Mr. Dickens is not a reader. He did not look upon his books but once last evening' (at the Springfield Music Hall, Massachussetts): 'He is simply and emphatically a very natural and delightful actor.' The difference between an actor and a Reader is that the former works without a book. Dickens was neither quite one nor the other. He had his prompt-copy in his left hand or resting on the desk, and although he would turn the pages regularly, his eyes were on his audience throughout, not on his text. By 1867 he had learned his Readings off by heart, as he said, in order to have 'no mechanical drawback in looking after the words'. The material book had become an impediment.

In formal terms Dickens kept the event just this side of theatre. He kept himself always behind his little velvet-clad desk and ensured that the copy of the book was always either in his hand or on the desk before him. This format gave him symbolic anchorage in the polite milieu of the drawing room. But he did not need the book. He probably did not need the desk. He could have relinquished both, just as he could—and often did—let slip his role as gentlemanly narrator in order to 'assume' one of his characters. That book—the prompt-copy itself—needs examination now, in the context of negotiating that staged transition from private reading to recitation, and to acting out the text, because the copy Dickens read from was not the book he had originally written. The novelist was speaking 'not through the dead pages of a printed volume, but in his own person', as *The Illustrated London News* put it. His prompt-copies were adapted as performance scripts, and in this process Dickens took great pains.

THE READING TEXTS—NOVELS INTO SCRIPTS

Dickens's planned or impromptu alterations to his more familiar texts sometimes disconcerted his audiences. Here is the *Manchester Guardian* humorously reproaching Dickens with changing what had become a familiar national monument—*Pickwick Papers*:

Surely Mr. Dickens has not been tampering with his text? What are the undergraduates of Cambridge who a few years ago passed so satisfactory an examination in the 'Pickwick Papers,' what are the countless thousands who fondly imagine they could at any moment stand a similar test, to think and to do if the author himself introduces (as we thought in two cases he introduced on this occasion) *variorum* readings? 'Pickwick' cannot be improved—even by Mr. Dickens.

Improvement or not, Dickens's Reading versions of his own work kept changing, long after he had completed, and sometimes published, the initial Reading version. The sight of new texts of old Dickens stories first happened in 1855. In December of that year, after a charity Reading of *A Christmas Carol* at Sheffield, the local newspaper observed that Dickens's Reading copy consisted of pages of the *Carol* pasted on large paper in a red morocco cover, and that he flourished a large paperknife 'with which he divided the leaves when they proved obstinate in turning'. A copy of the 'Carol' Reading text corresponding exactly with this description is in the Berg Collection, in New York Public Library. When Dickens prepared the Berg copy-text he used an 1849 edition of the story and inlaid the text into large octavo pages. The whole was bound in three-quarters red morocco. It is thought to be the only surviving prompt-copy of the 'Carol'. Philip Collins, who has done more than any other scholar to clarify the history of the Reading texts, considers it very likely that this was indeed the copy on which Dickens first worked for his 'Carol' Readings of December 1853. It was certainly in use near the start of the professional Readings, in 1858, because the flyleaf contains Dickens's jottings about the various provincial hotels planned for the tour in October 1859. Collins is sure that it was the same 'Carol' copy that he took to America fifteen years later for the tour of 1867–8, since the Boston trade edition was set up from it. The *Sheffield Times* report does seem to confirm that the Berg copy was in use some years before Dickens became a professional Reader.

Dickens's preparation of all his Reading texts has been very fully described by Philip Collins in his edition, *Charles Dickens: The Public Readings* (1975), both in the general introduction and in the headnotes to each printed Reading text. My own discussion of the texts is indebted to Collins's work. Rather than attempting a summary of his invaluable findings (see especially his Introduction, sections 3 and 4) across the full repertoire, I shall concentrate on just two of the best-known Readings, 'David Copperfield' and 'A Christmas Carol', to illustrate the characteristic tailoring job Dickens undertook in order to adapt a text written for private reading into a form suitable for histrionic recital. In the first Dickens is pulling different strands from a big text and weaving a concentrated and narrowly focused narrative; in the second he is simply distilling a short story. They make good contrasts in other respects, as reviewers noted with appreciation: 'David Copperfield differs as much from the Carol as tragedy differs from *vaudeville*.' The general style of 'Copperfield' was 'serious and pathetic', and in contrast to the 'Carol' it was conducted as a first-person narration. I begin with the 'Carol'. It had a longer history of development as a Reading text than any of his others and is one of the most interesting.

In many respects *A Christmas Carol* was, from the first, written to be read aloud. As 'a sort of improved child's story' (according to an Aberdeen reviewer) it had the widest appeal. It was popularly held to be the quintessence of Dickens: 'The great fires roar in its pages', wrote the *New York Tribune* when Dickens brought it to America in 1867, 'and bright eyes sparkle, and merry bells ring, and sunlight and starlight and joy wrap it round about in a delicious atmosphere of honest, ardent goodness.' The tone of address to the reader and the intrusive presence of the narrator made it seem as if one were listening to a compelling raconteur. 'It is a work of high finish, and has a certain exaggerated style that makes it especially fit for being acted', according to an East Anglian newspaper review of a Reading. This book made the ideal text for Dickens's distinctive Reading performances. As the reviewer for *The Liverpool Daily Post* remarked, 'On the whole, we think it quite safe to say that, as only Charles Dickens could have written these novelets [the Christmas Books], he only could read them as they deserve to be read.' The *Carol* was the first to be given the full trial of a public hearing. Indeed, with the exception of one recitation of the *Cricket*, it constituted his public repertoire for all the early Readings, from the winter of 1853 to the Spring of 1858; and, together with 'Bardell and Pickwick', it continued to dominate the repertoire through to the end of his Readings career.

Over the years Dickens cut the Reading down from about three hours (in 1853) to two and a half hours (for a memorial London Reading on Douglas Jerrold's death, in June 1857) to about two hours for the first provincial tour in the summer and autumn of 1858: this included a ten-minute interval taken at the close of Stave Two. From late October onwards during that tour he further reduced it so that it could be coupled with 'Bardell and Pickwick' for an evening's performance of just over two hours and twenty minutes. By the autumn 1861 series he had brought that whole programme down to two hours. At that first public Reading in Birmingham in December 1853, he had evidently already done some pruning. *The Times* congratulated him on some admirably 'judicious curtailment' in the way 'he had lopped off everything to which the knife of the critic would have been applied': 'His tendency to exaggeration and overcolouring became subdued, and the truthfulness of his delineations, thus sobered down, grew more strikingly powerful.'

Although deletions in the Berg prompt-copy are made in different coloured inks, it is still not easy to be sure of the sequence of cuts as the text was gradually reduced over the years. As Charles Kent described it, 'the pages came to be cobwebbed over with a wonderfully intricate network of blots and lines in the way of correction or obliteration'. He evidently worked rapidly. Ink blots occasionally appear on the text where it faces heavily inked deletions on the opposite page: Dickens has turned over to the next opening before the ink has dried (see Frontispiece 'Sikes and Nancy' for instances of such blots). The significant pattern of cuts in the final Reading version is summarized as follows by Collins:

the only episode which, conspicuously, is left almost entire is the Cratchits' Christmas dinner. The beginnings and endings of most of the Staves are much cut, and the fourth and fifth are run into a single Stave. In Stave II, Scrooge's schooldays are omitted, as is much of the episode concerning his fiancée. In Stave III, the long descriptions of Christmas Day in the London streets and among the miners and mariners are deleted, and the jollifications at Scrooge's nephew's house are much abbreviated. The deathbeds of Scrooge and of Tiny Tim in Stave IV are virtually eliminated, and the re-entry in Stave V of the portly gentleman collecting for charity is omitted.

The evolution of the Reading text results in a version of the *Carol* that is both more benign and less oriented towards topical social problems. The text increasingly plays up the comedy and jolly sentimentality, and plays down the social criticism. The Cratchit Christmas dinner, as already noted, was hardly touched, whereas the episode involving those emblematic victims of social neglect, Want and Ignorance, disappears.

By the time Dickens began his *professional* public Readings in 1858, the 'Carol' was already fifteen years old. Parts of it had dated, other parts had become assimilated into English folk culture.

The Reading text of 1858 responded to this historical evolution, and further editorial modifications over the following twelve years continued both to reflect it, and in some ways to promote it. So too did Dickens's platform improvisations, as he made impromptu cuts during performance—cuts never recorded in the written text. As he remarked to someone curious to know whether there were printed copies of the performance texts:

There are no printed abridgements of the Carol, Dombey, &c as I read them, or nearly as I read them. Nor is there any such abridgement in existence, save in my own copies; and there it is made, in part physically, and in part mentally, and no human being but I myself could hope to follow it.

In fact he had all his Reading texts specially printed to his specifications. The 'Carol' prompt-copy evidently provided the ideal format. Each page of that text, taken from that 1849 edition, contained 22 lines, as did all his Christmas Books in their original editions. Whether it became a form of superstition, Dickens directed subsequent Reading texts to follow the same format. Thus, when in 1861 he was adding Readings from *Nickleby, Copperfield*, and *Pickwick* ('Mr.Bob Sawyer's Party') to his repertoire, he ordered copies of each to be printed with precisely 22 lines per octavo page. While the font size is quite small, the leading is generous and must have helped to give a kind of visual ventilation to the text.

Over fifteen years the 'Carol' Reading kept changing in the author's own hands. One of these changes, the subduing and excision of the social criticism, was sometimes explained by Dickens in introducing his Reading:

On making his appearance, Mr. Dickens addressed his audience in a few prefatory words to the effect that the book which he was about to read, was written several years previously, in consequence of certain circumstances which seemed to him to render a few words of earnest remonstrance necessary. Though the cause for this remonstrance was now to some extent removed, and, in part, he hoped, by aid of his little work, yet a plea for the poor and distressed was never out of season.

It was probably simpler, as the 'Hungry Forties' receded in memory, for Dickens just to shed much of the element of 'remonstrance' from the text and performance, than to have to repeat explanations of the fading topicality of the 'Carol'. The fabular timelessness of the 'Carol', rather than its specific, historical propagandist programme, was the important point for subsequent generations of readers. That much is clear from Paul Davis's fine study of the story's typological history as 'the first gospel in the "secular scripture" of Victorian fiction' and as a protean 'culture-text' for the next century and half. Little by little, as he shows, through revisions and theatrical adaptations highlighting the Cratchits and their Christmas dinner, the 'Carol' came to resemble that 'soft', popularized ghost story we know today from countless versions for film, theatre, television, cartoon, and children's books. Dickens himself, as he developed his Readings through the 1850s and muted the social criticism, was to a great extent complicit with this evolution.

Another kind of change Dickens worked on as he shortened the Reading was to increase the dramatic element. In 1869, after his return from America, such changes were remarked on:

The *Carol*, we may remark, was the first of his writings he selected (now nearly ten years ago) for the exercise of his "reading" powers, and was then so little curtailed as to be sufficient for a two hours' entertainment. He has now cut it down to briefer dimensions, and made it less of a narrative and more of a drama than it was.

Dialogue between contrasting characters enabled Dickens to display his skills as an impersonator; and bit by bit his pruning favoured the speaking characters at the expense of narration and description. He also converted indirect discourse to speech. The 'Carol' prompt copy shows this in the exchange in Stave 1 between Scrooge and Bob Cratchit, when the latter is asking for Christmas Day off work (square brackets indicate deletions; bold type indicates handwritten additions):

[The clerk smiled faintly] "**Yes Sir**"

"And yet, [" said Scrooge, "] you don't think *me* ill-used, when I pay a
day's wages for no work."
[The clerk observed that] "[i]It [was] is only once a year [.] **Sir**."

The choice to go for more drama gave Dickens the opportunity both
to concentrate more on his character impersonations and also to
ensure rapid transitions. Where narrative was retained at any length,
it was usually narrative at a high level of energy (as in the excitement
of the Cratchit dinner description) and of the kind where the narrator
is especially self-assertive—in other words performing like one of
the story's characters. This was not hard to achieve in the *Carol*,
nor in the other early Christmas Books. *The Cricket on the Hearth*
was described as a 'dramatic monologue', and that is a useful way of
styling the *Carol* too as Dickens's Reading intensified the dramatic
presence and personality of the first-person narrator, as in these
snatches from the narrative of Fred's musical evening in Stave Three:

For they were a musical family, and knew what they were about, when they
sung a Glee or Catch, I can assure you[. . .]. And I no more believe Topper
was really blinded than I believe he had eyes in his boots . . .

Dickens's Reading text for the 'Carol' carried his margin directions
to himself. These are brief jottings to prompt him to 'run on' (past
deleted text) and to establish a change of key at certain points in the
narrative. Thus, for example, as can be seen in the illustration (Fig
2), when in Stave Two, Scrooge is taken to Fezziwig's by the Ghost
of Christmas Past, as he recognizes first the warehouse, then his old
employer, and then his fellow-'prentice, the margin prompts run:
'Scrooge melted'. . . 'Melted'. . . 'Melted'. . . with double underlining
each time. Elsewhere there are signals to 'Tone down to Pathos',
followed soon after by 'up to cheerfulness', again doubly underlined.
After the first nine paragraphs of the 'Carol', establishing Marley's
death and Scrooge's mean-spirited character, the Christmas story
begins in traditional fashion: 'Once upon a time—of all the good
days in the year, [on] **upon a** Christmas Eve[. . .]'. Against this,
Dickens writes 'Narrative' (doubly underlined) to prompt a change
of tone. We know how the tone changed at this point. One

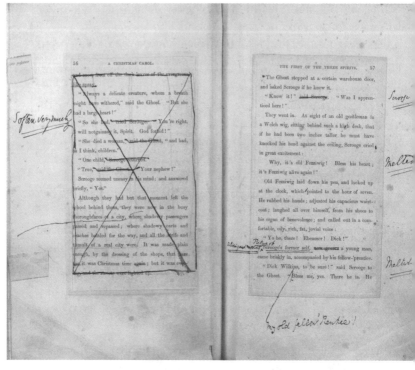

2. 'A Christmas Carol': Dickens's prompt-copy, pp. 56–7. Henry W. and Albert A. Berg Collection of English and American Literature, New York Public Library, Astor, Lenox and Tilden Foundations..

assiduous eyewitness, a journalist, Rowland Hill, attended several 'Carol' Readings between 1868 and 1870 (including the very last Reading): 'I used to take my copy of the book, and note, in pencil, any alterations he made, seemingly on the spur of the moment.' Hill records that when Dickens began 'Once upon a time [...]', he did indeed change his tone 'suddenly to a rich, mellow note, splendidly inflected'. Hill reports that Dickens 'constantly omitted phrases describing who spoke and how they spoke, by making marvellous changes of tone and changes of facial expression'. Many, but not all, such phrases are shown as deletions in the prompt-copy.

Dickens also added text in performance, and this was not always written into the prompt-copy. Rowland Hill meticulously records several instances of Dickens's amplification of the original text (Hill did not, of course, have access to the prompt-copy) with material that was never incorporated in the Reading text. One example comes at that point in the Reading (mentioned earlier) where Scrooge rediscovers old Fezziwig (and where Dickens has his margin prompt, 'Melted'). In the original text, and in the Reading text, Scrooge exclaims, 'Why, it's old Fezziwig! Bless his heart; it's Fezziwig alive again!' In performance this was expanded to 'Why, LOR! it's old Fezziwig! Bless his DEAR OLD HONEST heart; HE WAS DEAD AND GONE; but it's Fezziwig alive again!' Dickens's purpose behind the additions here was, one presumes, partly expository; to characterize Fezziwig's benign nature, and to reinforce the wonder of the old man's visionary resurrection. Elsewhere, Dickens ad libs touches of zestful hyperbole, as when the over-heated fiddler at Fezziwig's ball 'plunged his hot face into a pot of porter': to this Dickens added that the face 'POSITIVELY HISSED' as it hit the liquid.

Dickens had great difficulty in designing a Reading from *Copperfield*. He had been trying to adapt it since at least January 1855:

I have been poring over Copperfield (which is my favorite), with the idea of getting a reading out of it, to be called by some such name as 'Young Housekeeping, and Little Emily'. But there is still the huge difficulty that I constructed the whole with immense pains, and have so woven it up and blended it together that I cannot yet so separate the parts as to tell the story of David's married life with Dora, and the story of Mr. Peggotty's search for his Niece, within the time.

His practice in devising the other Readings had been to condense a complete short story ('A Christmas Carol'), to extract a single episode ('Bardell and Pickwick'), or to concentrate on a character study ('Mrs Gamp'). With *Copperfield* he was trying to do all three, to varying degrees: he wanted to encompass a developing narrative (the story of Emily and Steerforth); he wanted to feature some of the famous characters (the Micawbers, Mr Peggotty); and he wanted some strong single episodes (most notably the storm at Yarmouth). In simply practical terms he needed a text that could be read in under a couple of hours. Philip Collins has calculated that the printed text of the Reading copy contains about 26,500 words; the corresponding parts of the novel from which he drew his Reading text total about 35,500 words. So there were economies within economies. It started as a 2-hour performance (including a 10-minute interval) and was whittled down to about an hour and a half in the American tour of 1867–8. In fact there was an unpredictable elasticity in these Readings: Dickens could cut or add in an improvisatory way during performance. His matinee performances of the Reading were often shortened slightly.

He organized it first into five and then into six chapters. In 1974 E. W. F. Tomlin came across Dickens's own summary of the six-chapter version. It reads as follows:

Chapter I. Copperfield (as a young man of 19 or 20) takes his friend, Steerforth, to the old boat where Mr. Peggotty lives, and introduces Steerforth to Little Emily. It is foreshadowed in this chapter, that Steerforth admires her in a profligate way, and begins to form designs upon her.

Chapter II. Copperfield goes alone to the old boat, to pass with the family, the last evening of Little Emily's single life; because she has engaged herself to be married to Ham (Mr. Peggotty's nephew) that day fortnight. Ham suddenly brings the news that she has eloped with Steerforth—a last letter from her is read—and Mr. Peggotty sets forth to seek her 'through the world'.

Chapter III. Copperfield describes his love for Dora, and the dinner he gave to Mr. and Mrs. Micawber and Traddles.

Chapter IV. Mr. Peggotty returns from his search, unsuccessful, and relates where he has been in France and Italy.

Chapter V. Copperfield describes how he made proposals to Dora—how he married Dora—and what their little ménage was.

Chapter VI describes the storm at Yarmouth, in the words of the book, and the Death of Steerforth.

The Reading follows the novel's sequence of events, except in one respect. David's falling in love with Dora and the meal with the Micawbers are placed after the news of Emily's elopement. In the novel this chronology was the other way round. The reason for the relocation is clear. The Reading's first two chapters build the Emily–Steerforth relationship and elopement rapidly and yet contrast in mood: Chapter 1 is brimming over with joyous hospitality, community, and comedy; Chapter 2 is short and grim, concentrating on the announcement of the catastrophe, and dispersal of the boat-house family. The chronologically displaced Chapter 3, a long one, is a contrast again and a parallel to Chapter 1: it features Dora and David in love, and the Micawbers—sentimental and comic celebrations of new love and family solidarity. Chapter 4 is very short and sombre: the chance meeting in London with Mr. Peggotty, whose quest to find his niece has failed. Chapter 5 is romance and comedy again, with David and Dora's hopeless housekeeping. Chapter 6 is tense and builds to the climactic storm and deaths of Ham and Steerforth. The organization of the Reading is masterly. Dickens had shaped the narrative into a sequence of striking scenes, finely adapted for performance—'a series of tableaux', as one reviewer put it.

The Reading seems to have accentuated David's complex feelings about Steerforth. The text underlines Steerforth's confessed remorse at not having been better guided by his parents, and adds a sentence not in the original novel: 'You know my mother has always doted on me and spoilt me.' Steerforth's struggle with his conscience was evidently very forcefully enacted by Dickens: his 'visibly wrestling with his good angel had touches of art as magically suggestive as anything imagined of Faust.'

Dickens had from the first wanted to concentrate on the two love stories: to be called by some such name as 'Young Housekeeping, and Little Emily'. The two are counterpointed—as it were, sacred and profane love, child love and adult love: David and Dora, and Steerforth and Emily. It has an appealing symmetry. This alternation of comedy and pathos, the light and the dark, was clearly what

Dickens was after. And he succeeded. Here is his report on its reception, particularly by Macready:

(last night) I read Copperfield, and positively enthralled the people. It was a most overpowering effect, and poor Andrew came behind the screen, after the storm, and cried in the best and manliest manner. Also there were two or three lines of his shipmates and other sailors, and they were extraordinarily affected. But its culminating effect was on Macready at Cheltenham.You know that he is not too prone to praise what comes at all in his own way; but when I got home after Copperfield, I found him quite unable to speak, and able to do nothing but square his dear old jaw all on one side, and roll his eyes (half closed), like Jackson's picture of him. And when I said something light about it, he returned 'No—er—Dickens! I swear to Heaven that as a piece of passion and playfulness—er—indescribably mixed up together, it does—er—No, really Dickens!—amaze me as profoundly as it moves me. But as a piece of Art—and you know—er—that I—No Dickens! By God!—have seen the best Art in a great time—it is incomprehensible to me. How it is got at—er—how it is done—er—how one man can—well! It lays me on my—er—back, and it is of no use talking about it!'—With which, he put his hand upon my breast, and pulled out his pocket handkerchief, and I felt as if I were doing somebody to his Werner.

Macready recorded in his diary, 'The humour was delightful, and the pathos of various passages gave me a choking sensation, whilst the account of Emily's flight brought tears to my eyes.' This single Reading encapsulated the kind of varied programme Dickens aimed at when he presented an evening of different Readings.

There is a biographical interest in Dickens's crafting and launching this particular Reading at this juncture in his life. In 1860 Dickens began his series of *Uncommercial Traveller* papers in *All The Year Round*. In these reflective pieces Dickens enjoys projecting his Uncommercial persona in first-person narration. He invites some intimacy with his thoughts and feelings. The series comes to an end in October of that year—exactly at the time when Dickens realizes he must intervene in *All The Year Round*'s falling circulation with a new serialized novel—*Great Expectations*. The reflective first-person Traveller modulates into the reflective first-person Pip; and *that* persona carries Dickens into June 1861. *Great Expectations* finished its serial run early that August. Having said farewell to Pip, the self he had inhabited for nearly a year, Dickens begins to devise new Readings, amongst them 'David Copperfield', which allowed him to continue to address his public, now face to face, in the first person. But there was a new twist here. Unlike with *Great Expectations*, the world had long suspected that *Copperfield* had some thinly disguised material from Dickens's own life history. Now, in 1861, Dickens the international celebrity was launching in public a Reading of a text in which the 'I' was audibly and visibly both David the narrator and Dickens the professional Author–Reader. Perhaps also, as a conflation of these two, that 'I' was Dickens the private man himself, up there on that platform, disclosing confidentially, in first person, a barely fictionalized private self through a semi-autobiographical text? I suspect that gave a special resonance to the Reading of 'Copperfield', not least for Dickens himself.

None of the novels after *Copperfield* yielded public Readings. Dickens worked on *Great Expectations* and *A Tale of Two Cities* to produce Reading texts, but they were never delivered. The only fiction from the period 1850–70 to be drawn into the repertoire were the Christmas Stories from *Household Words* and *All The Year Round*. By far the most popular of these—at least the ones Dickens chose to perform most often—were 'Boots at the Holly-Tree Inn' (1858) and 'Doctor Marigold' (1866). When such later writing was paired with an early Dickens item for a single evening's entertainment, the stylistic contrasts sometimes jarred. Thus when in April 1866 Dickens read 'Nickleby' after 'Marigold' (published at Christmas just four months earlier) in Edinburgh, *The Scotsman* commented on the former's comparative crudity contrasted strongly with the carefully mellowed tone and effect of 'Marigold'. Conversely, the *Yorkshire Post*, reviewing Dickens's Leeds Readings early in 1867, was 'painfully struck' by what it felt to be the inferiority of 'Barbox

Brothers' and 'The Boy at Mugby' (both premiered that January)
to Dickens's earlier writings, and complained of their forced and
false pathos and extravagant humour. Dickens may well have read
this review: 'Barbox' disappeared from the repertoire after this
February. 'Marigold' remained and was usually very well received.
'The Signalman' from *Mugby Junction* was prepared for Reading,
but never performed. One more text, 'Mr. Chops, the Dwarf', from
Household Words's 1858 Christmas number, was introduced as a
Reading in 1868.

The very last item to be added to the repertoire was 'Sikes and
Nancy', first performed publicly on 5th January 1869. Dickens went
back (over 30 years) to his earliest fiction for this notorious Reading.
It has puzzled many a biographer and critic quite why Dickens made
this move when he did. Philip Collins has very plausibly suggested
that by the late 1860s Dickens was feeling competitive pressures
from other soloists who were having great success with sensational
Reading material, notably Thomas Hood's grisly poem, 'The Dream
of Eugene Aram', delivered in a passionately melodramatic manner.
Dickens's competitive nature would very likely have responded with a
tour de force piece. In devising 'Sikes and Nancy' he was determined,
as he told Forster, to leave behind him 'the recollection of something
very passionate and dramatic, done with simple means, if the art
would justify the theme'.

'Sikes and Nancy' is Dickens's histrionic contribution to the
'sensation' fiction and drama of the 1860s. Stories of treachery and
murder in a domestic setting were very popular in this decade: 'We
are thrilled with horror[...] by the thought that such things may
be going on around us and among us,' remarked a reviewer of this
kind of fiction in 1863. There was an extra frisson in this close
juxtaposition of savage violence and the comforts of ordinary life:
'It is on our domestic hearths that we are taught to look for the
incredible,' according to a reviewer in 1870 of what had come to
be known as 'The Sensational School': 'fiends sit down with us
at our table; our innocent-looking garden walls hold the secret of

treacherous murders'. Dickens gave a trial Reading of 'Sikes and Nancy' in November 1868, and one of the audience, the actress Mrs. Keeley, remarked to him afterwards: 'The public have been wanting a sensation for a few years—and now they've got it!' In resurrecting this particular sequence of events from *Oliver Twist* for consumption in the 1860s, Dickens was in key with popular tastes. 'Sikes and Nancy' combines the domestic and the savage in precisely the amalgam that would have appealed at that time. Rose Maylie, an Angel in the House, sheds her benign influence over Nancy, to make Nancy a surrogate middle-class Angel, who is then murdered at home in the most brutal manner. The appeal of this kind of spicy combination was recognized by Dickens when in 1867 he praised one of the finest Sensation novels of the decade, Wilkie Collins's *The Moonstone*: 'it is a very curious story—wild, and yet domestic'. Indeed, the very setting in which Dickens presented his own Sensation piece reinforced the frisson of this combination. As a Reader he established himself in a drawing-room ambience and there was to be seen releasing bestially savage forces in his evening dress as he impersonated the scene of the murder. I have tried later in this book to reconstruct, from eyewitness accounts, a sense of the impact of this notorious Reading.

All in all, the preparation of his chosen Reading texts never ended. As Rowland Hill recorded, the 'Carol' Reading was never quite the same, textually, from one performance to another, sudden cancellations and additions being prompted by Dickens's instincts in the act of Reading. Sometimes too, previously deleted text would be reinstated on the spur of the moment. The fluidity of the text made it fresh each time for him, as for his audience. The 'text' for a Reading is, anyway, more than the printed words on the script. It should include the performer's handwritten prompts. And then what about those prompts to delivery that were never written in—the pauses, pacing, and inflections that only become apparent in watching a performance? Since some of this 'mental' editing was conducted onstage, the performance text evaporated each evening, as Dickens took his farewell bow, and was renewed in slightly modified form whenever he next stepped onto his platform.

In a letter written a few weeks before his death, Dickens resisted some otherwise tempting requests to allow publication in America of some of the monthly parts of *Edwin Drood* very slightly in advance of their appearance in England. Under copyright legislation, prior publication in America of certain monthly numbers would have had the effect of securing American copyright on those numbers that had appeared before their English counterparts. Dickens would have ended up with only partial copyright control over his own novel, and this would have bizarrely restricted subsequent editions of his work. In pointing out the consequences of such partial forfeiture of copyright, he suggested a few imaginary analogies:

I said to him [the American publisher], 'Imagine a Copyright in Pickwick, with no Copyright in the Trial!' And I might have followed the absurdity into a Nickleby copyright excluding the Yorkshire School or the Country actors; or a Dombey copyright, excluding the child's death; or a Copperfield copyright without the young married couple or the storm.

He might have added, 'or the Carol excluding the Cratchit Christmas Dinner'. For what Dickens is drawing attention to here, in each of his novels, is precisely those episodes he had fashioned for the Readings: the Pickwick Trial, Nicholas at Dotheboys, the death of Little Dombey, the courtship of Dora and death of Steerforth. His Readings had made these episodes the highlights of their respective novels, just as he continued to modify the 'Carol' by highlighting the sentimental and joyous elements and dispensing with the social grievances.

Dickens's fashioning of his Reading texts and his rehearsal of them prior to performance were one and the same activity, one may assume. Just like his original composition of the novels, trying out characters and dialogue would have been conducted histrionically. It had to be clear not only that the narrative structure was right but that the material projected well. This latter criterion applied just as much to the narrative as to the dialogue. If the narrative element could work as a dramatic monologue, with a strongly coloured narrator-persona, so much the better. The first-person narration in 'Copperfield' fitted this ideally, as did, in a different way, the avuncular storyteller of the 'Carol'. In fact, three of the five Readings most often performed were first-person narratives: 'David Copperfield', 'Doctor Marigold', and 'Boots at the Holly-Tree Inn'. The other two were the 'Carol', with a narrator who asserts his personal presence throughout, and 'Bardell and Pickwick', which is predominantly a sequence of speeches in character, for which the minimal narrative acts as a pedestal.

The important point for Dickens, once he had, as it were, 'cast' his Readings, was to get the characters up there on the platform and audition them. Much pruning of the text must have taken place during these sessions; and the sessions were remarkably protracted: 'Every day for two or three hours, I practise my new readings, and (except in my office work) do nothing else,' Dickens told Forster. His rehearsals replaced his usual writing schedule, inasmuch as they took place in his study, in the mornings. The replacement, in *that* sanctum, was appropriate since Dickens was *composing* these Readings for performance, not just *rehearsing* them:

I have got the Copperfield Reading ready for delivery, and am now going to blaze away at Nickleby—which I don't like half as well. Every morning I 'go in' at these marks for two or three hours—and then collapse and do nothing whatever (counting as nothing, mad cricket and rounders).

The preparations were intensive. He told James Fields that it took him 'three months hard labour to get up one of his own stories for public recitation'. He told Charles Kent that if he had gone through 'Marigold' once he had 'gone through it two-hundred-times!'

By the time the Readings were ready for public performance, Dickens would have come to know much of the text by heart, and the cut-and-pasted, inkily 'cobwebbed' prompt-copies became increasingly superfluous aids. This was certainly the case with the last of the Readings, 'Sikes and Nancy'—and spectacularly so. At the trial Reading he came onto his platform before his invited audience of friends and acquaintances, text in hand, spoke to them briefly, opened the book and began to read. Then, 'gradually warming with excitement, he flung aside his book and acted the scene of the murder, shrieked the terrified pleadings of the girl, growled the brutal savagery of the murderer[...]'. That epitomizes the passage from reading to recitation to acting.

3

Impersonation

'Mr Dickens has invented a new medium for amusing an English audience.' Thus *The Illustrated London News* welcomed Dickens at the start of his professional career as a public Reader in 1858. Public Readings per se, as we saw in the last chapter, were not such a 'new medium' of entertainment: what was new was the inclusion in such recitations of virtuoso impersonation. *The Illustrated London News* was itself recording a range of such shows in London through the summer and autumn of this same year in its column devoted to theatrical events. For instance, its July 17 issue contained a notice of a Mr. Douglas Thompson lecturing in the Hanover Square Rooms 'on the present state of oratory and elocution in the different spheres of the Pulpit, the Bar, the Platform, and the Stage'. This included dramatic readings, 'rendered novel and amusing by each character being allotted to a well-known actor [...] with conversations involving rapid and frequent changes of voice'. On August 7, at the Egyptian Hall, there was an entertainment 'of a drawing-room character', called *Patchwork*, given by the Howards, a husband-and-wife team, in the course of which Mrs Paul Howard achieved 'no fewer than fourteen impersonations of character'. On September 18 at Exeter Hall a Mr Dolman recited *Macbeth* from memory, 'to, we regret to add, a small audience', who were nonetheless impressed by the extraordinary capacity of his voice to meet the range of characters in the play. On November 6, in the Strand Room, near Exeter Hall, the public was alerted to 'a new entertainment of the drawing-room kind', starring Adolphus Francis and Seymour Carleton. This consisted of a reading of *Hamlet*, accompanied by a spectacular display of 'dissolving views' representing various scenes and characters, and followed by 'Imitations of the Leading Professionals'. So, Dickens's own brand of Readings was keeping company with a curious range of solo or double-act shows, partly educational, partly virtuoso histrionics; and common to all of these were the ambitious feats of impersonation in which a wide range of characters were reproduced by just one or two performers.

This skill in mimicry was the cornerstone of Dickens's success as a Reader. It was also fundamental to his distinctiveness as a novelist, in that he had both a fine ear for nuances of accent and speech style and also a capacity to reproduce speech and behavioural idiosyncrasies on the page. Forster remarked that 'He had the power of projecting himself into shapes and suggestions of the fancy which is one of the marvels of the creative imagination, and what he desired to express he became.' Dickens's novels were generated by acts of impersonation. They were often *about* impersonation, in the broader reaches of the term. From Jingle to Jasper, plausible role-playing energized the fiction and its preoccupation with imposture, hypocrisy, disguise, personality splits, and identity quests. It is no wonder that Dickens took to the public platform to professionalize his talent for histrionic impersonation, for exploring other selves: it had always been seminal to his art.

'COMPOSING OUT LOUD'

In a speech to the Royal General Theatrical Fund on 29 March 1858, a month away from launching his career as a professional public Reader, Dickens observed that 'every writer of fiction, though he may not adopt the dramatic form, writes in effect for the stage'. The comment has often been taken, not quite accurately, as Dickens's confession that his fiction is peculiarly theatrical. The context of his remark makes it clear that he is actually thinking principally of qualities ideally shared by all creative writers and performers—'truth and wisdom', the ability to hold 'that great mirror [...] up to nature'—rather than any inherently theatrical disposition in the novelist. However, the initial proposition, as framed in Dickens's terms, does indeed point to the distinctively histrionic nature of Dickens's fiction, a quality that has long been recognized and variously regarded as part of the strength and the weakness of his writing. In the year that Dickens launched his professional Readings, John Hollingshead, a young journalist on *Household Words*, who later became a theatre manager, wrote an article for the *Critic* entitled 'Mr. Charles Dickens as a Reader'. He made the point that 'no original dramatic author, no writer of dramatic fiction in the form of novels, whose characters impress their forms upon the page in their own language out of their own mouths, can fail to be in heart, mind, and soul a natural mimic, or actor.' Dickens's fiction was born from habits of impersonation, and therefore to convert the fiction into platform performances was simply to rehearse those originating impulses—a point made by Hollingshead. His article, incidentally, was read by Dickens, 'with very great gratification'. One may suppose therefore that Dickens would not have dissented from the following account, which is very specific about the part played by impersonation in the composition of his fiction:

Every character in Mr Dickens's novels, drawn in the first instance from observation, must have been dramatically embodied—acted over, so to speak, a hundred times in the process of development and transference to the written page; and the qualities of voice, nerve, and presence being granted, Mr Dickens merely passes over that ground, in the face of a large and attentive audience, which he has often passed over before in the undisturbed privacy of his study.

Forster remarked, in recounting the story of Dickens's missing an early opportunity to become a professional actor and of his subsequent early success as a writer of sketches, 'he took to a higher calling, but it included the lower'. Forster believed that Dickens's talents for the 'lower' calling manifested themselves, as already mentioned, in his 'power of projecting himself into shapes and suggestions of his fancy,' and he added, 'The assumptions of the theatre have the same method.' Dickens did not forsake acting in the quarter-century after the disappointment of the missed audition; he simply diverted his enthusiasm for it into his creative practices as a writer (and, of course, he also exercised those gifts in occasional amateur theatricals). The impulse behind the launch of his career as a professional public Reader in 1858 was not a new discovery of a talent. It was the boisterous resurgence of a hitherto largely subterranean channel of energy, with its source far back in his childhood.

Acting and writing had been partners in Dickens's development from the earliest days. He facetiously boasted to a friend, 'I was a great writer at 8 years old or so—was an actor and a speaker from a baby.' During his Chatham childhood, at home and in visits to the Mitre Inn with his father, he used to perform parts of plays, popular songs, and recitation pieces: 'the little boy used to give with great effect, and with *such* action and *such attitudes*', according to the family servant Mary Weller. In *David Copperfield*, the child David comforts himself for the upsets in his life by retreating into those fictional worlds that his own reading had brought alive:

It is curious to me how I could ever have consoled myself under my small troubles [. . .] by impersonating my favourite characters in them [his favourite books]. I have been Tom Jones [. . .] for a week together. I have sustained my own idea of Roderick Random for a month at a stretch.

Young David brought these characters to life by impersonating them. He then enlisted the Murdstones into the cast, thereby creating a hybrid world populated by factual and fictional characters. Referring to these passages in the novel, Forster confirmed that 'every word of this personal recollection had been written down as fact, some years before it found its way into *David Copperfield*', so we may take this as further evidence of Dickens's early, developing appetite for impersonation. We may also recall that David's boyhood reading and enacting of fictional characters led to his being recognized as a talented storyteller during those long nights in the Salem House dormitory; and that gift matured to make the adult David a celebrated novelist.

Dickens's continual exercise of his imaginative identification with other characters, down to the smallest details, and the translation of that into bouts of impersonation, became crucial to his compositional method. His fictional characters were alive to him, whether or not they had 'originals', and they proved their vital existence as Dickens painstakingly impersonated them into life. His early years were partly spent not just in absorbing fiction or inventing stories but in vivifying and inhabiting those imaginary worlds and other characters. When he left Chatham and the real scenes that had become imaginatively grafted onto his favourite fictional settings, he felt forlornly (as he told Forster) as if he were leaving behind a host of friends.

At school in London, at Wellington House Academy, Dickens was an enthusiastic initiator of various theatrical events: 'always a leader at these plays', recalled one of his schoolfellows. The fondness for theatricals continued into his first job, when he was 16 or 17. A fellow clerk at Ellis and Blackmore, George Lear, recalled Dickens's talent for mimicry:

He could imitate, in a manner that I have never heard equalled, the low population of London in all their varieties, whether mere loafers or sellers of fruit, vegetables, or anything else. He could also excel in mimicking the popular singers of that day, whether comic or patriotic; as to acting, he could give us Shakespeare by the ten minutes, and imitate all the leading actors of that time.

He evidently had great confidence in both his powers of observation and his capacity to impersonate those he observed—key factors in his writing and in his fascination with acting and studying other actors. Dickens in his late teens became addicted to the theatre:

I went to some theatre every night, with a very few exceptions, for at least three years; really studying the bills first, and going to where there was the best acting; and always to see Mathews whenever he played. I practised immensely (even such things as walking in and out, and sitting down in a chair): often four, five, six hours a day: shut up in my own room, or walking about in the fields.

Dickens's priority was the quality of the acting, not so much the plot or scenic spectacle or particular playwright, but the quality of individual performances of character. How much of this applies to his priorities as a novelist? Could one not say of the fiction that, whatever other novelistic shows there were in town, Dickens's always had the best acting—that his books were platforms for great dramatic character performances? To spend hours at a time in studying the simplest functions—exits, entrances, sitting down in a chair—indicates his intense fascination with details of behaviour traits, not only observed but personally enacted and re-enacted. The scale of his devotion to observation and imitation of character traits is quite extraordinary. How many ways *are* there to sit down in a chair? Open a Dickens novel and it is clear that how people sit down reveals much about them. The same applies to handshakes, soup-drinking, walking, letter-writing. Any trivial activity is unwittingly, treacherously idiosyncratic in Dickens's world and flashes up as a piece of revelatory stage business.

Dickens once told G. H. Lewes that 'every word said by his characters was distinctly *heard* by him'. The creatures of Dickens's imagination had an auditory reality, but they were often also start-lingly visualized as they formed themselves before him. In 1865, tired with writing *Our Mutual Friend*, he sat down one day to try to find some ideas for the annual Christmas story for *All The Year Round*. From what seems to have been almost an inspiration, he created the figure of the little adopted daughter of Dr. Marigold. He described the moment of creation to a friend: 'Suddenly the little character that you will see, and all belonging to it, came flashing up in the most cheerful manner, and I had only to look on and leisurely describe it.' These characters appeared spontaneously, caught in performance, as if Dickens were not creator but audience. Such experience became for him a touchstone of the reality of fictional beings. In giving some advice to a young author he stressed the need for the writer to believe in the fiction he was creating, and cited his own experience: 'when I am describing a scene I can as distinctly see the people I am describing as I can see you now.' He made much the same point in a letter to Forster, written at a time when he was undergoing considerable distress, of a kind that might have threatened his concentration as a novelist:

But may I not be forgiven for thinking it a wonderful testimony to my being made for my art, that when, in the midst of this trouble and pain, I sit down to my book, some beneficent power shows it all to me, and tempts me to be interested, and I don't invent it—really do not—*but see it*, and write it down.

Dickens is simply transcribing what already exists. However, the apparently spontaneous creation, in visual and auditory terms, of his imaginary characters was consolidated, or even helped into being, by his own impulse to play their roles. His daughter Mamie famously recalled one occasion (most probably during the time of writing *Hard Times*) when she watched him in the heat of composition:

I was lying on the sofa endeavouring to keep perfectly quiet, while my father wrote busily and rapidly at his desk, when he suddenly jumped from his chair and rushed to a mirror which hung near, and in which I could see the reflection of some extraordinary facial contortions which he was making. He returned rapidly to his desk, wrote furiously for a few moments, and then went again to the mirror. The facial pantomime was resumed, and then turning toward, but evidently not seeing me, he began talking rapidly in a low voice. Ceasing this soon, however, he returned once more to his desk, where he remained silently writing until luncheon time [. . .]. He had thrown himself completely into the character he was creating, and [. . .] for the time being he had not only lost sight of his surroundings, but had actually become in action, as in imagination, the creature of his pen.

Further confirmation of this strong link between acting and composing comes from a witness late in Dickens's life. The 13-year-old George Woolley worked on the gardens at Gad's Hill, and recorded his memories some years after Dickens's death:

Opposite the house was a sort of wood the master called the Wilderness. He used to go over there to write [in the Chalet] [. . .]. I used to hear what sounded like someone making a speech. I wondered what it was at first, and I found out it was Mr. Dickens composing his writing out loud. He was working on *Edwin Drood* then.

While 'composing his writing out loud', he may well also have been performing the evolving characters, as he certainly did for Luke Fildes, the illustrator to *Drood*. Fildes used to go down to Gad's Hill over this period in order to discuss the illustrations for each part. Sometimes, he recalled, Dickens would act out the particular scene to be depicted. Presumably the scene had been so precisely visualized (and heard) by the novelist, as it came into being, that he could not conceive of its being portrayed in any other way. Again, when he invited James Fields into his study at Gad's Hill to hear the first number of *Drood*, on 10 October 1869, some months before its publication, he 'read it aloud acting it as he went on'. Even when he was not reading aloud, but just conversing anecdotally with friends, that irrepressible histrionic instinct fluttered into activity, as Percy Fitzgerald described:

It is difficult to give an idea of Dickens's 'bearing' in conversation; for he regularly *acted* his stories, and was irresistible. He called up the scene, his eyes became charged with humour, the wrinkles at the corners of his mouth quivered with enjoyment, his voice and richly unctuous laugh contributed, with his strangely grotesque glances, and so he told the tale.

The extraordinary scene recounted by Mamie bears out Forster's point about Dickens's 'power of projecting himself' into his imaginary characters; 'what he desired to express he became'. These characters were intensely realized acoustically and in terms of facial expression. Dickens's verification of the reality of his imaginary characters had to be histrionically conducted. The characters he generated from observation, drawing either from individuals or isolated features in the world around him or from what that 'beneficent power' miraculously showed to him in his study, were auditioned for their roles in the novels by submitting to Dickens's impersonation of them. The creative process Mamie describes closely resembles Dickens's private rehearsals for his public Readings. Both as a writer and as a Reader, he performed his fictions into being.

Composition for Dickens, as he often remarked, was less burden-some than might have been expected, since so many characters came spontaneously before his imagination. His impersonation of these fledgling characters was a recreational indulgence. He relaxed into it. Late in his life he could spend hours in mimicry. During the exhausting winter tour of America, 1867–8, on evenings when he was not performing on the platform he would perform impromptu, in private, with friends. Annie Fields's diary records several occasions when her husband James and Dickens would spend such evenings together: 'He [Dickens] had been giving imitations and making pan-tomime all the evening until they were choked and convulsed with laughter.' Dickens made a confession on one occasion that reveals a lifelong inclination: 'Assumption has charms for me—I hardly know for how many wild reasons—so delightful, that I feel a loss of O I can't say what exquisite foolery, when I lose a chance of being some one, in voice &c not at all like myself.' The Readings ensured that he gave himself as many chances as he wanted to indulge what he here calls the 'exquisite foolery' of impersonation.

'MOST PEOPLE ARE OTHER PEOPLE'

As I remarked earlier, in addition to being a compulsive mimic him-self, Dickens's fiction was preoccupied by the motif of impersonation. However fascinated he himself was with the charms of 'assumption', he also played to the contemporary curiosity about the complexities and instabilities of social identity, the role-playing that featured so much in the popular literature of the period. The early decades of the nineteenth century marked a time of accelerating social mobility and of the accumulation in towns and cities of a socially very diverse population. The projection of a 'self', 'making a figure' in society, especially in the concentratedly heterogeneous society of the city, naturally engaged the interests of a 'parvenu civilisation' (as Robin Gilmour has termed it), one for whom 'Silver Fork' fiction, with its heyday in the later 1820s, offered both voyeuristic entertainment

and a species of 'conduct' literature for those aspiring to consort
with patrician circles. The 1820s and 1830s also saw the proliferation of 'foundling fiction', narratives chronicling the progress of
protagonists with no known social and familial background. *Oliver
Twist* (1837–9) is the classic in this context. The wide appeal of
this subgenre tapped into the contemporary preoccupation with
the question of how identity is constituted in a society increasingly
susceptible to social mobility and therefore increasingly fascinated
by symptoms of origins. The orphan could assume—indeed could
be—any kind of identity: Oliver himself commutes for much of the
novel between Fagin's gang and the genteel homes of Mr Brownlow
and the Maylies. Because we do not know his social background, we
have no way of knowing for sure to which of these social milieux
he belongs by birth. Dickens's emphasis on the arbitrary 'power of
dress' in this novel reinforces the sense that identity is a social construct, where agreed codes of signification rather than any inherent
individual identity become paramount:

Wrapped in the blanket which had hitherto formed his [the baby Oliver's]
only covering, he might have been the child of a nobleman or a beggar; it
would have been hard for the haughtiest stranger to have assigned him his
proper station in society. But now that he was enveloped in the old calico
robes which had grown yellow in the same service, he was badged and
ticketed, and fell into his place at once—the orphan of a workhouse [. . .].

Clothes, like theatrical costume, can bestow identity just as much
as express it. 'Clothes gave us individuality [. . .] Clothes have made
Men of us', writes Professor Teufelsdröckh in Carlyle's *Sartor Resartus*
(1833–4), the book that evidently inspired Dickens's play with the
'clothes philosophy' in *Oliver Twist* three years later: 'Society, which
the more I think of it astonishes me the more, is founded upon Cloth.'
Markers of social class—clothes, carriages, gesture, gait, epistolary
style, accent (all those things the young Dickens studied)—could be
bought or learned by those with more money than pedigree, much as
actors could acquire mimic skills and the necessary stage accessories
in order to project a certain kind of social identity. Jingle, the rogue

actor in *Pickwick Papers*, performs just this kind of trick to insinuate himself into social acceptance among those who are not his social peer group, and it is chiefly Jingle's protean identity that energizes the action in the early months of *Pickwick*.

The 'right' kind of accent could certainly be cultivated, in order to assume a persona—to 'impersonate'. As one historian of nineteenth-century forms of speech has observed, 'Anxiety about pronunciation was associated with anxieties about social class at a time when many of the old demarcations were being eroded by newer types of capitalist economy with its opportunities for sudden rises and catastrophic falls.' In 1836, the same year as the publication of *Sketches by Boz*, B. H. Smart, the author of *A New Critical Pronouncing Dictionary* was promoting the consolidation of 'standard dialect': 'that in which all marks of a particular place of birth and residence are lost and nothing appears to indicate any other habits of intercourse than with the well-bred and well-informed, wherever they may be found.' Several of Boz's 'Sketches' comically exploit parvenu anxieties about lowly origins, for instance 'The Tuggses at Ramsgate' and 'Horatio Sparkins'. In the face of social pressures of this kind for a genteel linguistic homogenization, linguistic motley and idiosyncrasy acquired fresh curiosity value of just the kind that the young Dickens provided in *Sketches*. Dickens was very conscious of an effort to preserve the fading picturesque in London's street life, as for instance in 'The Last Cab Driver and the First Omnibus Cad': 'Improvement has peered beneath the aprons of our cabs, and penetrated to the very innermost recesses of our omnibuses. Dirt and fustian will vanish before cleanliness and livery. Slang will be forgotten when civility becomes general.' Live exhibitions of such picturesque types and their spicy language were a gift for journalists, novelists, and professional impersonators.

The jostling of a great variety of dialects in the early nineteenth century would have been particularly conspicuous in the large cities, especially London, as they became centres for a huge and diverse cosmopolitan population. In the mid-1830s it was reckoned that there were, 'on an average, 120,000 strangers at all times, staying only for a few days in London'. This number excluded non-English settlers in the city: e.g., 130,000 Scots, 200,000 Irish, 30,000 French. London was a polyglot phenomenon, and that is where the teenage Dickens honed his skills in mimicry. Journalists and other writers revelled in reproducing the speech idiosyncrasies of London's many types. As we saw in the previous chapter, police reports in popular newspapers were often cast in the form of dialogues between magistrates and plaintiffs or accused, in which each would be distinguished by his or her particular speech style, phonetically rendered. This encouraged the reading aloud of such reports, in which the reader would vocally reproduce the accents of the criminals and judiciary.

One way and another, there was a heightened alertness to the range of speech styles and voices, and hence perhaps the growth in popularity of entertainments in which acts of multiple impersonation featured prominently. 'Most people are other people,' wrote Oscar Wilde: 'Their thoughts are someone else's opinions, their lives a mimicry, their passions a quotation.' This formulation lifts the issue of impersonation into another dimension. The precariousness of social identity and the consciousness of the self as a congeries of roles rather than a unitary being are symptoms of the condition of modernity. One historian of modernity summarizes the predicament (seeing the self as a kind of permanent impersonator):

Becoming a self could be said to involve a 'rehearsal' of identity, a taking-on and casting-off of roles, which are tried on, worn, almost like clothes; the self becomes a series of such identities, never really assimilated to them, yet clearly marked by them [. . .]. Using the theatrical analogy, we can say the self is both actor, and audience or spectator; actor and spectator become part of the structure of self-identity.

The preoccupation with rehearsing an identity, in the terms sketched out above, became conspicuous in the early Victorian period, and particularly in Dickens. Impersonation as a public entertainment effectively theatricalized a predicament warily recognized as part of the cultural condition of nineteenth-century England. Because impersonation was most spectacularly evident in the theatre—in the actor's professional role-playing—the theatre was branded a kind of 'pariah', as we saw in Chapter 1: theatricality, in Nina Auerbach's words, 'connotes not only lies, but a fluidity of character that decomposes the uniform integrity of the self'. What Dickens and the brood of professional impersonators mentioned at the opening of this chapter managed to do was to continue to indulge the fascination with role-playing, the mobility and fluidity of identity, but to distance such performances from the 'theatrical'. They were offering those 'reverent Victorians' drawing-room entertainments, within which 'theatre' was distanced both by establishing a polite parlour ambience and by the accomplished imitation and ridiculing of professional actors. The most celebrated prototype for such forms of entertainment was the actor whom the young Dickens went to watch on every possible occasion, Charles Mathews the Elder and his 'At Home' entertainments.

CHARLES MATHEWS

Charles Mathews was the greatest professional impersonator of the age and a powerful influence on Dickens in a number of ways. I have already alluded briefly to Dickens's early flirtation with the theatre as a career. It was in April 1832 that the twenty-year-old Dickens made an arrangement to be auditioned at Covent Garden Theatre before the stage manager George Bartley and the actor Charles Kemble. On the appointed day he developed such a bad cold that he had to cancel the audition, intending to renew his application in the following season. The disappointment was something of a turning point in his career: 'See how near I may have been, to another sort of life', he wrote to Forster years later, indicating that he had been thinking of the theatre 'in quite a business-like way'. Before he could renew his application, his literary career began to shows signs of greater promise: 'I made a great splash in the gallery soon afterwards; the Chronicle opened to me; I had a distinction in the little world of the newspaper, which made me like it; began to write [...]'. 'Began to write': as biographers are prone to remark, we nearly lost Dickens the Novelist to Dickens the Actor. 'Fancy Bartley or Charles Kemble now!' he mused in 1844, recalling the auditions scheme of twelve years earlier: 'And how little they suspect me!'

He did not, of course, relinquish acting. When, later in life, he took part in amateur theatricals, he revelled in opportunities for impersonation of a variety of characters. In Montreal in May 1842, he joined the Garrison Amateurs in a production of three plays, taking a role in each of them. He was occasionally so completely disguised as to delay recognition by the audience for some time. *The Montreal Gazette* found his acting style 'a sort of mixture of the late Charles Mathews and Mr. Buckstone's'. In a production in 1852 of a short farce co-written with Mark Lemon, *Mr. Nightingale's Diary*, Dickens played a character who appeared at various points in the play in a medley of disguises. One who saw him in this role remarked, 'As *Mr. Gabblewig* he assumed four or five different disguises, changing his look, voice and dress with a completeness and rapidity that no Lingard [W.H. Lingard, actor and vocalist] or MacCabe [Frederic MacCabe, the ventriloquist and impersonator] on the regular boards has ever excelled.' The various disguises included a cockney 'Boots', like Sam Weller, and an elderly woman very much like Mrs. Gamp. For several of those watching, he was hard to recognize for some time in each of these impersonations. Years later, in 1867, a reporter for the *New York Times*, in reviewing one of Dickens's New York Readings, recalled that performance in *Mr. Nightingale's Diary* as 'inimitable': 'we certainly have rarely, if ever, seen comic acting equal to it. It was easy, graceful, never overdone or overdrawn; and its effect was irre[s]istible.' In 1850 Dickens took the part of Sir Charles Coldstream in Boucicault's farce *Used Up* at Knebworth and Rockingham. Once again he played a character who is required to disguise himself as another: Sir Charles must become a ploughboy in Act II. The technical challenge of role-playing within role-playing was profoundly appealing for Dickens.

The piece the twenty-year-old aspirant had chosen to perform at Covent Garden was an item from the repertoire of Charles Mathews himself. Dickens claimed that he 'knew three or four successive years of Mathews's At Homes from sitting in the pit to hear them'. Mathews was more to Dickens than an inspirational mimic. The conduct of his performances as narrator–presenter offered a model for the relationship Dickens the novelist cultivated with his readers, and it is time to examine this more closely, in the context of Mathews's career. Paul Schlicke has done more than most, in *Dickens and Popular Entertainment*, to investigate Mathews's relationship to Dickens, especially where the Readings were concerned. He identified three particular 'areas of consonance' between Dickens's and Mathews's entertainments: the role of the solo performer in generating a special rapport with his audience; the soloist's ability to embody a wide range of characters through impersonation and make these impersonations very 'natural'; the status of the entertainments as 'rational amusements', embodying both social satire and moral uplift. These are useful pointers. I shall be exploring some of their implications in the following discussion of Mathews.

Mathews began his career as a comic actor. By the time he was 27, after a busy three years with the prestigious York Company, he had become a very proficient impersonator of the leading actors of the day, and could perform ventriloquism. His London debut was in 1803. In 1807, a leading comic actor at Drury Lane, Jack Bannister, won critical acclaim by performing a monologue entertainment with songs, called *Bannister's Budget*. This involved impersonations of half-a-dozen different characters. Mathews was impressed and devised a near-solo entertainment of his own—near-solo in the sense that the only other performer was his wife who offered (in her own words) just 'occasional assistance' with some songs. This was performed every season from 1808 to 1811. Between 1811 and 1817 Mathews wrote and performed similar entertainments with a variety of partners (including Edmund Yates) and his reputation as a virtuoso soloist grew. In 1817 his one-man show, the prototype of an immensely successful series of what he called 'At Home', made its London debut. These were the shows that the young Dickens followed so avidly in the late 1820s.

Although the 'At Home' performances were modified over the years between 1817 and Mathews's death in 1835, they followed a basic two-part structure. The first part (often in two 'acts') consisted of songs and recitations, frequently with a travel motif: e.g., *Mail Coach Adventure*, *Trip to Paris*, *Trip to America*. Mathews would play himself as the central figure subjected to the diversions and follies of a range of colourful characters (all impersonated by Mathews) encountered on his journeys. The second part was the 'monopolylogue', a one-man farce, with Mathews playing each of the half-dozen or so characters. The staging for the musical-recitation section consisted usually of a drawing-room set, with a centre-stage table, covered to the floor with green baize, a piano, and a large screen, behind which the performer would make his rapid costume changes. Mathews would initially appear in formal evening wear.

Mathews's art evidently attracted a diverse audience, from all social and intellectual levels. Its high level of histrionic sophistication called into question popular assumptions about 'mimicking' and 'imitating'. For many of those who saw him, Mathews's talents went far beyond mere mimicry, as Paul Schlicke has emphasized. Thus, for example, *Blackwood's Magazine* asserted:

It is idle and invidious to attempt to distinguish this kind of acting from any other, by calling it *mimicry*. Who thinks of calling [David] Wilkie's pictures mimicry?—And what are they but just representations of individual character and habit, under peculiar circumstances? And what does it require to produce them but plastic bodily powers working under the direction of a mind possessed of a fine talent for general observation, and an exquisite taste for discrimination between that which is common and essential to a class, and that which is peculiar to a particular individual of that class. And these are precisely the qualities which Mr. Mathews possesses in common with all successful actors.

Mimicry, according to this estimate, suggests something too mechanical, too superficial a dexterity, to apply to Mathews's performance.
There was an intelligence and social perceptiveness that marked off
his histrionic talents from those of the mere mimic. Byron is reported
to have remarked that 'Mathews's imitations were of the *mind*', and
that those who pronounced him a mimic should rather consider him
'an accurate and philosophic observer of human nature, blest with
the rare talent of intuitively identifying himself with the minds of
others'. As *Blackwood's* remarked, 'his faculty is so decidedly that of
[. . .] creating character, instead of merely aping the tones, or gestures,
or countenances, of individuals'. That is an important distinction.
Mathews was not copying a subject; he was not simply what we
would call an impressionist. He was building characters meticulously
and thoroughly and this vivid creativity would have had great appeal
for the young aspiring actor–writer Dickens. Mathews himself was
emphatic about distinguishing his art from that of the mere mimic
entertainer: he was, he said, an 'imitator of manner' and his speciality
was 'imitative satire'. He was not to be thought a coarse lampooner.
In his prefatory address to *Country Cousins* in 1820 he made the
point very clearly:

Before I enter upon my task, permit me, however to utter a few words in
explanation of the epithet *imitation*, or, as it is sometimes in carelessness,
and sometime in hostility, called *mimicry*. I look upon this talent when
applied to the body, to be what satire is when applied to the mind [. . .].
It is my purpose to evince, by *general* delineation, how easily peculiarities
may be acquired by negligence, and how difficult they are to eradicate when
strengthened by habit; to show how often vanity and affectation steal upon
the deportment of youth, and how sure they are to make their possessor
ridiculous in after life; in short, to exemplify the old adage, that 'No man is
contemptible for being what he is, but for pretending to be what he is not'.

Mathews is making some fine discriminations here in attempting
to dissociate the essential personality from the mannerisms ('peculiarities') that grow upon it, either by negligence or by cultivation.
His satirical art is designed to draw attention to this process of

accretion, to ridicule by imitation those parts of the personality that have formed as late and distorting growths, through vanity and affectation, and thereby encourage people to shed them. His description of his comic art is remarkably similar to the theory of laughter developed at the end of the century by Henri Bergson. Bergson's contention that we laugh at the 'mechanical' in human behaviour, at the rigidities that form themselves on otherwise 'elastic' organic human beings, focuses at one point in his essay on gestures, especially where they become rigidified and artificial. One test of whether such gestures are a natural, organic expression of their owner is their imitability:

This is also the reason why gestures, at which we never dreamt of laughing, become laughable when imitated by another individual. The most elaborate explanations have been offered for this extremely simple fact. A little reflection, however, will show that our mental state is ever changing, and that if our gestures faithfully followed these inner movements, if they were as fully alive as we, they would never repeat themselves, and so would keep imitation at bay. We begin, then, to become imitable only when we cease to be ourselves. I mean our gestures can only be imitated in their mechanical uniformity, and therefore exactly in what is alien to our living personality. To imitate any one is to bring out the element of automatism he has allowed to creep into his person. And as this is the very essence of the ludicrous, it is no wonder that imitation gives rise to laughter.

Like Dickens, and especially like the early Dickens of *Sketches by Boz* and *Pickwick Papers*, Mathews's comic exposure of vanity and affectation must have focused on those rigidified idiosyncrasies.

What drew the young Dickens to attend so many of Mathews's shows was the extraordinary technique of impersonation, Mathews's capacity almost to efface himself in the act of embodying one of his characters: it was tantamount to a faculty for 'creating character' as *Blackwood's* had described it. This is what Dickens was to do, not only in his Readings, but also as a writer in the process of composition, as we have seen. The commitment to full impersonation and the consequent disappearance of the soloist narrator into his characters were testified to again and again by those who saw

Mathews in action. 'As an actor, Mr. Mathews possessed the rare art of extracting his personal nature from his assumptions; and he was *Sir Fretful* or *Morbleau*, without one shade of *Mathews* about him.' The question about how to define precisely what he did might best be addressed by constructing a terminological gamut: mimicry—imitation—impersonation—assumption. *The Observer* was concerned to draw fine distinctions between such terms:

There never was a greater mistake made than that Mathews was a mere imitator. He was, indeed, an imitator, but he kept his powers of mimicry in due subjection; he made use of them as accessaries [sic] towards effecting his main object. He has also been called a caricaturist. This is not true: the caricaturist exaggerates and distorts; Mathews, on the contrary, was always natural.

Mimicry is the imitation of external traits; impersonation is the fuller entry into the character of someone else; assumption suggests the complete absorption of the self in another. At the mimicry end of the gamut, the performer remains the principal presence, ostentatiously drawing attention to his powers of imitation. At the assumption end the performer has gone, having transformed himself into a different identity. Mimicry, as the *Observer* remarks imply, is just a technical means to a more complex end. Mathews was evidently not a caricaturist in the sense of confining his impersonations to exaggerated mimicry of isolated traits. He represented the whole personality along with its various behavioural excrescences. Dickens as a soloist seems to have aimed for the same rendition; that was not surprising since as far as his craft was concerned he had grown up on Mathews. Compare the *Observer*'s eulogy of Mathews's ability to transcend caricature with this 1859 review of a Dickens Reading: 'Mr. Dickens never in his imitations allowed himself to overstep the line which separates imitation from caricature.' More importantly, what the *Observer* said of Mathews, that he was 'always natural', was also said of Dickens in his platform impersonations, and said with some surprise, since the early works from which he mostly drew his Readings were so strongly associated with caricature. We will return to this critique in a later chapter.

What Dickens learnt from Mathews was incalculable, both for his art as a novelist and for his public Readings. Of course, he had an innate talent for impersonation in the first place, as he had acknowledged, 'I believed I had [. . .] a natural power of reproducing in my own person what I observed in others.' His study of Mathews enabled him to develop this talent by close attention to the actor's technique and by sustained practising of the arts of character acting. This was always more than a matter of mastery of technique. Dickens had a passion for sinking himself into his characterizations. Simply to *be* someone else, for a brief period, was intoxicating for Dickens, as we have heard him confess ('Assumption has charms for me'). The vocal and physical contortions involved in impersonation stretched and toned his imagination, and refreshed his spirit. It took him out of himself, almost literally. I shall be exploring later the broader significance of this in relation both to Dickens's composition of his fiction and to his career as a public Reader. My purpose here is to underline the affinities between Dickens and Mathews as masters of the art of projecting themselves into other characters, so as to make those characters live as people, not caricatures.

Mathews's extraordinary capacity to concentrate in one person an apparently infinite variety of social types—dynamic demonstrations of the fluidity of identity—must have had a special attraction in the cultural climate of the 1820s and 1830s, when, as already suggested, there was such a marked interest in questions of identity, class status, and the changing composition of society. Mathews's art was just one of several contemporary enterprises designed to nourish and tease such curiosity. Forms of entertainment based on the reproduction of a miscellaneous gallery of social types, from all classes, with their dress, physical mannerisms and speech patterns accurately caught, are precisely what Mathews and Dickens were offering to the public in the early 1830s, in, respectively, 'At Home' and the newspaper sketches by Boz. However, Mathews was not just the impersonator; like Boz he was also the presenter–narrator. The crafting of that role for 'At Home', the relationship developed between Mathews and his characters and between Mathews and the audience, may also have influenced Dickens in less obvious ways, both in his writings and in the Readings.

Let us look at the kind of material Mathews used and the way he presented it. Here is an extract from one of his shows, *Trip to Paris* (1819). It is an extended satire on the fashionable 'Galomania' in England in the years immediately following the opening up of Europe to the tourists in 1815. It depicts an English provincial family (father, mother, daughter), evidently newly rich and concerned to acquire some cultivation. It is a fair example both of the kind of material and of the role of the observer–narrator. The family join the narrator-Mathews figure in the coach bound for Dover and the crossing to France. The father opens conversation with the narrator:

'Good morning, sir, are you going across?' 'Across? [says Mathews] Yes, sir.' 'Aye, suppose you are going to Paris?' 'Yes, sir.' 'So are we; wife and *daater*, there they be, sir, that's my wife, and that's my *daater* up in the corner; *daater* speaks French.' 'Astonishing.' ' Learnt it of a German, that learnt it at Dunkirk; talk, Polly, talk; ax the gentleman if he's going to Paris in proper French?' 'La, pa, don't be so disagreeable; how can you be so?' 'Talk, I say, Polly, what's the use of me laying out *sich* a sight of money in your *hedication*, if you won't show off; talk, Polly—talk, I insists upon it.' '*Ouly vou poor Parie, Mounseer*?' 'There sir, what do you think of that? That's what I call French; that'll do, I think!' 'Pray, sir,' said his fat wife, from the other side of the coach, 'is the sea-bathing good at Paris?'

One would need only to add a little facetious narration to make this material into one of Boz's sketches. 'The Tuggses at Ramsgate', for instance, tells much the same story, with the same fondness for comic exposure of details of such pretensions, especially in speech styles. Much of Dickens's early comic work springs from the same source. Since he had learned several of Mathews's most popular routines by heart, it is not surprising he wanted to recycle some of it as he made his literary debut.

Dickens's literary debt to Mathews was explored some years ago, notably by Earle Davis and by Ana Laura Zambrano. Davis argued forcefully for the degree to which Dickens's characters are, through Mathews's influence, largely constituted by their idiosyncratic speech styles. Both critics demonstrate echoes in certain Dickens characters of speech idiosyncrasies exploited in Mathews's performances. Zambrano saw Mathews's use of comic dialects, exaggerated and eccentric characters, digressions from the main narrative into songs and tales, and the 'travelling from town to town whenever the action slows', as fundamental to the design of *Pickwick Papers*. To this list of correspondences I would add two or three points. Firstly, Richard Klepac, in his study of the 'At Home' events, has drawn attention to the frequency in Mathews's entertainments of characters with reiterated tag lines—a device that became very common in Dickens. Secondly, Dickens and Mathews seem to have shared literary influences, perhaps even script-writers, to some extent. Mathews's 'At Home' sketches were written both by himself and by contemporary dramatists and theatre practitioners, and they included John Poole and Richard Brinsley Peake. Contemporary reviewers of *Pickwick Papers* quickly recognized the similar comic milieu from which Dickens's writings came. The first monthly number was greeted by *The Atlas* as stale, overfamiliar humour, from 'that melancholy region of exhausted comicality, which Hood and Poole [...] have reaped'. Furthermore, Dickens had acted in plays by Peake in the early 1830s, and *Pickwick Papers* clearly bears the legacy. One of the incidents in Mathews's 'At Home' entitled *Air, Earth and Water* is a sketch of two Cockney sportsmen out shooting crows on the first of September.

The third point concerns the writer-as-performer. To watch a Mathews monopolylogue was both to be amused by the range of colourful character types presented in a racy narrative and to marvel at the technical virtuosity of the soloist. This is also true of Boz in *Pickwick Papers*. As the narrator Dickens was the gifted, virtuoso, hyperactive literary performer. This sense of Dickens's fiction as a species of theatrical performance was well put by Robert Garis in *The Dickens Theatre*:

In theatrical art the primary object of our attention is the artist himself, on the stage of his own theatre, performing his brilliant routines. The characters he 'creates' on this stage will come to us, and be consistently known to us, as the embodiments of his brilliant gift for *mimicry*.

Dickens was ebulliently self-conscious of his roles as editor–impresario (he calls himself 'Mr Pickwick's Stage-Manager') and single-handed animator of this vast cast of characters. Each monthly instalment of *Pickwick* was a literary 'At Home'.

I am suggesting that Dickens's narratorial relationship with his readers was influenced by Mathews's combination of narrator and impersonator in a variety of subtle ways. Consider the staging of the 'At Home' performances. As noted earlier the musical-recitation section of Mathews's 'At Home' was performed in a drawing-room set, with a central green-baize table, a piano, and a large screen, behind which the performer would make his rapid costume changes. Mathews would initially appear in formal evening wear (as did Dickens for his Readings). The 'At Home' performances were to be redolent of 'Home' entertainment rather than 'Theatre'. Mathews publicly insisted that his 'At Home' series was 'not an entertainment of the stage'. So that proverbially disreputable site for histrionic performance transformed itself under Mathews's management to a genteel drawing room. These are important details in the light of Dickens's management of his public Readings. Mathews's centrally placed green-baize table might have been consciously echoed in Dickens's centre-stage Reading desk, which at an early period was covered in green velvet. Dickens's platform set, while not a drawing room, was composed of domestic furnishings—the elegant little desk, the carpeting, the matching fabric backdrop. This scenic distancing of the genre from 'the stage' was reinforced by the particular rapport Mathews developed with his audience, as one reviewer remarked:

It is true the room in which he received his company was very theatrical in *form*,—otherwise, it was substantially the private drawing-room of the most entertaining gentleman of his age; and had it not been for the spikes in front of the orchestra, the pit must have shaken hands with Charles Mathews, Esq. before it wished him good-night. His performances, indeed, [. . .] were so personally directed to the audience, that the latter was rather a participator in than witness of what was said and done by the 'gentleman at the head of the table;' and who, at least, was as far removed from the company of a stage as from the 'ladies and gentlemen' who form the company in front of it.

The title 'At Home' asserted the domestic base from which all these imitative excursions departed, to which they returned, and by which all that did not belong to 'Home' was to be judged. Much of Mathews's material came from his travels abroad. His audiences were invited to share Mathews's particular comic relish of a range of colourful types, in a complicitly homely recognition of norms of behaviour from which the miscellaneous characters entertainingly deviate.

How did this strategy of cultivating a personal and informal relationship with his audience nuance the presentation of Mathews's material? The types of social pretension illustrated in that *Trip to Paris* scene would have been very familiar to Mathews's audiences, and it is notable that those audiences represented a full cross section of British society. He was admired as a consummate artist (not just a popular entertainer) by Byron, Scott, and Coleridge. His 'At Home' shows were great events in the London season, and at his death many obituaries drew attention to his extraordinary appeal across all classes. His audiences were drawn by the performance strategies to laugh *with* Mathews, the drily ironic satirist, at the crassly expressed social and cultural aspiration of these naïve folk, while at the same time candidly or covertly aware of correspondences with the behaviour patterns of their own families, or their friends or themselves. The relationship between their 'true' selves (as they thought) and the social selves they might sometimes assume (the behavioural codes they subscribed to) was histrionically projected as the relationship between Mathews *in propria persona*, the detached gentlemanly narrator, and Mathews the polyphonic medley of impersonated types. The distinction was reinforced by the way Mathews engaged his audience's complicity, according to the comment quoted earlier. His often costumed impersonated characters belonged to 'the company of a stage', but Mathews belonged to the 'private drawing-room', together with the ladies and gentlemen of his audience: he was one of them. This segregation, however, was a masterly illusion, because Mathews, ostensibly alienating his medley of ridiculous characters to the other side of the footlights (figuratively speaking), was also, of course, assimilating himself to them through the act of impersonation. The carefully calibrated relationship between performer, audience, and impersonated characters seems to have been mastered by Dickens in his Readings. The *New York Times* remarked on this in reviewing his first Reading of 'A Christmas Carol' in New York: 'His face relaxes into a smile, never marked enough to interfere in the least with the impersonation, but indicating and establishing a strong and hearty sympathy with his audience.' One of the first things noted by the New York reviewers was Dickens's 'putting himself *en rapport* with his hearers and becoming one of them—while occupying his own position as story-teller'.

Mathews's complicity with the audience, therefore, the sense that he was a gentleman among ladies and gentlemen, created a subtle intimacy that more deeply engaged his audience (throughout its various levels of sophistication) and gave the illusion of distancing the gallery of eccentric characters whom he paraded in impersonation. In a review of the relative merits of Mathews and one of his famous rivals, the ventriloquist showman, Alexandre Vattemare, this point about Mathews's distinctive relationship with his audience came out strongly: 'A great advantage the former [Mathews] possesses over his competitor is that "conversational web", by which he ingratiates himself with his company, gives relief to his entertainment, and comparative repose to himself.' This 'conversational web' spun by the performer to secure his audience's sympathetic companionship is similar to the circumstances stipulated by Henri Bergson as a necessary precondition for laughter:

Our laughter is always the laughter of a group [. . .]. However spontaneous it seems, laughter always implies a kind of secret freemasonry, or even complicity, with other laughers, real or imaginary.

The entertainer, theatrical or literary, and particularly the comic entertainer, must create the community culture that is going to be supportively responsive to the material. Mathews did this. Dickens, as we saw in the first chapter, worked hard, both as writer and Reader, to develop the close, personal relationship with his readers and audiences so as to establish this 'freemasonry'. We are aware, for instance, of Dickens spinning just such a conversational web in the opening paragraphs of *A Christmas Carol*; and in Stave Two he describes the presence of the Ghost of Christmas Past at Scrooge's bedside, 'as close as I am now to you, and I am standing in the spirit at your elbow' (a passage deleted from the Reading text, since Dickens was indeed physically in the company of his readers). Throughout the 'Carol' he is the ingratiating, teasing, avuncular narrator, explicitly underlining his close companionship to the reader.

Dickens's habitual persona in so much of his fiction is that of the virtuoso narrator, 'performing his brilliant routines', in Robert Garis's words. He plays to his readers in his fiction, carefully cultivating their sympathies and coaxing them into active responsiveness: cajoling, facetious, hectoring, buttonholing. Dickens the narrator *projects* his narration much as an actor is taught to project his lines in a theatre. The act of narration becomes just that—an act—histrionically amplified. It sometimes amounts to another form of impersonation. In straddling the divide in this way, in being the gentlemanly narrator–observer as well as virtuoso animator by assumption of a vast range of highly coloured characters, Mathews created a model for the relationship Dickens developed with his readership in the early years and reinforced later as a public Reader before his audiences.

The appeal of Mathews's shows was not just the bifocal enjoyment now of the narrator–presenter and now of the impersonated dramatis personae as each gave way to the other. It was also based on that shifting, sleight-of-hand relationship, on the mystery of the ingenuity of transformation. How could one person so rapidly and so plausibly assume several different personalities, not just mimic accents? What might such a performance suggest about the constitution of personality and the capacity to inhabit several different identities? We have already seen the delight Dickens had in assuming a variety of roles as an actor. But it went deeper than that. He drew for his fiction on his sense that he himself had the potential for more than one identity. The fissility of the self was exploited creatively.

Dickens's narratorial persona, though not ostensibly a 'character' (except, of course, in first-person narration), was nonetheless instinct with histrionic self-awareness, now spinning the conversational web to trap the reader's relaxed confidence, now partly entering character by sidling into free indirect discourse, now subsumed wholly in character. And even those characters seem touched by this colossal histrionic vitality. Robert Garis made some subtle discriminations between types of theatricality among Dickens's own fictional characters. 'All of the typically Dickensian characters can best be thought of as "performing" their own personalities or the emotions characteristic of their "roles".' He goes on to distinguish two types of 'performing people': those self-consciously playing a certain role and expecting us to be the audience for the performance (Skimpole is his chief example), and those who 'generate "behaviour" in a copious and continuous flow, never showing the slightest concern about the effect they are making on other people'. This second type is the one that Dickens represents in his most famous characterizations, according to Garis. While the distinctions between the two seem less sharp than this summary implies (for example, to which category does Micawber or Mrs Gamp belong, each being concerned to project a certain social or professional persona, but not to the degree of Skimpole's self-projection?), the idea of Dickens's characters' 'performing' their own personalities, with greater or lesser degrees of self-consciousness, is highly suggestive in the context of our present discussion. For there are layers of role-playing in a Dickens novel. There is the bravura narrative performance (as Garis remarked, 'Dickens's presence in his prose takes the form of an impulse to applaud'), and there is the sense we may have of a consciousness in the characters themselves of their self-projection (applicable to the muted Arthur Clennam and Esther Summerson, just as much as to the Bounderbys and Sparsits). Dickens's powers of impersonation summon them into being in the first place, in all their idiosyncratic distinctness—shape, size, gestures, voice. Once launched, many of them seem to have caught some of the surplus histrionic energy of their creator and take pains to keep up the performance. An obituary tribute in *Fraser's Magazine* caught exactly this sense in its observation that Dickens's 'figures impress one rather as impersonations than as persons'. Their superabundant personalities, their heightened colouring as identities, relate, as it were, to their capacity for sustained self-impersonation. The characters project themselves and thereby ready themselves for reproduction through theatrical impersonation.

Oddly, though, they don't survive theatrical reproduction too well without their narrator. Dickens was indispensable to his characters, not just in the obvious sense of his being their author in the first place, but also in his mediation of them to the reader in the course of their career in the novel. Percy Fitzgerald observed this dependency in his assessment of the degree to which stage adaptations impoverished some of Dickens's leading characters: 'another feature [of Dickens's humorous inventiveness] lies not so much in making the characters, as in "bringing them out" by the curious comments, hints, and remarks of the novelist himself.' This was lost in theatrical adaptations, but preserved in Dickens's Readings. They may have seemed larger than life and independent of the novel they happen to inhabit (and thus endlessly extractable for costumed reproduction in Dickens festival parades), but they were not independent, as Fitzgerald remarked. Remove the impersonator Dickens and they turn into costumed dummies. They belonged in their creator's hands, symbiotically. They were his impersonations of them.

Charles Mathews on stage, in his drawing-room set, established the framework for this fluctuating coalescence of actor and spectator, self and other, narrator and characters, in a sustained exercise of impersonation. He offered, 'At Home', both a laboratory for armchair sociology and a compendious satirical spectacular. He himself was a formidable personal presence in his kaleidoscopic virtuosity and solo command of so much material. Given each and all of these distinctive characteristics, it is no wonder the teenage Dickens was enthralled and pursued him night after night in the London theatres, at the same time as he was honing his own skills in impersonation, as aspiring writer and actor. Charles Mathews was the prototype of Charles Dickens. Indirectly, in April 1832, at that missed Covent Garden Theatre audition, Mathews's influence had nearly sucked that young man's life into his own professional orbit. Just over a quarter of a century later, the 46-year-old novelist and journalist decided to offer himself for another audition, before the national audience, as a gentlemanly soloist with a special capacity for impersonating a wide range of character types. The aspirant performer no longer needed to rely on a piece from Mathews's repertoire. Like Mathews, he now worked wholly from his own material. But that material and the narrator's mediation of that material already bore the impress of the great impersonator.

4

Celebrity on Tour

People in their thousands came to look at Dickens as he travelled all around Britain; they came 'to hear him roar or shake his literary mane as one of the largest lions of the day'. Once Dickens had reconciled himself and his readership to his new profession he had two principal tasks to address: the practicalities of staging the Readings, and the rewards and difficulties of being a hugely popular celebrity. In the 1860s, and particularly in America in 1867–8, he consolidated his status as one of the first great international celebrities in history. It was a type and scale of celebrity more easily associated with rock stars of the 1960s. For Dickens this raised tensions between privacy and public expectations, even though it was the direct outcome of his lifelong courtship of a close relationship with his readers. We begin, however, with the staging of the Readings, and the extraordinary (though typical) pains Dickens took over perfecting the Reading 'set', which he and his entourage took all around the country.

THE SET

There is a photograph of Dickens reading to his daughters in the garden at Gad's Hill (Fig. 3). It was taken in about 1865. Dickens sits on a garden chair, which has been reversed to allow him to use the chair-back as a book-rest. Mamie kneels close beside him, one hand on the chair-back, and Katey stands behind his left shoulder, looking down at the book, with her hand resting lightly on her father's right shoulder. Dickens sits, ramrod-straight, with an almost

3. R. H. Mason, Charles Dickens with Katey and Mamie, Gad's Hill Place (?1865). Photograph. Courtesy of the Charles Dickens Museum.

military air, posing with the open book. The *tout ensemble* is rather stiff and formal: no one looks as though he or she is relaxing over a book. Of course, the camera has not crept up to capture a family reading already in session. This is one of several photographs taken of the family and friends at home, and the three of them would have had to organize the pose and hold themselves still for some time, even though exterior photography, in full natural light, allowed a shorter time for exposure than interiors.

Nonetheless, it captures a family moment—Dickens reading to an audience of two. At this time in his life he was also reading to audiences of two thousand. As Dickens became a public Reader his needs in terms of set and props gradually expanded. In the first place he was to stand, not sit; so a chair-back was no use as a book rest. He also needed to be seen clearly, as well as heard clearly, in halls seating around two thousand listeners. So lighting and acoustic enhancements were developed. Since he read in halls rather than theatres he needed to be able to bring all this equipment to the venue, rather than rely on there being a ready-made set for him when he arrived. I shall be considering the key elements in this set, as Dickens prepared his platform for performance: the desk, the lighting and the screens. All these together ensured maximum focus on the solo reader, visually and acoustically, and control of the audience's viewpoint. No one, on such occasions, was allowed, like Katey, to look over the reader's shoulder. In fact, Dickens seems to have had a particular dread not only of anyone sitting behind him on these occasions but of listeners encroaching on either side of him. This became apparent years before he turned professional. What must have been one of his first Readings to a group outside his own house or (as in the case of his December 1844 Reading of *The Chimes* at Forster's house) the house of a close friend took place in Genoa, at the house of the British Consul, in the early summer of 1845. On that occasion Dickens was reported to have been particularly nervous, and he insisted that no one should sit behind him.

The Desk

At the Genoa reading, when he read the *Carol,* Dickens arranged for a reading table to be placed near a doorway. It carried a reading lamp, a glass of water, and a paper bag of raisins, by Dickens's special request. The raisins were presumably to fortify the reader's sugar level, when energy flagged, though it is hard to imagine Dickens taking time off, still at his table, to chomp the fruit. It is not known whether he sat or stood to give this Reading; most probably he sat, as he had done for the Reading of *The Chimes* at Forster's the previous December. The first public Readings came eight years later, at Birmingham Town Hall, where over three nights in December 1853 he read the 'Carol' (twice) and 'Cricket on the Hearth'. For that occasion he must have stood, in order to reach audiences of around two thousand, and he possibly used a lectern. The scale of the enterprise here dwarfed home Readings, or Readings to small circles of friends, though Dickens was concerned to preserve as much of that kind of intimacy as was compatible with reading before thousands. But clearly these large-scale Readings needed different furniture accessories.

The success of the Birmingham Readings (reported in *The Times* and other papers) brought many invitations from other institutions, a few of which he obliged the following December. One of his Readings took place in Sherborne, on 21 December 1854, and he wrote in advance to his old friend Macready, wondering what accommodation for Reading was provided at the hall there:

Because our illustrious countryman [Dickens] likes to stand at a desk, breast-high, with plenty of room about him—a sloping top—and a ledge to keep his book from tumbling off. If such a thing should not be there, however, on his arrival, I suppose even a Sherborne carpenter could knock it up, out of a deal board.—Is there a deal board in Sherborne though?

He was very precise about what he wanted, and it was to be a high desk. When he read (for charity) at Bristol just over three years later (on 19 January 1858) he was reported in the local paper as having been distinctly fussy about the exact size of the desk required. This suggests that he was still relying on the organizers of local Readings to provide him with his furniture, rather than travelling with his own equipment.

His Sherborne specifications seem to have been met in the high desk illustrated in one of two paintings of Dickens Reading by Robert Hannah (Fig. 4). No firm date has been assigned to this picture, which was apparently painted the morning after the artist went to a Dickens Reading. The desk depicted here corresponds to a description of a charity Reading given by Dickens at Peterborough, 18 December 1855:

4. Robert Hannah, Portraits of Charles Dickens Reading (?1858). Oil Paintings. Courtesy of the Charles Dickens Museum, London.

Dickens himself came down and superintended the arrangements, so anxious was he as to the result. At one end of the large Corn Exchange [. . .] he had caused to be erected a tall pulpit of red baize, as much like a Punch and Judy with the top taken off as anything. This was to be the reader's rostrum, but as the tall red pulpit looked lanky and very comical stuck up there alone, two dummy pulpits of similar construction were placed, one on each side, to bear it company. When the reader mounted into the middle box, nothing was visible of him but his head and shoulders, so if it be really true, as was stated afterwards by an indiscreet supernumerary, that Mr. Dickens' legs shook under him from first to last, the audience knew nothing of it [. . .]. The whole character of the stage arrangements suggested that Mr. Dickens was sure of his head, but not quite so sure of his legs.

Walter Dexter wrote an article in *The Dickensian* in 1941, on the occasion of the Dickens House's having been presented with this portrait and its companion picture (both by Hannah) of Dickens reading at his more familiar desk. Dexter mentioned inscriptions on Hannah's paintings by both the artist and Georgina Hogarth, to whom the paintings were given in 1904. Neither inscription can be found today. Dexter, however, presumably reporting on the information on the inscriptions, writes that this portrait 'represents Dickens giving his first Reading, presumably that in aid of the Hospital for Sick Children'. Dickens gave a Reading in London on behalf of the Hospital on 15 April 1858. If this dating of the painting is correct, then Dickens was still prepared to use the 'pulpit' lectern on the eve of his launching his professional career as a Reader (the first paid Reading was 29 April). However, by the start of his provincial Tour, in August of that year, he was using the small desk that was to serve him for all his subsequent Readings in Britain and America. This is illustrated in Hannah's second painting. The most likely time, therefore, for the change to the new desk is the spring or early summer of 1858. Georgina Hogarth, according to Dexter, wrote on Hannah's second painting, 'Date uncertain, probably about May 6th [1858]'. The date in square brackets may be Dexter's. May 6 was the second of Dickens's paid Readings, at St Martin's Hall, Long Acre, London.

Dickens designed his desk with great care. His drawing and written instructions for the design are on a slip of paper held at the Charles Dickens Museum, London (Fig. 5). The instructions are: 'X The parts marked thus to be of a greyish green not too dark—The fringe to match. There should be fringe round the little desk for the book.' The whole Reading desk, legs and all, were to be covered with this greyish-green material. Several newspaper reports from the first series of the Readings confirm this description; 'a singularly-shaped table also covered with green baize' matched the green-baize-covered platform. 'A small table, covered with green cloth' stood backed by a 'chocolate-coloured screen' for the Dublin performances. 'The back-ground is of a well-chosen brown, the carpet is green, the desk is green.' Prior to this, Dickens seems to have favoured a desk (perhaps the pulpit model) covered by a crimson cloth. When and why he changed to green baize is not clear. It was still green for the London

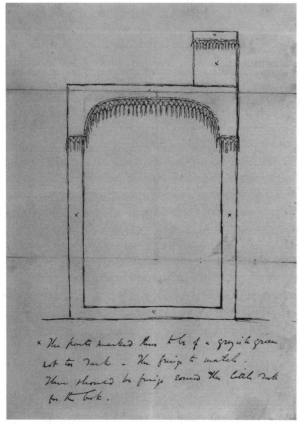

5. Charles Dickens, Design for his Reading Desk (?1858).
Drawing. Courtesy of the Charles Dickens Museum, London.

Readings in the early 1860s, but at some point thereafter it changed
again, to the maroon velvet familiar to most audiences.

The drawing does not include the little shelf, on the Reader's
right, which held a water bottle and a tumbler, nor one sometimes
reported (by Dolby among others) as being on the Reader's left on
which Dickens laid his handkerchief and gloves. These refinements
may have been added later. They certainly provided economies of
space: Dickens used to have a separate small table with carafe and

glass, standing beside the tall lectern, as illustrated in the first Hannah portrait.

The desk is preserved in the Charles Dickens Museum, in London (Fig. 6). It was nearly lost to posterity. Once Dickens had agreed to give up the Readings, he thought to destroy his desk:

Neither Charles Dickens nor his daughter Kate [Mrs. Perugini] set any store on possessions, as such. During breakfast at Gad's Hill—in the presence of Mamie and Miss Hogarth—her father said: 'I must destroy the reading-desk,' adding somewhat sadly, 'I have no further use for it.' 'Don't destroy it, papa,' said Mrs.Perugini, 'give it to me.' He appeared touched and pleased, not to say surprised, that she should want to possess it, and immediately gave it to her. Henceforth the famous red-plush-covered desk found a place in her home.

Katey gave it to B. W. Matz in 1920, and Matz left it to the Dickens House (now the Charles Dickens Museum), where it now stands, minus its little side shelf and the raised prop for the book. Matz wrote at the time, 'We believe it was first used in the drawing room of Gadshill at a trial reading, being specially sent down from London for the purpose.' Again, this may well refer to the spring and early summer of 1858, when he was finishing the London series (the last Reading there was 22 July) and devising and rehearsing new Readings for the first provincial tour, and no doubt trying them out on family at Gad's Hill.

The Reading desk at the Dickens Museum is $37\frac{1}{4}$" high. Its flat top is horizontal, not sloped, and measures 2' wide and 20" deep. The four legs are braced by cross-pieces at floor level, to give extra stability. The whole is covered with dark red velvet cloth, stretched tight, here and there glued and tacked. The seams between the separate velvet panels show stitching. The arches are ornamented with a fringe secured by brass-painted studs. On the desk-top is a small hole near the Reader's left-hand corner. This was the slot into which the raised book-rest block could be fixed. It stood probably about 8"–10" high. On the (Reader's) right side of the desk, about 8" below the top and beside each spring of the arch, are two small

6. Dickens's Reading Desk. The Charles Dickens Museum, London. Photograph by Jaron Chubb.

metal-fronted sockets into which the shelf for water bottle and glass would have been inserted.

The colour of the velvet has darkened and dulled to the colour of dried blood. However, here and there, under a fold or where the studs have dropped off, something like the original colour is visible. It is a lustrous maroon. Under intense lighting it could easily pass for crimson, as some contemporary accounts described it. The desk is surprisingly unbattered, given that it travelled back and forth across the Atlantic, on innumerable trains in America and Britain, and was hauled in and out of hundreds of Reading venues. Henry Scott, Dickens's devoted valet and superintendent of the luggage on the tours, is to be congratulated. There is one suggestive spot of wear. Along the (Reader's) left-hand edge of the top surface, the seam where the side and top panels of velvet join runs fairly straight. On the opposite edge the seam dips down a little, about a third of the way along (from the Reader), and then returns to follow the edge to the front of the desk. The dipped section, about 5" long, has been re-stitched. This suggests that the seam at that point was put under some strain, a downward pressure. It is just at the position where a Reader, with the book in his left hand, would rest his right hand, and on which he would press down when leaning forward over the desk.

The new desk is indeed 'singularly-shaped'. It tells us a lot. For one thing, Dickens would have gained in confidence, and thus been prepared to show more of himself—including his trembling legs (if indeed they did quake). 'The desk does not hide the speaker', wrote a somewhat carping reporter when Dickens was on his American tour, 'whose legs, not to put too fine a point on it, are not altogether as straight as those of the stand.' Dickens was releasing more of himself to take part in the whole visible narrative and enactment of the story and its characters: 'it is plain that Dickens believes in expression of figure as well as of face', observed Kate Field in her description and assessment of the stage set. A two-hour solo Reading is very demanding on the sustained attention of the audience, especially in a large hall, where for those of the audience about 20–30 yards back from the platform the lone figure of the performer would be much reduced. If all that these distant viewers could see was Dickens's head bobbing about above the 'pulpit' desk, for two hours, one could imagine their stamina draining away fast. Dickens had to use all possible resources to command attention. The redesigned desk would have achieved much in that endeavour. With so much more of him visible, he could project himself physically, with arm gestures and body movement, just as he was learning to project his Readings vocally. The new desk enabled him to amplify his histrionic skills.

The reduced height of the desk meant that the Reading text could not so easily rest before the performer's eyes. Dickens solved that partially by having the raised block or prop (clad in the same grey-green or maroon cloth) positioned to the left side of the horizontal desk top: this acted as a book-rest or arm-rest, thus bringing the book closer to the Reader's eyes without obstructing the view of the Reader's upper body in action. It was a clever compromise. The 'pulpit' desk had been designed to enable the reader to work closely with the script, inches away from his eyes. By the time Dickens turned professional, he was already partly independent of his script, so the book in his hand could be lowered away from time to time, and even rested down on the prop. That meant he could engage his audience more directly, without the intervening of either the high fence of the pulpit desk or the book thrust in front of his body.

Props

By the late 1860s Dickens had learned all his Readings by heart and his books had become props. They lay on the Reading desk. Dickens glanced at them from time to time, and would flick pages over, but he was no longer reading from them. He had few other props, though one or two deserve mention.

The *Sheffield Times*'s report on a Reading of 1855 mentioned his flourishing of a large paperknife, which he used now and again to divide the leaves of his text. This is an odd prop. It seems to have been used habitually, in the early years of the Readings, as part of Dickens's repertoire of gestures, and not just to ease the turning of pages. It is shown in Dickens's right hand in the stereoscope photographs by Watkins (Fig. 7). A somewhat sneering review of an October 1858 Reading deplored Dickens's descending to 'the most artificial conventionalities, even to the display of a monster paper-knife—we presume in case a book, which has been read a score of times and which the Reader evidently knew well nigh by heart, should require to be cut open'. Dickens persisted with the knife long after he really needed it for its proper services. It had become a theatrical

7. Stereoscope of Dickens giving a Reading, based on a photograph by Herbert Watkins (?1858). Courtesy of the Charles Dickens Museum, London.

accessory. In reading the 'Carol', when he came to Fezziwig's dance and described how the dancer 'appeared to wink with his legs', he gave an expressive look and a wave of the paperknife. In later years when he had dispensed with the knife, he used to perform the actions of the dance with his fingers on the Reading desk.

The knife was still in use in 1863, if the long-term memory of an eyewitness can be trusted. Writing in 1911, W. Ridley Kent recalled a performance of 'Mrs. Gamp' in 1863, towards the end of which Mrs Gamp is described as sitting close to the fender and drowsily amusing herself with sliding her nose backwards and forwards along the brass top. Dickens reproduced the action by rubbing his nose to left and right along the paperknife.

The little shelf to the side of the desk held a flask of water and a glass, and was also the resting place for Dickens's gloves and handkerchief. The water glass was occasionally called into play during performance, as when he read the dinner-party scene in 'David Copperfield'. In his impersonation of Mrs Micawber and her confidential disclosures over a glass of punch, 'Mr. DICKENS leaned slightly on the desk, holding his glass in his hand and occasionally raising it to his lips, [. . .] and the audience seemed to see the estimable lady as well as hear her talk.'

The Platform

Because Dickens read in halls and Corn Exchanges rather than theatres, he had to go to some lengths to enhance the visual and acoustic focus. Where there was no stage, this often entailed the making of improvised platforms, to increase his visibility throughout the hall. The auditoria at such venues were not raked, by and large, so every effort was needed to keep sight-lines clear. Ladies in the reserved stalls were respectfully requested not to wear bonnets. He wrote home from Shrewsbury, during the first month of the first provincial tour in 1858, reporting his disappointment with the hall there, after his preliminary inspection: 'everything was wrong [. . .] I have left Arthur [Smith, his first tour manager] making a platform for me out of dining-tables'. Over the years the stage set developed in elaborate ways to compensate for auditoria with poor acoustics or inadequate lighting, or both. One refinement was a back-screen. He took all the components of his staging with him across the Atlantic for the American tour, where the set attracted much attention from the newspaper reporters. The back-screen was judged to be about fifteen feet long by seven feet high, and was positioned about four feet behind the desk. It was probably a folding screen, to make transportation easier. Even so, it suffered some battering in its time and at least one replacement had to be made. It was constructed as a series of wooden frames covered with canvas, and this was itself covered again with maroon cloth (or a 'brown-crimson color') to match the Reading desk. It served two purposes. One was to act as a sounding board, the other was to throw the figure of the Reader into higher relief. An additional, mischievous suggestion was that the deep maroon backing helped to 'relieve' Dickens's 'very red face'. The more experience he had of the Readings the more adamant Dickens became about these devices. In agreeing to give a Reading

8. G. Sargent, 'St Martin's Hall, Long Acre' (1853). Drawing. Guildhall Library, City of London.

at London's St Martin's Hall in 1865, he had clear ideas as to what he needed. The Hall had a tiered orchestra gallery spanning the full width of the far end of the room (Fig. 8). The platform set thrust forward from the bottom step of the gallery would have taken up only part of that width, so Dickens wanted to mask the spaces to either side of his platform:

as I have had much experience in this regard, I trouble you by mentioning what is indispensable to *me*. [. . .]the platform must be advanced into the hall to its utmost limits, the empty sides of the Orchestra being screened or curtained off. My servant has a screen of my own to be placed behind me, and assist the voice[. . .]. Such aids are indispensable, or the most practised speaker cannot be long heard, and the audience will be restless and disappointed.

The forward positioning of the platform, where possible, was something he always favoured, in order to bring himself closer to his audience and yet still isolate his set. When Dolby went to America to reconnoitre the Reading venues, he reassured Dickens that he knew exactly what was wanted: 'Your public close to you, and you able to do with them exactly as you like.' Manchester's huge Free Trade Hall, for example, could be adjusted as an auditorium in this way:

The scene at Manchester last night was really magnificent. I had had the platform carried forward to our Frozen Deep point, and my table and screen built in with a Proscenium and room Scenery.

The screen compensated for the fact that Dickens did not have a powerful voice: 'With a sounding board at his back not a word was lost, not a tone or inflection of speech, but had its weight and due value in portraying the characters and carrying the story onwards to its end.' But it could not solve all the acoustic problems. At St George's Hall, Liverpool, he instructed staff to hang up 'banners' at strategic points in the room to stifle echoes. At Torquay's Royal Assembly Rooms, he was disgusted by the acoustics: as a result, 'the whole unfortunate staff have been all day, and now are, sticking up baize and carpets'. In the vast Steinway Hall in New York, as we saw in the chapter 'Premiere', even greater sacrifices had to be made: the Hall held two-and-a-half thousand, but some 400 seats had to be withdrawn and two balcony recesses were closed off in order to rectify the acoustic problems. Even so, a third of that Steinway audience, according to one first-night witness, heard Dickens 'very imperfectly'. St James's Hall, Piccadilly, where Dickens gave most of his London Readings, was on a similar scale. The first-floor, grand concert chamber of this highly ornate, Gothic-Revival hall had been opened in 1858 (and was demolished in 1907), just when Dickens began his professional Readings (Fig. 9). It was 60 feet high and 136 feet long. It had eccentric acoustic problems as Dickens reported (unless his friends, the Priestleys, were hard of hearing):

As an instance of that part of St. James's Hall which it is impossible to touch, — the Priestleys (Wills says), I think on the 19th row of stalls, could

9. 'St James's Music Hall, London.' *Illustrated London News*, 10 April 1858.
Courtesy of *Illustrated London News* Picture Library.

not hear; while the people behind them, and before them, were driving
them mad by hearing perfectly. So on the 8th. row at the Crystal Palace the
Music is all confused. On the 7th. and the 9th. all right.

Dickens and his tour manager would test the acoustics as soon
after arrival in town as possible. This involved Dickens standing in
the room at the point where he was to perform and speaking in an
even or a low voice while his manager went from one part of the
room to another and into the corners to listen to the varying levels
of sound. According to Dolby, a hall that seemed bad for sound
had to be 'cured' by means of a method 'the secret of which he
alone seemed to know'. Since there was nothing particularly secret
about draping carpets, baize, and banners around an auditorium, nor
about the installation of the back-screen, Dolby may be referring to

something that Dickens did with his own powers of vocal projection. Dolby also sometimes went on a discreet acoustics patrol during the performance and reported back to Dickens during breaks in the Reading. He came to the side of one of the screens, and 'a brief conversation, carried on in an "aside" during the applause was held between the reader and myself':

MR. DICKENS: Is it all right?
MYSELF: All right.
MR. DICKENS: Hall good.
MYSELF: Excellent; go a-head, sir.
MR. DICKENS: I will, when they'll let me.
MYSELF: First-rate audience.
MR. DICKENS: I know it.

Despite all Dickens's precautionary preparations, there were some halls where the acoustic problems could not be overcome, and audiences in the rear seating were disappointed in being unable to hear much of the Reading. To judge from newspaper reviews this hardly ever happened, but then the reporters enjoyed good seats, generally. A letter in a Dundee newspaper in 1858 complained that 'over 200 in the back seats left in the interval, unable to hear' Dickens at the Corn Exchange Hall. Sometimes Dickens changed the planned venue in order to ensure not just audibility but that his finer effects would tell more distinctly. In the spring of 1863, for his London Readings, he forsook St James's Hall in favour of the Hanover Rooms in Hanover Square (Fig. 10) — 'quite wonderful for sound', he reported, 'and so easy, that the least inflection will tell anywhere in the place exactly as it leaves your lips'.

The back-screen was designed to throw the sound of Dickens's voice forward into the main chamber. It also functioned as a means of emphasizing Dickens's figure on stage. He was in dark evening dress and the screen was, for the later Readings, maroon. The colour contrast was enhanced by the stage lighting, so Dickens was thrown into strong relief. The overhead lighting system minimized any distracting shadows thrown onto the back-screen. At a later stage,

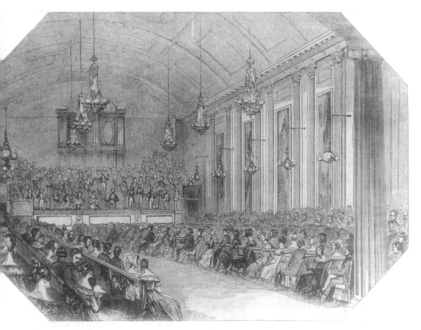

10. Hanover Square Concert Room. *Illustrated London News*, 24th June 1843.

after he had returned from America and was giving a trial Reading of 'Sikes and Nancy', he added two large maroon side screens to the set, like stage 'wings'. In addition there were curtains of the same colour used 'to close in any width of room from wall to wall', as he described in a letter to friends in America. Thus 'the figure is now completely isolated, and the slightest action becomes much more important'.

The whole development of the platform—back-screen, rug, and Reading Desk all in a rich maroon—increased the isolation and distinctiveness of the Reader. Dickens performed from within a warmly lit red frame. This was just as well, given the chilly conditions in some of the Reading venues, such as the Chester Music Hall, described by Dickens as 'like a Methodist chapel in low spirits, and with a cold in its head'. No matter how cavernous and draughty the hall, that small, glowing, maroon chamber must have focused attention and kindled a warmth of response on its own. The staging was simple but highly effective. It matched Dickens's histrionic aims for his performance as a whole, the use of simple means to achieve great effects. He did not depend on stage props to create an illusion, only on auditory and visual enhancements to his own dramatic skills. His (or Pip's) hilarious description of the tawdry, low-budget staging of Wopsle's London *Hamlet*, like so many of his descriptions of incompetent theatricals, shows how set and props can become perilous distractions rather than subtle reinforcements of illusion.

The lighting system contributed to this effect in a powerful but discreet way. Dickens would have grasped this before he became a professional Reader. At an 1855 Reading in Sheffield's Mechanics' Institute he was evidently supplied with a row of overhead gaslights, and as the local paper reported, the arrangement ensured that 'a powerful light was concentrated on the reader's face, and his features were distinctly seen all over the room'. Dickens must have been impressed by these fly lights: he seems never to have considered working before footlights. For one thing, footlights would have cast his face into shadow every time he held his book up before him. For another, they would have thrown the magnified shadow of Dickens onto the back-screen in a distracting way. Properly positioned overhead lamps would have eliminated most of these shadows.

Dickens developed his own lighting rig, which was certainly in place by 1858. We have already heard him assure one correspondent who was trying to organize St Martin's Hall in London for a Reading, 'My servant has a screen of my own to be placed behind me, and assist the voice; also, my own gas-fittings.' The 'gas-fittings' consisted of a high batten, running horizontally about twelve feet above the platform and forward of the desk, supported by two vertical battens at either end, secured with copper-wire guys (Fig. 11). These were slim cylindrical pipes through which gas was run, in a flexible cable, from the hall's main supply. The battens had gas-jets, one positioned about halfway up each vertical pipe and screened by green shades,

11. Dickens's Reading Set. *Harper's Weekly,* 7 December 1867.

and a row of them along the top one. Sometimes a metal reflector was positioned along the top row. Just before Dickens entered, the gas-jets were turned up to the appropriate level. Dickens scrutinized the levels carefully, though not obtrusively, as he stood receiving the initial applause on his entry. The overhead lighting was shielded from the audience by drapery of the same colour as the rest of the set. As one American reporter observed: 'The whole is artistically designed to concentrate the attention of the audience upon the reader; there is no vacant space behind him for the eye to wander away.'

The portable lighting arrangements were potentially hazardous. At a Belfast Reading in 1858, while Dickens was describing the high-spirited party at Scrooge's nephew's, someone accidentally stood on the flexible gas feeder tube, strangled the supply, and extinguished all the lights. There was a break in the Reading while a ladder was fetched, the gas supply restored, and the jets re-lit. On another occasion there was a gas leak in the top batten that threatened to burn the copper wire holding up the heavy reflector and send it crashing down onto the front stalls. The fault was hidden from the audience, but Dickens, Dolby, and the gasman saw it and watched in agony: all three agreed it would just last until the end of the Reading, which it did, though 'the whole thing was at its very last and utmost extremity'. In America, at a Reading of the 'Carol' in Washington one night, the gas pressure was so low that Dickens felt he had to acknowledge the problem at the start: 'I began with a small speech to the effect that I must trust to the brightness of their faces for the illumination of mine; this was taken greatly.' On another occasion in America, at a Reading in Worcester, Massachussetts, the hall had been prepared for a three-day exhibition organized by the New England Poultry Club. About 250 fowls were lodged overnight in premises just off the main hall. As the gas-lights came up in the hall and particularly when the stage lights were on to full, the birds, who had bedded down for the night, saw the light seeping into their quarters, assumed it was dawn, and a crescendo of crowing accompanied Dickens's Reading for some time.

The whole arrangement testifies to the iron control exercised by Dickens in maximizing the effect of these performances. He always preferred evening to matinee Readings. 'I have a great antipathy to daylight reading.' One reason was that by night he could exercise more control over the lighting: 'It is a tough job', he explained to Macready, 'and I own that I want night and false light.' False light bestowed an aura on the figure and the occasion, making both unforgettable. Having attended one of the London Farewell Readings in February 1870, *The Graphic* observed, 'It will be impossible hereafter to avoid looking back [...] to that effective figure thrown out like one of the Moroni portraits by the deep, violet background, and lit up with such cunning and disguised effect.' It gave a literal force to Ruskin's famous remark in 1860 about the manner of Dickens's fiction, that he chooses 'to speak in a circle of stage fire'.

THE TOUR MANAGER AND CREW

Dickens, of course, was the ultimate tour manager, but even he, with his obsession for organization, recognized that once the professional Readings established themselves as an institution in his life he needed to hand over much of the management to a reliable aide.

Arthur Smith, brother and former manager of the showman Albert Smith, was enlisted by Dickens as his first manager, for the Readings of 1858. Smith was 'the best man of business I know', according to Dickens. According to Forster, Smith's 'exact fitness to manage the scheme successfully, made him an unsafe counsellor respecting it', by which Forster meant that Smith's already belonging to the world of show-business disqualified him as a judge of the propriety or otherwise of Dickens's undertaking professional Readings. That did not worry Dickens: he simply needed someone completely reliable and efficient. Smith, as business manager for the Readings, undertook arrangements for booking the venues, organizing seating and tickets, and dealing with all correspondence to do with the Readings. His duties covered a wide range of activities, as Dickens comically observed:

Arthur is something between a Home Secretary and a furniture-dealer in Rathbone Place. He is either always corresponding in the genteelest manner, or dragging rout-seats about without his coat.

One of his skills lay in maximizing seating capacity in the various halls. For instance, to Dickens's great approval, he was able to more than double the usual number of seats in St Martin's Hall. The more seats installed and sold for the Readings, the greater Smith's remuneration, since he earned ten per cent of receipts. In this show-business enterprise, Dickens was the show and Smith was the business. Smith enabled Dickens to keep his hands free of the business side of things—free to rub them in delight at the money pouring in from their astounding commercial success: 'Arthur bathed in checks [after a Liverpool Reading]—took headers into tickets—floated on billows of passes—dived under weirs of shillings—staggered home, faint with gold and silver.'

The fullness of Dickens's schedules and the travelling arrangements to meet those schedules were very demanding on the logistical skills of the managers, especially when there was no Standard Time for Great Britain. Dickens gave a Reading at Stonehouse near Plymouth on 4 August 1858 having travelled down from London two days before. He began promptly at 8 p.m., as usual, to a disconcertingly thin house. After about a quarter of an hour the room began to fill. Local time was about seventeen minutes behind London (Greenwich) time, and Dickens's team had forgotten to allow for that. Equally demanding was the business of getting clearance from local officialdom for the Readings to take place on the provincial tours. There was the occasion when the Town Clerk of Blackburn insisted on having full particulars in advance of 'the nature of Mr. Dickens's entertainment'. Highly amused, Dickens replied through Dolby: 'the subject matter of Mr. Dickens's Readings is to be found in a long row of books published by Messrs Chapman and Hall, in Piccadilly, London.'

When Smith fell ill in the summer of 1861, Dickens engaged his assistant, Thomas Headland as temporary manager, and then, on Smith's death (1 October) as manager. Within a month and a half Dickens was regretting the appointment: 'it is the simple fact that he has no notion of the requirements of such work as this.' Headland muddled the Readings schedule and misjudged distribution of tickets to local agents. Early in January 1862, Dickens had reached a point where he could only describe Headland as 'damned aggravating'. Fortunately that provincial tour came to a close at the end of the month. Dickens gave a short series of Readings in London between March and June 1862, and another one over the same season in 1863. The consistency of venue for these two series took pressure off both Dickens and Headland. There were no more professional Readings until the spring of 1866. The long break, and the making of a new contract with the impresarios Chappell, enabled Dickens to relieve Headland of his duties, and appoint another manager.

12. Dickens and George Dolby in America. Cartoon Sketch (?1868). Courtesy of the Charles Dickens Museum, London.

In November 1858, Dickens received a letter from Charlotte Dolby, the celebrated contralto, with whom he had had a very brief correspondence eight years earlier. She suggested to Dickens that her brother, George, might be a very suitable person to perform the kind of role then being undertaken by Arthur Smith. Dickens at that time had no thought of replacing Smith. Eight years later, he signed up with Chappell for a new series of Readings. 'Messrs. Chappell proposed that I should accompany the Reader as their representative and manager throughout the tour,' recalled Dolby. George Dolby was manager of the Readings, in Britain and America, from 10 April 1866 to 15 March 1870 (Fig. 12). He was a bluff and boisterous new presence in Dickens's life, and much to

Dickens's liking. He was more exacting and interventionist than Arthur Smith had been—'none the worse for laying about him in a slashing manner on the least sign of any thing amiss', noted Dickens. Dolby's vigorous personality and his devotion to his 'Chief' gave Dickens a sense of security vital in conserving his energies, especially during the American tour. His robust dealings with ticket agents, touts, and aggrieved ticket buyers, his bonhomie and readiness to drink time away with officials whose goodwill towards the Readings he courted, his command over the hefty correspondence incurred during and between the tours, and his sensitivity towards Dickens's needs—all contributed to his indispensability for Dickens. Dolby' s commission on the American tour amounted to £2,888, according to Dickens's calculation. According to one well-disposed American biographer of Dickens in 1912, Dolby 'certainly earned more than that sum, if we merely compute what an honest man should properly charge for being privately and publicly denounced as a rogue and a ruffian'. He became Dickens's personal friend and confidant. He was involved in discussions as to whether Ellen Ternan should accompany Dickens to America. He was quite prepared on occasions to risk his Chief's fury in offering advice which he felt to be in Dickens's longer-term interests though contrary to his immediate wishes. On many occasions Dickens had cause to reflect gratefully on this man's support: 'Dolby is as tender as a woman and as watchful as a doctor.' Without Dolby, the scale of achievement in meeting commitments during the later Readings might have been very different.

Dolby, like his predecessors, headed a small crew of assistants for the Readings. There was Henry Scott, Dickens's valet and dresser:

As a dresser he is perfect. In a quarter of an hour after I go into the retiring-room where all my clothes are airing and everything is set out neatly in its allotted place, I am ready, and he then goes softly out, and sits outside the door. In the morning he is equally punctual, quiet and quick. He has his needles and thread, buttons and so forth, always at hand; and in travelling he is very systematic with the luggage.

So very scrupulous was Scott about the luggage that on one occasion, on a train journey from Boston to New York, he was discovered leaning his head against the side of the carriage and weeping because he had witnessed the railway staff's irreverently rough handling of their trunks. His tearful conscientiousness was both endearing and irritating for Dickens. On another occasion, on tour in the Midlands in England, he thought he had left behind some of Dickens's prompt-copies for 'Boots', 'Sikes and Nancy', and 'Mrs.Gamp':

We immediately telegraphed to the office. Answer, no books there. As my impression was that he must have left them at St. James's Hall, we then arranged to send him up to London at seven this morning. Meanwhile (though not reproached), he wept copiously and audibly. I had asked him over and over again, was he sure he had not put them in my large black trunk? Too sure, too sure. Hadn't opened that trunk after Tuesday night's reading. He opened it to get some clothes out when I went to bed, and there the books were! He produced them with an air of injured surprise, as if we had put them there.

George Allison was the man in charge of the gas-fittings. Dickens regarded him as the 'steadiest and most reliable man I ever employed'. He was responsible for the lighting rig and for preparation, with Richard Kelly, of the venues. Kelly was the least reliable of the team. He had been recruited in order to help with the arrangements in America over advance bookings. However, he was caught speculating on the tickets and eventually discharged by Dickens.

This team was enlarged for the American tour:

We have a regular clerk, a Bostonian whose name is Wild. He, Osgood [James Ripley Osgood, a partner in the publishing firm Ticknor and Fields], Dolby, Kelly, Scott, George the gas-man, and perhaps a boy or two, constitute my body-guard. It seems a large number of people, but the business cannot, be done with fewer[. . .]. You may get an idea of the staff's work, by what is in hand now. They are preparing, numbering, and stamping six thousand tickets for Philadelphia, and eight thousand tickets for Brooklyn. The moment those are done, another six thousand for Washington. This in addition to the correspondence, advertisements, accounts, travellings, and the mighty business of the reading four times a week.

It was indeed a mighty business, mightily profitable, and mightily exacting on all concerned. The pressures of Dickens's perfectionism were everywhere apparent as this enterprise took shape. A part of all the infrastructure was the managing of Dickens's public image in what was then a new, very public, and somewhat controversial role for a distinguished author.

MANAGING CELEBRITY

Dickens gave himself to his public, and that public had to become used to seeing and assessing the man behind all those famous books. Dickens now had to manage not only the way he projected his stories from behind the little reading desk, but also the way he projected himself as a celebrity. Here is one episode that is symptomatic of the scale and nature of Dickens's celebrity towards the end of his Reading career. It highlights media manipulation of the image of Dickens, a topic I shall be discussing more extensively a little later.

Dickens arrived in New York for his first Readings in that city on 7 December 1867. On 14 December he sat for the photographers J.Gurney and Son, to whom he had promised exclusive rights to take photographic portraits of him during the American tour. However, on 12 December the *New York Daily Tribune* had assured its readers that a rival photographer, Mathew Brady, had also taken Dickens's portrait, and would 'have this noble lion netted'. The next day the paper announced the exhibition of 'The Latest Photograph of Mr. Dickens' at Brady's gallery, No. 785 Broadway:

Mr. Dickens's character, and the world of imaginative [sic] ones he has created, live in every line of his brow, in every furrow of his features, in every angle and contraction of his penetrative eyes. These lines, these furrows, these angles, these contractions, Mr. Brady has reproduced, with a rare degree of artistic skill, in the three-quarter length, full imperial photograph.

13. Mathew Brady, 'Charles Dickens' (?1867). Photograph. Courtesy of National Archives and Records Administration, Washington, DC.

Dickens is portrayed in three-quarter profile, looking solemn though fairly fresh (Fig. 13). The freshness is less in the expression than in his hair. Both beard and hair have a thickness and lustre not evident in any of the many Gurney portraits of this period. The silky moustache is disconcertingly long, as if Dickens has been competing with General Custer. It is also badly angled, nearly parallel to the picture plane, instead of following the tilt of the head. In addition the Gurney portraits all show the temple hair brushed forward into those characteristic tufts above his ears. In the Brady portrait, the temple hair (at least on Dickens's left) is brushed back. In the Gurney portraits Dickens is in day-wear, collar and tie, and wide-lapelled coat. In the Brady portrait he is in evening dress, with a flower button-hole.

There is a mystery about this portrait by Brady. George Dolby had formally agreed, in a letter of 10 December 1867, that the photographers J. Gurney and Son should have exclusive rights to photograph Dickens during his American visit:

I will guarantee your various likenesses of Mr Charles Dickens to be the only portraits for which he has sat or will sit, in the United States. I do this with the knowledge and sanction of Mr Dickens.

When the Brady portrait was exhibited on 13th December the Gurneys responded with some indignation in notices in various New York papers:

We beg to assert thus publicly that Mr Charles Dickens has not, and will not sit to any other Photographers but ourselves in the United States; that any picture of Mr Dickens, either exposed to view or offered for sale, and not having our imprint, are *copies* of pictures taken in Europe, and that any attempt to advertise them, either by payment or by editorial notice, 'as originals', is a fraud and imposition on the public.

The *New York Herald* was comically vituperative about such embargoes: 'Alas for those artists ruthlessly forbidden to meddle with that face [. . .] those locks are "private" [. . .] the jaw is subject to contract! We know not if the sun will be permitted to shine on the novelist, lest it might be in league with opposition photographers.' There are two portraits of Dickens in the Brady collection, the exhibited one and another, also three-quarter length, which shows the seated Dickens looking very worn but distinctly younger than in any of the 1867 Gurney photos. While his beard is thin and straggly, his hair is more abundant than in the Gurney portraits, especially that on the crown of his head. This photograph actually derives from an 1861 photo-portrait by the Watkins brothers, most likely by John Watkins. On 28 September 1861 Dickens wrote to John to acknowledge receipt of some photographic cartes-de-visite, amongst which is one (now in the Charles Dickens Museum) that may well be the 'No. 18' that was greeted with a 'howl of horror' by the family at Gad's Hill, as Dickens reported: 'It has a grim and wasted aspect, and perhaps might be made useful as a portrait of the Ancient Mariner.' A print of this 1861 portrait, or a photograph of a print (Brady's is considerably more flecked and coarse-grained than the Watkins originals in the Dickens Museum), must subsequently have come into Brady's possession. It was not in the public domain, so it is unclear how he came to acquire it.

A closer examination of the exhibited 'Readings' portrait by Brady suggests that it might well actually be a manipulation of the 1861 photograph. The sitter's pose in each portrait is identical. It is in the cosmetic details that differences emerge. The 'Readings' portrait appears to have remade Dickens's 1861 beard and moustache, tidied up the straggly hair, smoothed lines on his face, and re-dressed Dickens for his evening Readings. The day waistcoat in the 1861 photo has been cut in order to paste in or paint over a dress-shirt front, and a buttonhole has been added to his lapel. Otherwise, as already mentioned, the portraits are nearly identical. He sits in the same chair, with the same configuration of sharp highlights on its wooden arm (perhaps enhanced with a paintbrush in the 'Readings' version). The left hand in the Readings photo grasps the handkerchief at exactly the same angle, to produce exactly the same handkerchief folds as in 1861. The clinching evidence lies in the fact that the reticulation of creases all down Dickens's left arm in the Readings portrait matches precisely that in the 1861.

The indignant suggestion by the Gurneys that any non-Gurney photographs of Dickens are copies or fakes is distinctly plausible in the case of the Brady portrait. Dickens probably never did sit for Brady. It would indeed have been strange if he had broken his pledge to the Gurneys. To meet the great demand for images of Dickens in New York in 1867, Brady probably made the best he could of the earlier photograph already in his studio, and presumably felt safe in so doing since it was not in the public domain.

The pains Brady went to in order to cash in on Dickens's presence in America are some indication of the scale of Dickens's celebrity. The image-making industry was a powerful factor in constituting this celebrity, but the information offered in the products of this industry was problematic. 'Looking at this portrait [by Brady]', remarks the *Tribune*, 'we see Mr. Dickens just as he is in his Readings.' This means not just in the matter of dress, but in the projection of personality: '[Brady] has indicated all the mobility of Mr. Dickens's features, and preserved all the force of the countenance.' The claims are hard to credit. Dickens looks distinctly unanimated. Kate Field said of the many photographs of Dickens in circulation during the American tour, 'Dickens looks as if, previous to posing, he had been put under an exhausted receiver and had had his soul pumped out of him.' Whatever 'mobility' the features may have had (and it was just that facial mobility that held audiences during the Readings) has been subdued in the studio, maybe partly due to use of the concealed headrest designed to help freeze the sitter during the long exposure time. Even those 'penetrative' eyes have dulled.

Illustrations of Dickens—engravings from painted portraits in the early years, and then, later, photographs—circulated vigorously once he started his Readings. Audiences prepared themselves for Dickens's coming in a variety of ways. For instance, in his earliest days as a Reader, prior to his becoming a professional, Dickens visited the town of Reading to give a performance of 'Christmas Carol'. It was December 1854. The local newspaper reported, 'Some consulted Mr. Dickens's portraits prefixed to his writings, in order that they might distinguish him at a glance; some re-perused David Copperfield that they might trace the resemblance they imagined to exist between the author and the hero of the tale.' Once Dickens became a visible presence in various parts of Britain, as a result of his Readings, his personal appearance became a matter of great curiosity. There was at that time little visual information on the Dickens of the 1850s. It is hard for us now to imagine that dearth of images of celebrities. Most people in the early 1850s drew their impressions of his looks from the Maclise portrait of 1838, engraved for the publication of

Nicholas Nickleby, when Dickens was in his mid-twenties. They were in for a shock when they saw the same man now in his early forties, bearded and furrowed. Thus when Dickens went on from Reading to Sherborne, two days later, to give another performance of the 'Carol', the *Sherborne Journal* remarked with some disappointment on his difference from the Nickleby portrait, now that he was wearing a moustache. Dickens had a fuller beard by the time the professional Readings began, and this was seen to have several disadvantages. The addition of quite light-coloured hair to the lower face and a receding hairline above contributed to 'the vague expression of the face when seen from a distance.' The beard also concealed the mouth and thereby jeopardized the play of one of Dickens's most expressive features. Several journals produced new portraits of Dickens, but (according to the *Wolverhampton Chronicle*), 'As yet we have failed to meet with a portrait which was sufficiently accurate to have enabled us to recognise him when we meet him in the public streets.' That may have been some relief to Dickens. There was a miserably inept engraving of him at his Reading desk in the *Illustrated London News* for 1858. In the same year, the *National Magazine* produced one, as did the London *Critic*, on a specially tinted sheet. The latter portrait was taken from a photograph by Herbert Watkins, and was judged to be the best representation of Dickens then in circulation. When Dickens arrived in America his face was reproduced everywhere, according to the *Boston Tribune*:

At every turn in the illustrated newspapers, in the hotel office, and in all the shop windows, the new portrait of Mr. Dickens is to be seen, showing a man somewhat past middle life, with thin grey hair, a scanty beard, and eyes downcast reading a book

The photographic presence of the author and its relationship to his works was a topic of some controversy in the middle and later years of the nineteenth century, as Gerald Curtis has shown in his book *Visual Words* (2002). He suggests that the proliferation of images of Dickens reading from his works 'further cemented in the public imagination that his "voice" and persona were one and the same with the narrative voice in the texts'. These commercial images were yet further projections of Dickens's multifaceted persona that had begun with the voice, or voices, of Boz back in the 1830s and were to culminate in the physical presence of the man before his public, impersonating a range of characters from his books, including the persona of the intensely companionable narrator. Curtis's point about amalgamation of image and voice bears closely on the Readings project. Was that evening-suited Reader up there on the platform the real Dickens, the one behind all those literary, engraved, and photographic self-projections, or was there another Dickens—the *Ur*-Dickens, as it were—concealed even behind that poised gentleman-recitalist? His Reading tours made it seem obviously the former. Those of Dickens's friends who tried to discourage him from professional public Reading were partly protecting him from damaging the dignified mystique of authorship, which did give an illusion of there being a single source, the well-spring of literary creation, which could be experienced only by the author in the privacy of his study. This was not the way Dickens saw it. His imagined readership-cum-audience was there with him in his study. He implicitly played to it as he made his faces in the mirror, and muttered out lines in the voices of his imaginary characters. His narrative and descriptive manner in the novels and shorter stories frequently solicited the reader's personal attention: they were part of the communicative performance essential to his mode of fiction. Photographs of Dickens ostensibly at work at a desk, sitting demurely with quill in hand, catch none of this activity, nor the effort expended in establishing and maintaining the close rapport with his readers that so energized his writing.

Photography was, nonetheless, endlessly curious about the appropriate postures for creativity. The London *Critic* had given a hostile review to the first appearance, in 1855, of Walt Whitman's *Leaves of Grass* ('We had ceased, we imagined, to be surprised at anything that America could produce'). It remarked that there was no name on the title page; instead the reader met a portrait 'of the notorious individual who is the poet presumptive'. Young Whitman, in an idling pose, open-necked shirt, hand in pocket, gazes with calm defiance at the reader, as if he were inviting a cult of personality. The named identity of the author is replaced by this new kind of information—expressed in clothes-style and body posture. 'A photograph likeness sells a book', remarked a Dublin reporter on the occasion of Dickens's visit to that city in August 1858. The reporter continued to meditate on the changing attitudes to literary celebrity—particularly that curiosity about the subject's appearance—changes which Dickens's new career was influencing:

A literary man may, like the corncrake, whose mystical voice we hear at the twilight hour booming from some sequestered nook in the meadow, derive additional importance and interest from the mystery of his movements; but it is a thoroughly English propensity to make money, and now-a days [sic] the public must know all about your domestic relations, your personal appearance, your age, the number of your children, the colour of your eyes and hair—must peep into the arcana of your social existence.

Dickens was increasingly exposing his private self to public scrutiny, and for that public the experience was akin to visiting a rare creature in a zoo:

Mr. Charles Dickens is 'starring it' in the provinces; we use a common-place expression to publish a very common-place fact [. . .]. Poor Albert Smith [the solo showman of the *Mont Blanc* spectaculars] has much to answer for in drawing out of the retirement of their studies our popular authors to gratify the curiosity of their readers and admirers, with the sight of the man with whom they are familiar only as a writer. It is something to see a 'live author'—to see the man, not simply the portrait, and above all to hear that author read his own writings. People will go to see the exhibition just as they go or used to go to see the lions in the Tower; and if popular authors choose for a 'certain consideration' to travel through the country as 'sights' there's an end of the question.

Dickens did not need a 'photograph likeness' to sell either his books or his Readings. Nonetheless, the portraits by Gurney and Brady were designed to cash in on the popularity of the Readings and to satisfy the craving for insights into the appearance and personality of the man. It was on the same scale as the demand for autographs. Dickens had not been in America for more than a few days when a mountain of correspondence accumulated, including over 200 requests for his autograph. These portraits met a public demand, but also raised certain expectations. The New York photographers contributed their skills in bringing the man himself into close-up, with carefully focused detailing of all those legible furrows inscribed on Dickens's 55-year-old face. At the start of the new year 1868, *Harper's Weekly* was advertising the Gurney portraits in three sizes, 25 cts., 50 cts. and $3. They proved to be very popular. However, they were in some competition with the journalists who reported on the Readings, and who, in offering their own portraits, often disparaged the visual portraits. 'We think the generality of people were rather disappointed in the size of the great novelist,' pronounced the *Syracuse Daily Standard*: 'He is certainly not above the medium height—if indeed he reaches that. We had thought him a large man. His pictures certainly give that impression.' 'His photographs give no idea of his genial expression', insisted another reporter while describing Dickens's appearance on the platform at Portland, in April that year. Kate Field styled her written record of the Readings as *Pen Photographs*, to emphasize that she relied on her own on-the-spot impressions to convey a better sense of Dickens in action than any photographic still could achieve: 'when it is remembered that the best photographs fail to do justice to their originals, and that the most interesting subjects generally receive the worst treatment, I hope to be exonerated from so grave a charge.'

The press revelled in extended descriptions of Dickens's looks. How ought a human genius to look?

We don't know what those people would have who talk about his not coming up to their ideal, and wish they had never seen him. Did they expect to see a solemn, dignified personage, or a demi-god?

The *New York Tribune* printed an extract from a Boston lady's private letter, expressing her disappointment with Dickens's appearance—'small and slim-legged—a dapper little fellow[. . .]and small

14. Charles Lyall, 'From Whom We Have Great Expectations' (1861). Courtesy of the Charles Dickens Museum, London.

eyes, bird-like, glancing, and restless'. A solemn, dignified person is exactly what the photos transmitted, as Dickens had to steady, if not freeze the natural mobility in his expression while the shutter gaped at him. The photographic 'netting' of the lion captured the carcass but lost the vital energies that went into the creation of those hundreds of imaginary characters and then into the histrionic recreation of them at the Reading desk. But then how could any single portrait reproduce Dickens's creativity? One of Dickens's own favourites, as he told a friend, was the 1861 caricature by Charles Lyall, 'From Whom We Have Great Expectations':

I hope you may have seen a large-headed photograph with little legs, representing the undersigned, pen in hand, tapping his forehead to knock an idea out. It has just sprung up so abundantly in all the shops, that I am ashamed to go about town looking in at the picture windows—which is my delight. It seems to me extraordinarily ludicrous, and much more like than the grave portraits done in earnest. It made me laugh when I first came upon it, until I shook again, in open sun-lighted Piccadilly.

Dickens enjoys the greater likeness partly, perhaps, *because* it is not grave or earnest: it does not take him too seriously; it catches him in action, and also appeals to his sense of humour. It has a vitality lacking in most of the studio portraits. He turned down numerous requests from photographers and others who wanted him to sit for portraits. 'I declined, and still must decline, to sit for any new photograph,' he wrote to one applicant in 1864; 'firstly, because I very much dislike that operation; secondly, because my doing so would involve me in the redemption of a dozen other conditional promises; and thirdly, because three London photographers can supply me in all manner of shapes and sizes.' One reason for his loathing of being photographed was that, as he said, 'Somehow I never "come like" in these productions.' Another reason may well be related to his horror of statues. His Will famously prohibited his friends from making him 'the subject of any monument, memorial, or testimonial whatever', and his reaction to invitations to contribute to memorial effigies was equally adamant:

But I have no faith in statues, and no desire to help towards the remembrance of any man in that manner. The existing abominations in that wise fill my soul with grief and despair. I will be one of any committee to take any public statue down, but cannot be a committee-man to set one up.

Was it the leaden immobility of memorial statues that so appalled Dickens, as well as their pompous gravity? Statues of eminent persons consolidated that 'buttoned-up' respectability that Dickens so often pilloried in the novels; such subjects seemed dismally inflexible and immune to the sympathies that Dickens was trying to stimulate. A statue, like a photographic portrait, is the complete antithesis to the protean mobility that Dickens was celebrating in the Readings, night after night: a statue, like a photograph, would be a poor memorial to somebody who embodied such creative energy. But—again—how does one portray creativity?

There have been several attempts to amalgamate faithful portraiture and fanciful allegory where Dickens is concerned, in order
to communicate some sense of his distinctive achievement. He is
probably unique in being portrayed in many capriccio drawings and
paintings (the most famous being R. W. Buss's *Dickens' Dream*) as
a solemn figure, a still, material presence, surrounded by dozens
of small figures emanating from his novels and drifting like ecto-
plasm around their author. In many of these pictures Dickens looks
bemused, exhausted, or simply asleep, upstaged by the boisterous
fictional offspring who have consumed most of his own energy. Perhaps this was the only way to realize Dickens's portrait—to 'net the
lion'—because Dickens's identity was inseparable from the world
he had created. These portraits could indeed function as allegor-
ical representations of the Readings, when Dickens, alone on the
platform, produced out of himself, seemingly by magic, a swarm of
characters, each with distinctive voice and physical expression.

Dickens knew the anatomizing gaze to which distinguished writers
were subject, as he indicated in 1855 when declining the offer to
Household Words of some anecdotes about the recently dead Charlotte
Brontë: 'I have a particular objection to that kind of interest in a great
mind, which prompts a visitor to take "a good look" at the mortal
habiliments in which it is arranged, and afterwards to catalogue them
like an auctioneer. I have no sympathy whatever, with the staring
curiosity that it gratifies.' Nonetheless, three years later, as a touring
celebrity, he offered himself up to precisely this kind of curiosity,
and he came to know well—and treat comically—the disappointed
expectations of those waiting to see him, as he told the painter,
W. P. Frith: 'then they look at you as if it was your fault—and one
for which you deserve to be kicked—because you fail to realize their
ideal of what you ought to be.'

Let us sample some of the fuller written portraits of Dickens; first,
as he appeared to audiences during the first series of public Readings,
in 1858:

[The head] of DICKENS is large and symmetrical, very high in the crown, remarkably broad in the forehead, which ascends in a lofty slope from the powerful ridge of observation along the brows, to the largely developed organs of judgment, wit, and imagination. His face is handsome, the features clearly cut and strong. One and all of which are expressive of great energy of character. The charm of the countenance, however, centres in the large, brilliant, and penetrating eyes, whose power and beauty is typical of that magical faculty of Observation, by which, in his earlier works, he has laid the basis of his fame. He wears a moustache and pointed beard, after the American fashion, but time is fast trimming the abundant locks which he bore when MACLISE drew his portrait [the Nickleby portrait of twenty years earlier]. Though he is only forty-six, his countenance bears the impress of age, and it is easy to read in the lineations about the mouth and eyes the chronicle of long years of persevering labour, of anxiety and care.

This observer is keen to analyse Dickens's character and history in his 'mortal habiliments'. He does so phrenologically, and by interpreting the lines deepening in Dickens's face. He very much wants to read authorial genius in or onto the physical features. So did most reporters as they published first impressions of Dickens on the day or two after he had given his first Reading in their town. That was inevitable. Dickens was not some new presence in their lives. By and large, his audiences around the country, and the press, wanted to reconcile the famous Dickens they already knew, or had inferred, from his books, with the individual who had come to perform before them. Dickens the man was arriving in the wake of long-fermenting expectations arising from knowledge of Dickens the novelist: he had visibly to live up to his invisible stature. For the analytical observer just quoted, Dickens obviously fulfilled expectations. The physical description is not particularly detailed or distinctive beyond its phrenological corroboration of the already known, highly developed faculties of observation and imagination and the life eroded by strenuous literary work. There is indeed an odd hollowness about this portrait: it describes individual features with some care, but Dickens's own identity is so much more than the sum of his facial features. The deep lines in his face in his later years were to one observer not just the result of labour, anxiety and care (most observers interpreted them thus), but rather the result of permanent high spirits and strenuous expressiveness. 'His face, latterly, from its extreme mobility, and from the constant and incessant way in which he worked it about, was a mass of lines and wrinkles.' Dickens's own vitality was incising those lines.

A written portrait is much more prey than a photograph to distortion by subjective agenda, and the press and other eyewitness descriptions, both published and private, of how Dickens looked to those first audiences vary considerably, even when reporting exactly the same event. Press reviews were, with few exceptions, constrained in publishing detailed personal accounts of Dickens's appearance. Private letters could be much more candid. One correspondent, Richard Stratford, after attending a London Reading in January 1859, confessed privately to being disappointed with Dickens's appearance, though delighted by the performance:

Mr. Dickens appears to be at least 45, while he wishes to appear 10 years younger. I rather think he rouges his cheeks, at all events he is very much got up[. . .]. Of all men I think an author should not be a fop[. . .]. Dickens is really rather like a smart waiter, and one cannot help identifying him to a certain extent with Sam [Weller].

Why single out an author 'of all men' as especially unsuited to assuming a youthful or foppish appearance? What would be considered appropriate authorial dress and demeanour? Foppishness suggests too much susceptibility to fashionable opinion, too much attention to personal appearance in someone who should be essentially concerned with the life of the mind. Stratford's subsequent comments suggest also that this particular author comes across as more the 'Gent' than the gentleman: the disparagement becomes a class one.

Disappointment with Dickens's appearance was always going to be related to the nature and scale of whatever expectations people had about the famous name on the title pages of the famous novels. As an example, here is one witness recalling in detail Dickens's appearance at a Reading in Boston:

Dressed in a suit of faultless black, with two small flowers, one white and the other red deftly attached to his left lapel, a profusion of gold chains festooned across his vest, his earlocks standing almost straight from his head, and a countenance still fresh, though no longer youthful, Charles Dickens stood, book in hand, before his audience and gracefully acknowledged the hearty greetings bestowed upon him. Those who saw him for the first time hardly realized, we think, their ideal of this gifted author. His countenance has not that soft, refined, pre-eminently intellectual look which one who so deeply stirs the finer feelings of our nature would naturally be thought to present. The mark of genius is not so obvious, at least by gaslight, as an admirer would expect. A dashy, good-natured shrewd English face it is, one that would be associated with the outdoor life of a smart man of business, not particularly troubled with fine sentiments and not unmindful of good cheer, brusque, not beautiful, wide awake and honest.

This gives an account of certain specific expectations of authorship: soft, refined, an 'intellectual' look, manifesting 'fine sentiments'. The *beau ideal* presumably derives from some Romantic stereotype of strong sensibility, a type long ago caricatured by the young Boz himself in his short sketch 'The Poetical Young Gentleman' and in the 'handsomely miserable' fraud Horatio Sparkins. The middle-aged Dickens, however, looked uncompromisingly worldly.

If young ladies expect a sentimental young man of the Byronic style, they will be disappointed; he is a capital specimen of a strong-built, large-boned, large-headed Englishman [. . .] and a bold, manly, independent port characterise[s] him. He steps upon the platform with the light quick step of the captain of an English ship of war, who has seen much service, and braved the billow and the breeze with a stout heart and unshaken nerve.

He seemed sharp, business-like and prosperous. So he was. There was actually something of contradiction about Dickens's appearance: 'There is a self-dependence and power in the face that does away with the little fopperies of dressing the beard and training the somewhat scanty hair into "beau-catcher" curls over the brow.'

Such first impressions of the visiting celebrity, often betraying disappointment, were common across a wide range of witnesses, in both America and Britain. This was the case with Mark Twain, who first heard Dickens read in New York in December 1867:

But that queer old head took on a sort of beauty, bye and bye, and a fascinating interest, as I thought of the wonderful mechanism within it, the complex but exquisitely adjusted machinery that could create men and women, and put the breath of life into them and alter all their ways and actions, elevate them, degrade them, murder them, marry them, conduct them through good and evil, through joy and sorrow, on their long march from the cradle to the grave, and never lose its godship over them, never make a mistake! I almost imagined I could see the wheels and pulleys work. This was Dickens—Dickens. There was no question about that, and yet it was not right easy to realize it. Somehow this puissant god seemed to be only a man, after all. How the great do tumble from their high pedestals when we see them in common human flesh, and know that they eat pork and cabbage and act like other men.

Dickens resisted indulging his personal celebrity on the platform. He was there to read his work, not to display his personality, and he would launch into his Readings without delay and with minimal introduction. Having announced that he is to have the pleasure of reading to the audience, 'he begins as it were in the same breath'. It was consistent with the emphasis he made in his Will, in insisting that it should be on the basis of his works, not himself, that he be remembered by his country. His briskness in avoiding preliminaries upset many who had wanted to savour their first meeting with Dickens in the flesh:

If the truth were told, three-fourths of the audience would confess themselves agreeably disappointed. They had anticipated a treat, but more, perhaps, in the study of the author's personality than in the display of dramatic talent. There walks on to the stage a gentleman who gives you no time to think about him, and who dazzles you with twenty personalities[. . .]. He puzzles you with his complete abstraction from himself.

Dickens was amused by this bewilderment (especially marked in the American audiences) at the lack of any self-introductory overture:

The newspapers are constantly expressing the popular amazement at 'Mr. Dickens's extraordinary composure.' They seem to take it ill that I don't stagger on to the platform overpowered by the spectacle before me, and the national greatness. They are all so accustomed to do public things with a flourish of trumpets, that the notion of my coming in to read without somebody first flying up and delivering an 'Oration' about me, and flying down again and leading me in, is so very unaccountable to them, that sometimes they have no idea until I open my lips that it can possibly be Charles Dickens.

In nearly every case I have come across, where there has been initial disappointment, or something akin to disappointment with the first sight of Dickens at his Reading desk, such impressions have been overcome once he starts reading. Until that moment, he seems little more (and on occasions rather less) than a three-dimensional version of his photo-portraits. He transcends his sometimes disconcerting physical appearance, and any perceived mismatch between that appearance and his established distinguished-author status, through the charismatic power of his performance. A new Dickens then comes into being, a compound of the familiarly named author of old ('This was Dickens—Dickens', as Twain kept telling himself), the neat bearded newcomer in evening dress, and now something else: a magician—a storyteller who suddenly fractures into different individuals up there on the stage, who reaches into his listeners like an invasive force. This was way beyond anything that a photograph could capture. However much one might have felt inclined to carp at the first appearance of Dickens as he stood silently up there on the platform, the cynosure of thousands of gazes, receiving the audience's greeting, it was hard not to be gradually swept towards and into the vortex of his histrionic power once he began to read. Lady Westmoreland, attending a London Reading of 'Little Dombey' early in 1862, was one of those initially put off by the first sight and sound of Dickens:

Nothing can be less prepossessing than Dickens's appearance. His action is not graceful, his voice is not musical, and rather hoarse; and yet he moves masses of people of all ages, and of all kinds alternately to tears and laughter, to a degree I never saw equalled.

Once this power had been experienced, once word got around that the famous novelist was also a wonderful reader, and that what was happening in town halls around the country as he proceeded on his triumphal Reading tours amounted to historic events, to be transmitted down the generations—once all this had happened, day-to-day living for Dickens had to change radically. Celebrity on this scale, especially on the American tour, necessitated strict regimes to ensure as much privacy as possible. Dickens's life during these periods stretched into extremes of solitude and crowds. It must have been the strangest of experiences. This was a man famished for intimacy: he was one who also needed both absolute solitude in order to compose his novels and the company of thousands of devoted listeners under the sway of his voice and imagination. The regime devised to accommodate this split life is the focus for the final section of this chapter.

'A CONVICT IN GOLDEN FETTERS'

'A convict in golden fetters' is how George Sala described Dickens's life while on the Readings tours. Dickens's celebrity in the 1860s was something more than his fame as an author, more than the kind of aura attached to Sir Walter Scott or Thackeray. The audiences waiting for the moment of the Reading were excited by the twin prospect of seeing a literary giant and greeting an old friend. Novelty and familiarity were oddly associated:

The advent of Mr Dickens was most affectionately awaited. Curiosity we had in plenty—but it was that curiosity which we have in the desire to see a friend whom we have thoroughly known through mutual acquaintances, and whose genial qualities we have tested through intimate correspondence, yet one whose face we have not looked upon. It was curiously blended with recognition.

Dickens and his readers were old friends who had never met. That relationship gave a sharply distinctive turn to the general adulation and curiosity about the touring celebrity. It was a relationship that Dickens directly invoked right at the start of the public Readings, when, as we saw earlier, in the spring of 1858 he was urging Forster to drop his objections to the enterprise: 'Will you then try to think of this reading project (as I do) apart from all personal likings and dislikings, and solely with a view to its effect on that peculiar relation (personally affectionate, and like no other man's) which subsists between me and the public?' This comes a few sentences after he has been talking about the failure of his marriage ('It is all despairingly over[. . .]. A dismal failure has to be borne, and there an end'). One long-term intimacy ended, miserably, and so Dickens turned to that other 'personally affectionate' relationship he had been cultivating for as many years as his marriage. As John Butt and Kathleen Tillotson long ago put it, serialization launched Dickens on 'his lifelong love-affair with his reading public; which, when all is said, is by far the most interesting love-affair of his life'. The Readings offered him something like a consummation of that love. Later in 1858, after the summer announcement of his separation from Catherine, he wrote to Angela Burdett Coutts, three-quarters of the way through his first Reading tour of the provinces:

the manner in which the people have everywhere delighted to express that they have a personal affection for me and the interest of tender friends in me, is (especially at this time) high and far above all other considerations. I consider it a remarkable instance of good fortune that it should have fallen out that I should, in this Autumn of all others, have come face to face with so many multitudes.

The emotional consolation gained through the Readings fuelled an intensification of the mutual dependency Dickens had spent years fostering in his readers, as we saw in Chapter 1. Ten years before he launched his first series of paid Readings, he had analysed his reputation in terms of professional status and the public warmth towards him personally: 'Go where I will, in out of the way places and odd corners of the country, I always find something of personal affection in people whom I have never seen, mixed up with my reputation. That is the best part of it, and it makes me very happy.' So, when Dickens asked Forster to take this particular circumstance into account in reconciling himself to the Readings, he was using it to overcome the sense of impropriety in a gentleman's performing for money, and to emphasize the Readings as continuous with, not a derogation from, the Writings, so far as relations with the public were concerned. To recite professionally would, he argued, make no essential difference to the relationship that had grown up over the years of publishing the novels. The special friendship between readers and writer was already established: the Readings would simply improve it.

The phrase 'personal affection' comes like a refrain in letters to friends and family in the first month of the first provincial tour. It was more important than celebrity (he had that anyway). In Exeter, at only the second Reading of the tour, 'I never beheld anything like the personal affection which they poured out upon me at the end.' Three weeks later, in Dublin, the 'greatest personal affection and respect' had greeted him everywhere. Two weeks later, in York, came a startling tribute: 'I was brought very near to what I sometimes dream may be my Fame, when a lady whose face I had never seen stopped me yesterday in the street, and said to me, *Mr. Dickens, will you let me touch the hand that has filled my house with many friends.*' All in all, by October of the year in which he had launched his paid public Readings, he could assemble abundant evidence for Forster that he had not only not jeopardized his standing by becoming a professional performer, but actually enhanced it, especially where the sense of personal friendship with his readers was concerned: 'As to the truth of the readings, I cannot tell you what the demonstrations of personal regard and respect are'—though of course he does, again and again. Significantly here he writes of the 'regard' and 'respect', whereas in letters to others he had emphasized the ardent affection of the public. He needed to be able to prove to Forster, in terms that were important to Forster, that those initial anxieties about Dickens's dignity and reputation were proving groundless.

Following the reassurances about this 'personal regard', Dickens described the variety of effects his Readings had had:

How the densest and most uncomfortably-packed crowd will be hushed in an instant when I show my face. How the youth of colleges, and the old men of business in the town, seem equally unable to get near enough to me when they cheer me away at night. How common people and gentlefolks will stop me in the streets and say: 'Mr. Dickens, will you let me touch the hand that has filled my home with so many friends?' And if you saw the mothers, and fathers, and sisters, and brothers in mourning, who invariably come to 'Little Dombey', and if you studied the wonderful expression of comfort and reliance with which they hang about me, as if I had been with them, all kindness and delicacy, at their own little death-bed, you would think it one of the strangest things in the world.

Dickens is careful to let Forster know that people of all ages and from all stations in society are responding in the same way. It was not just a matter of his courting the lower classes in these performances: he has the enthusiastic support of that class of people who might have been most inclined to stigmatize the public Readings. And so it went on. 'Success attends me everywhere, Thank God, and the great crowds I see every night all seem to regard me with affection as a personal friend[. . .].' 'The audience, though so enormous, do somehow express a personal affection, which makes them very strange and moving to see.'

The arrangements for the tours ensured that Dickens was protected as far as possible from the oppressive consequences of both his celebrity and the intimacy that he courted. In London he simply retreated after the Readings to his apartment at the offices of *All The Year Round* where he would despatch the office boy to neighbouring restaurants to fetch him ices. Wherever he went on the tours, he stayed in hotels, hardly ever at the homes of friends. As he explained apologetically to one such friend, during his Reading commitments, 'I am in lavender on a shelf all day.' As far as possible he declined invitations to dine in company, and ate in his own room, alone or with his tour manager. His reasons for sticking to this regime were varied. It gave him seclusion, quiet, and rest to recharge his energies and save his voice from extra wear. It also established a system with his entourage (valet, gas-man, and others) ensuring the punctual discharge of their duties: 'knowing that I am never away, they are always at their posts.' In New York, as we saw earlier, he found the ideal accommodation in a hotel where he had private access between his suite of rooms and the street. A young boy, one of the hotel staff, was detailed to sit outside his rooms and keep visitors at bay. 'Silence, a darkened room, and an unsociality very foreign to my nature, are the sequel of my readings every night': and every night, from silence, darkness, and unsociality, he went into a brilliantly lit, tumultuous room to meet a thousand or two people. This pattern of extremes during his Reading tours is extraordinary. It stretched to his commuting between the guaranteed privacy of his Gad's Hill retreat and hotel life in dozens of towns around England: 'I miss the quiet of my own desk, but I look forward to resuming it—and it is a great sensation to have a large Audience in one's hand.' It also had its counterpart in Dickens's writing life. Dickens in the solitude of his study wrote to reach out to multitudes. From the lonely desk, he 'circulated' among tens of thousands of readers, and germinated that special personal relationship that he discovered in riotous blossom once he took to the road.

Between these extremes of solitude and rapturous multitudes, the private self and the public self, Dickens conducted his usual business as novelist and journalist. The second series of provincial Readings ran from 10 to 27 October 1859. These were followed by three Christmas Readings in London. No further Readings were planned for 1860. In January of that year he was contemplating a series of occasional papers for *All The Year Round*, and came up with the idea of the Uncommercial Traveller as a narrative persona. Mr Uncommercial is a third kind of self—one that steps anonymously out into public life, often under cover of darkness, and becomes the observer rather than the observed. It must have been a welcome recreation both from the high-profile self that toured the country and from the closeted self trying to protect his privacy on those occasions. Mr Uncommercial has been described as a 'flexible alter-ego' for Dickens. It was indeed that, and the persona is chosen at a time when Dickens is having to maintain not only private and public selves, as already suggested, but also a host of other parts as he enters his own characters, night after night, on the Reading platform.

Mr Uncommercial luxuriates in a profile so low that he can often seem to assimilate himself tracelessly into whatever he observes on his rambles ('what he desired to express he became'). Thus he delights in sinking himself into the restless, motley body of a theatre audience in the essay 'Two Views of a Cheap Theatre', and surrendering himself with zest to the materials and spinning processes involved in the great rope-making shed in Chatham Dockyard: 'Sauntering among the ropemaking, I am spun into a state of blissful indolence, wherein my rope of life seems to be so untwisted by the process that I can see back to very early days indeed [. . .]'. This freedom to unravel the strands of selfhood or dissolve the self into the larger social body is the recreational obverse of the controlled solitariness that was one part of Dickens's life and analogous to the recreational projection of the unitary self into other imagined selves (his characters) that constituted for Dickens so much of the lure of the Readings. The Readings were thus both lonely and gregarious, a firm flexing of power from the isolated platform and a surrender to being tossed on the emotional turbulence generated in that sea of people watching and listening. The Readings, while promoting his celebrity, were also a relaxation from being the famous individual, Charles Dickens. 'The platform absorbs my individuality', he remarked once, enigmatically. I take this to mean that in the Readings he could disappear into his imaginary worlds and characters, and revel in becoming other personalities. Individuality means indivisibility: etymologically it denotes the unitariness of identity. But Dickens spun many identities out of himself. Nowhere was this gift more spectacularly exercised than in the Readings. Charles Kent, who attended many, many performances, marvelled at the transformations as the solitary man submerged himself into a cast of characters, and he used the term 'individuality' in much the same way as Dickens had done:

Watching him, hearkening to him, while he stood there unmistakably before his audience, on the raised platform, in the glare of the gas-burners shining down upon him from behind the pendant screen immediately above his head, his individuality, so to express it, altogether disappeared, and we saw before us instead, just as the case might happen to be, Mr. Pickwick, or Mrs. Gamp, or Dr. Marigold, or little Paul Dombey . . . .

The Dickens of these years paced the cage of his own celebrity, one man, but also a compact mass of unruly energies held at bay behind those bars. 'I am as restless as if I were behind bars in the Zoological Gardens,' he confided to Dolby in 1869: 'and if I could afford it would wear a part of my mane away as the Lion has done by rubbing it against the windows of my cage.' In America his eye seemed to one observer 'like a comet in a cage'. He could not afford (even with 'golden fetters') to wear that literary mane away, when thousands wanted to see him shake it and hear him roar, 'as one of the largest lions of the day'.

5

Performance

*The Reading is due to begin at 8 p.m. At about 6.30 Dickens arrives
at the hall. In the room set aside as his dressing room, his valet Scott
has laid out his evening clothes to air. Everything is arranged neatly
in its allotted place. The slightest irregularity at this stage would upset
Dickens's studied composure. Within a quarter of an hour, with Scott's
help, he is dressed. Scott then goes softly away, and sits outside the door.
In the empty auditorium George Allison is checking over the platform
arrangements, and especially the gas rig. Dolby comes and goes, now
talking to the front-of-house staff as the time nears for doors to be
opened to the public, and now quietly putting his head in at Dickens's
dressing-room door to make sure all is well. An abstracted smile and nod
from Dickens.*

*Shortly before eight the vast hall is filled and noisy. There is a hush as
Allison comes on to the platform, turns up the gas-jets, pauses to check
the lighting level, and pads away. The desk glows brightly in its maroon
frame. The bubble of noise returns. At eight precisely Dolby appears
by the platform (another lull in the noise—is this Charles Dickens?),
scans the auditorium quickly, and retires. Dickens is standing by in the
darkness, waiting, bolt upright, book and gloves in hand. Dolby nods
and murmurs. Dickens strides out into the sea of faces.*

*From the back of the auditorium one sees a small figure marching
briskly into the bright radiance of the platform. As he stops by the desk,
turns and bows to the applause, hundreds of opera glasses are raised to
inspect the famous features. Those at the back without glasses register a
presence but see little detail. When the voice comes, announcing in rather
flat, measured tones that the performer is to have the pleasure of reading*

A Christmas Carol, it seems to take time to travel; and when it reaches the back seems to have picked up bits of acoustic debris in its passage. Neither face nor voice is as distinct as had been hoped.

Dickens went to extraordinary lengths to project himself, his gentlemanly, evening-dressed self, his voice (or voices), his facial expression, and his actions, to the remoter regions of great cavernous halls. In some senses he had been practising such projection all his writing life, throwing his voice into hundreds of different characters, and amplifying even the quietest tones of his narration. The Readings were the final and most extravagant effort of his life to touch his devoted public, in the remotest recesses. He reached out to them all as they gathered to listen to him retelling his stories. His performance style before audiences of two thousand had to be amplified to the utmost limit of what he felt could and should still work as a fairly intimate encounter between a storyreader and a group of rapt listeners. Near the start of his professional Reading career a Sheffield newspaper judged the fine balance that Dickens had to strike in his performances:

he has chosen a happy medium between what would be pleasing in a private circle and what would be requisite on the stage[. . .]. Any attempt to display great dramatic power in the presence of a dozen persons only, would be simply ridiculous[. . .]. Mr. Dickens, having to read, not to act, before large audiences, so tones his manner that, whilst every varying change of character or incident is so strikingly marked as to arrest and fix the attention of his hearers, there does not appear to be the slightest tinge of exaggeration.

Dickens worked very hard to achieve this toning of manner without apparent strain or artifice, and seems to have been particularly concerned to avoid charges of exaggeration. He used the Readings not to project himself, but to tell his stories, bring his characters to life, and draw his listeners into his imaginary worlds. An American newspaper acclaimed him as 'an artist who produces his scenes to our perfect satisfaction, and with the slightest obtrusion of himself'. The technical virtuosity—the well-judged expressiveness of voice, face, and gesture—was a means not an end in itself. He judged just how much in the way of vocal and gestural expression would be necessary to achieve those ends and seems to have taken pains to preserve the naturalism that so many eyewitnesses remarked on, while at the same time ensuring sufficient amplification, without distortion, to reach the most distant spectators. 'The greater the room and the larger the audience, the more imperative the necessity for something dramatic,' he reflected: 'Remember the little unchanging figure, seen from afar off, and the very little action that can be got into a bird's-eye view of that table.' He knew that he was risking some overprojection. To one criticism that he had overaccented the difference in address when, as Steerforth, he greeted Mr. Peggotty and then, with a distinctly and tellingly different look, Ham, he replied, 'Is she sure, sitting in the first, second, or third row, that she[. . .] makes artistic allowance enough for what it is to be when it reaches the end of the caravan in a great desert like the Steinway Hall?' That was one of the greatest difficulties he faced. Subtle nuances of voice or gesture would simply be lost by those near the back of the very large halls in which he chose to read. Yet, to pitch his effects to the back rows would have entailed undue histrionic amplification for those in the front rows. It is something like the difference today between small-screen acting and stage acting: the twitch of a facial muscle in a tense close-up is a type of histrionic eloquence that would be lost in a theatre.

The art lay, as a Dublin reviewer observed, in 'hiding the art by which he enthrals attention, elaborately studied as it undoubtedly is [so that the] keenest eye fails to detect the least preparation for the effect about to be created, and when it comes it strikes like Nature'. We know from the prompt-copies that Dickens signalled to himself, in margin notes, that he should start preparing for particular effects. But this preparation was to be invisible to everyone else. Like the conjuror that he was, Dickens on the Reading platform projected his illusions without displaying the secrets behind them, and he evidently had a particular relish in being able to surprise his audiences in this way. He defied people to catch him working the pulley-systems as he moved his audiences this way and that.

When he gave a special performance of his Reading of 'Sikes and Nancy' to professional actors and actresses, on 21 January 1870, he confided to Wills, 'I set myself to carrying out of themselves and their observation, those who were bent on watching how the effects were got:—and I believe I succeeded'.

15. Anon., Dickens giving a Public Reading (most probably at St James's Hall, March 1870). Watercolour. Courtesy of the Charles Dickens Museum, London.

Did he succeed, and if so how did he manage it? We need now to get a sense of how Dickens sounded in performance and what he looked like as he put actions to words. How did he engage his audience for two hours at a time? How did he come across? Because his Readings developed textually and histrionically over the years, and because, even within a single week, no two performances of the same Reading were the same, there is no single record that will stand for them all. That said, it is still possible to get a good idea of voice and gesture, characterizations, narrative manner, and rapport, even without any sound or visual record of Dickens in action on the platform.

VOICE

As will by now be apparent, Dickens was a shrewd judge of the reach and range of his voice and how to make the best of it in large halls, even though he failed on several occasions to sustain audibility. The three points of advice he gave to his son Henry when he was due to make a speech at Cambridge University could hardly be bettered: 'Open your mouth roundly and well. Speak to the last person visible; and take your time.' 'Speak to' is a masterly choice of words here: it implies amplification of the voice without (as far as possible) altering the register. Simply to raise the volume to a near shout would distort the speech, offend those near, and soon exhaust the speaker. It is a matter of projecting the voice. As we have already noted, when Dickens and Dolby tested the acoustics in the halls, with Dickens standing at the desk, they would talk to each other in a low tone as Dolby walked to all parts of the auditorium. The low tone established a vocal baseline for the Reading: if that became inaudible in parts of the hall, then the whole performance, including gestures, would need to be pitched a shade or two higher. Perhaps this was what Dickens meant by 'enlarged' when he reported his vocal triumph in the formidably huge Manchester Free Trade Hall in 1869: 'Without much greater expenditure of voice than usual, I a little enlarged the action last night; and Dolby (who went to all the distant points of view) reported that he could detect no difference between it and any other place.' This question of the right volume and tonal level was important to the whole project of the Readings. They were to preserve as much as possible of the drawing-room occasion, although translated to very different milieus. We shall see, in examining the performances themselves, how Dickens worked to develop this unique mode of recitation.

'Open your mouth roundly and well.' By all accounts, Dickens had a very mobile mouth, embedded though it was behind his beard, so it perhaps came fairly naturally to him to open it 'roundly' in order to gain maximum articulation. He was also, of course, quite an experienced actor and public speaker. The final advice, to 'Take your time', was a considerable challenge in the face of a nervous ordeal, but an important point to stress was the taking of *your* time, and refusal to be hurried into 'getting through' the speech or Reading. It was a token of the speaker's retention of absolute control, as he set his own pace and rhythm. Dickens's margin prompts to himself in the Reading texts remind him now and again to go at the pace determined by the unfolding story, not to be rushed by extraneous pressures.

Dickens gave some very detailed attention to the vocal techniques that might be required in reading to a large group of people when he wrote in 1864 to the curate of his local (Higham) church, who had asked for some advice. His letter is worth quoting at length:

> Mrs. Cay having mentioned to my sister in law that you would be glad to compare notes with me on likely means of ensuring audibility in reading to a congregation, I very readily offer you a few slight words of suggestion out of my own practice and experience.
>
> The main point is difficult to express, and will have, I am sensible, a very odd appearance on this paper.—If you could form a habit of finding your voice, *lower down*—in other words, of reading more from the chest and less from the throat—you would find yourself immensely relieved, and your voice greatly strengthened. When you experience any little distress or difficulty now, I think it is in the throat; and I think that is, because the strain is in the wrong place. If you make the trial, reading aloud alone, of placing your hand on your chest, and trying as it were to originate your voice behind the hand, you will probably soon find a capacity in it almost new to you, while the ease of speaking will be correspondingly increased.
>
> I should have supposed your perfectly unaffected reading of the Lessons to be generally audible throughout the Church. If it be not so, it may pretty surely be made so, by addressing the last persons in the building and by being always watchful and careful not to drop the voice towards the close of a sentence or a verse, but rather to sustain and prolong the distinctness of the concluding words. Always supposing the words to be well separated and never run into one another, I believe that a very moderate voice, observing this method, may be heard with ease and pleasure in a large place, when a very powerful voice, neglecting it, might be quite ineffective. The habit of reading *down-hill,*—or dropping the voice as the sentence proceeds,—is so

extremely common, that perhaps even if Mrs. Cay were to happen to read a few pages to you by the fireside, you would detect yourself asking what this or that lost word towards the close of a sentence was. Imagine how fatal the fault must be to distinctness, when there are listeners at various removed distances.

I should be even more diffident than I am in offering these simple hints, if I had not habitually acted on them, with the result that I am said to be always heard.

Dickens was very familiar with the strains on the voice after too much Reading—or rather, as he implies, of protracted recitation using the wrong vocal technique. Chest-production of the voice can give a more rounded and resonant tone as well as take the pressure off the throat. It also engages more of the body by bringing the torso into play as a source of energy. In the third paragraph of the letter, Dickens reiterates the advice he had given to his son Henry when he recommends 'addressing the last persons in the building'. The rest of his advice in that paragraph bears on sustaining audibility through the complete sentence. He had offered similar advice to Henry Chorley: 'If you could be a little louder, and would never let a sentence go, for the thousandth part of an instant, until the last word is out, you would find the audience more responsive.' The common tendency, he suggests, is to drop the voice as it nears the end of a sentence, either with a diminution of volume or with a falling inflection. The important point is to round each sentence clearly, just as one should complete each word in it with distinctness, especially in concluding consonants. Dickens seems to recommend even a kind of overcompensation to correct the '*down-hill*' tendency by prolonging the distinctness of the concluding words. This has intriguing implications for what many listeners found to be an odd feature of Dickens's own Readings, his obtrusive use of the rising inflection at the end of sentences. It was remarked on in the 'Premiere' chapter of this book. Dickens's voice 'runs up at the end of a sentence, when the rules say it ought to come down[. . .].' 'He closed each sentence with a rising inflection,—quick and sharp on the ear, like the rapid crack of a whip.' As far as I know, this trait was not observed in his ordinary speech. Might it be that Dickens was practising what he had recommended to Christopher Cay, and deliberately speaking 'up-hill', especially in the opening paragraphs of a Reading, to make sure he carried to the last person visible in the large hall?

Dickens did not have a particularly distinctive or full-bodied voice. Kate Field, who heard him on many occasions during his American tour, said that he had a 'naturally monotonous voice', though others described it as sonorous and expertly modulated. It was subject to very few mannerisms, apart from those oddly rising inflections at the ends of sentences which have already been noted, the 'sing-song tone, ascending from a low to a high key'. He had to overcome a hint of a lisp, a slight thickening of the 's' and 't', as if his tongue were rather too large for his mouth. He hissed his sibilants somewhat; and 'country' could sound like 'counthory'. This 'slight but pleasant and conversational' lisp seemed to some an attractive idiosyncrasy: 'It carries out that direct man to man impression which his writings inspire, and is evidently one of those things which he neither cares to disguise or exaggerate.' He tended to roll his 'r's rather too abrasively for some tastes. He shed the slight aspiration (more common then than now in English speech) in the 'wh' of 'when' or 'where'. Otherwise it was an unremarkable voice, trained into an extraordinary instrument.

Newspaper reports on his Reading voice made little allowance for the special pressures under which Dickens was performing, and therefore it would be unwise to generalize a vocal character from their verdicts. The sheer strain of the Readings regime on his stamina meant that Dickens was often husky or gruff at the start of a Reading, especially during the American Readings, when he had to contend with persistent catarrh as well as a very taxing schedule. He sometimes carried a box of lozenges with him on to the platform. His frequent resort to a raw egg beaten up in a glass of sherry would have benefited not only his energy level but also his tired voice: it was a well-known specific, as was a glass of good bottled stout drawn long enough for the froth to have subsided. The huskiness usually wore off, or was deftly camouflaged, once he began to change voices for each of his characters. The voice was also affected by the simple matter of ageing. Some of those who heard him several times in the 1860s sensed a slight deterioration in clarity in the last three years. This may have been due to the inordinate demands on his voice during the years of touring as well as latterly to the effects of possible small strokes on vocal articulation. In the many and often contradictory reports on his Reading voice, the majority verdict was that what he lacked in natural power and flexibility he more than compensated for by cultivating a clear enunciation and supple intonation:

His voice is not of a flexible nature: it is strong, sonorous, full; but it is not flexible[. . .]. It is a good, sound, English voice, carrying itself through, without much variation, except when it imitates the boyish treble, in which it is better than in advanced age: it is good in middle age; but it never attempts with success the feminine tone.

As one might expect from Dickens, it was a voice whose natural deficiencies were mastered by being subjected to the most rigorous training: it had to fulfil its duties, however arduous.

Dickens's voice needed to command attention in two ways. He had, as already remarked, to ensure audibility in large halls and he had also to maximize tonal variety and rhythm of phrasing to sustain the audience's full engagement over two hours. He practised hard to achieve both these, by projection without undue distortion or reliance on sheer volume, and by refining his distinctness of phrasing and expressive modulation. In the early days the pace was sometimes too hurried: 'he reads slightly too fast to be followed by the bulk of the audience', thought the *Liverpool Daily Post* when Dickens gave his first Reading in that city. It was easier to hold attention when performing a character part than in sustaining stretches of narration, so he had to take particular pains with the latter, especially in its pacing and phrasing. He succeeded, by and large: even in the 'level' portions of the narrative, remarked a Dublin reviewer, 'when the interest might be expected to flag, he keeps attention alive by the admirable distinctiveness of his tones, by the judicious pauses—the measured flow and variety of his vocal modulations'. The reviewer for the *Manchester Guardian* during the first series of Readings referred to Dickens's 'almost invariable monotone', and also detected some eccentric phrasing: 'the division of his sentences by no means accords with what is usually understood to be required by the rules of syntax or punctuation.' Dickens became a master of the dramatic pause, and he could vary the pace to an astonishing degree. One listener described the 'furious speed' with which he read, in the 'Carol', the flight of the spirit of Christmas over the rooftops: 'he never drew breath.'

Again and again Dickens returned to practising and perfecting his delivery of the Readings. Nearly ten years after he turned professional, when his extraordinary triumphs might have allowed him to relax into the routine, he undertook a wholesale refurbishment of the repertoire. He told Forster in the Spring of 1867, 'I have tested all the serious passion in them by everything I know; made the humorous points much more humorous; corrected my utterance of certain words.' By constant attention to the smallest details, he developed what one reviewer judged to be a perfect elocution, 'neither straining after undue effort nor lapsing into carelessness, but poising every sentence with nicest regard to its true interpretation'. In all this he seems to have been self-taught, beginning no doubt with his intensely close childhood observations of Charles Mathews. In an age of proliferating manuals on public speaking and recitation, he was not by any means a textbook elocutionist. This was a relief to most who heard him:

The great fault with professional readers is that they are teachers of elocution, and are in the habit of exaggerating the differences between various tones and qualities of voice by way of illustration to pupils; and they become possessed with this habit to the extent that it seems as if they were bound, in giving a public reading, to show the audience a full assortment of all the wonders a voice is capable of. Mr. Dickens's style is on the contrary easy, and harmonious with itself throughout, without being dull or monotonous.

While most of those who commented on the matter were pleased by his freedom from formulaic elocution or theatrical mannerism—'drum and trumpet declaration', as it was called— some were upset by the degree to which Dickens the Reader often positively offended against prescribed practice, by both omission and commission:

He laughs the '*Rules*' to scorn. He is as guiltless of inflexions as a Chinese noun. Sometimes every sentence, every clause in a long paragraph will turn up its toes, figuratively speaking, in a manner that would make Prof. Hows gasp with horror. Sometimes he is monotonous to that degree that every well regulated elocutional person must scorn him with inarticulate scorn. Sometimes he is quite indistinct in his utterance[...]. It is enough to make the sainted dead, Walker and Macready, and Kemble and Forrest, and Murdock and Russell, and the rest, rise from their graves, to see all their established teachings put to open shame by a reader who, by the mere force of simple, unaffected nature, without apparent art, without discoverable artifice, can make a thousand people laugh, shudder, tremble into sudden tears, freeze into moveless silence, or thrill with joy, of voice and hand, over meanness and cruelty rebuked and punished.

While not in thrall to professional elocutionist practices, Dickens did seem to have made a distinction in practice between his speech-making style and his Reading style, according to at least one observer, George Douglas, the Duke of Argyll:

As a speaker he was quite peculiar. It was the very perfection of neatness and precision in language—the speaking of a man who knew exactly what he was going to say, and how best to say it. But it was without fire, or tones of enthusiasm, or flights of fancy[...]. On the other hand, in dramatic reading and acting, he was really wonderful, full of the most varied powers in the expression of humour, and of pathos, and of ferocious villainy.

The circumstances of speech-making and public Reading are very different, of course. In the former Dickens was *in propria persona*, delivering his own opinions on public matters, and accountable for his views. In Readings and amateur theatricals he could bury his own self in other personalities, and roam altogether more freely in an imaginary world. His creative energies, which most readily expressed themselves in mimetic form, could be exercised in the most exhilarating and sometimes unnerving ('ferocious villainy') forms.

But whether he was impersonating or simply narrating, Dickens's orthodoxy in the Readings was an impassioned naturalness, in both voice and gesture.

GESTURE

'The Englishman is a reticent, undemonstrative creature, not predisposed even to vocal expression, and decidedly indisposed to pantomimic.' So wrote John Hullah, the composer who had written the music for Dickens's 1836 operetta *The Village Coquettes*. Hullah was a teacher of singing and speaking, and published his book on *The Cultivation of the Speaking Voice* in 1870. English reserve had to be overcome by the professional actor and singer, at least to the extent of giving proper expressive force to the sentiments of a song or recitation piece. Dickens, however, was not the kind of Englishman typified by Hullah. His highly expressive and mobile face, the eyes and mouth particularly, was attested to by many. Less well known is his body language. Sir Arthur Helps commented on Dickens's hands:

He had most expressive hands—not beautiful, according to ordinary notions of beauty, but nervous and powerful hands. He did not indulge in gesticulation; but the slight movement of those expressive hands helped wonderfully in giving additional force and meaning to what he said, as all those who have been present at his readings will testify. Indeed, when he read, or when he spoke, the whole man read, or spoke.

In terms of gestures, Dickens kept within the bounds of Reading, rather than acting. That seems to have been the general opinion, with some exceptions: 'We might object that the hands are used and the eyebrows wafted a little too much in the stagey way', thought a Liverpool reviewer in 1858. However, on his return from America, some observers felt his performances had become more theatrical in speech and gesture: 'Unless we are mistaken, Mr. Dickens makes his points a little more markedly than was formerly his custom [and his] gesticulations [...] have become almost the full gesticulations of the stage.' Dickens hardly ever moved away from the desk, but made full use of facial expression and arm gestures. The point has already been made that to stray beyond his desk would be tantamount to trespassing into theatre: the central presence of the elegant little velvet-covered desk—icon of authorship and redolent of the domestic drawing room—anchored him to the role of Reader rather than roaming actor. Once he had learned his Reading texts by heart and could let the book lie on the desk, the whole of his upper body was freed to reinforce visually what he delivered vocally, but to reinforce it within certain bounds.

There was a protocol for gestures in public performance, outlined by J. H. Hindmarsh, Henry Neville, and others in standard guidebooks on the subject. There were three kinds of 'radius', in ascending scale of histrionic expressiveness: the colloquial, the rhetorical, and the epic. For the colloquial, little more was appropriate than slight sweeps of the forearm only, well below the shoulder level, with the forearm and palm swivelling up or down ('supination' or 'pronation', respectively). 'The *stroke* of the gesture on the particular word, or accented syllable, is marked by the hand [and gestures] must be made *with the words*, neither precede nor follow them.' Modulation into the rhetorical radius takes the whole arm up, free to sweep at shoulder level or below, and epic sees the arm raised to full height (which Dickens would have done, of course, in murdering Nancy). By and large Dickens observed these protocols, and stayed mostly within the colloquial radius. One observer in America remarked, 'He hardly ever gesticulates from the shoulder, but only from the elbow, and generally in front of his breast—a sort of twisting of his hand, as if he were winding up an imaginary watch inside his waistcoat.'

Essentially Dickens seems to have settled for two distinct modes, or perhaps degrees of gesture, one for narration and one for character-impersonation. As third-person narrator (i.e., not when he assumes a character such as Magsman or Marigold or David Copperfield to deliver the narrative), he tended to restrain his gestures. In this capacity, and allowing for slight role inflections, he was after all Charles Dickens, the author and the gentleman-Reader, the

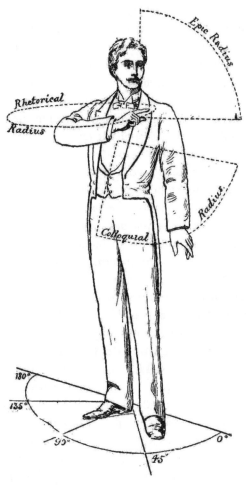

16. The 'Strokes' of Gesture. Illustration in H. Campbell et al, *Voice, Speech and Gesture* (1897), p. 131.

embodied principle of control over his creations, and not one of their number. 'His right hand moves continually upon the wrist, slightly indicating actions of movements which are described.' That represents the base-line, minimal gesturing mode, when Dickens is engaged in simple descriptive reading, and when, perhaps, he holds the text for a while in his left hand. But even his smallest gestures could be startlingly eloquent: 'Frequently a mere motion of his hand shed a hitherto undreamt-of meaning upon a whole passage, giving you the idea that this member is to Dickens what the wand is to the familiar fairy.' At the other extreme, the narrator disappears and Dickens transforms his whole demeanour, along with his voice, and becomes the gesticulating, grimacing character in the story. I want to deal first with his use of gesture and action as a narrator.

There is a strategic problem which most performing Readers must confront: to what degree should gesture accompany verbal description? What is the point of miming an action that is being described adequately in the Reading? For example, if the narrative announces, 'he went up and smartly rapped the door-knocker', is it not redundant for the Reader to mime the action of knocking? Gesture might well extend or underscore a narrated action of this kind, or even clarify a movement that may be slightly obscure in the text, but simply to carry out the same movement as that described in words can be mechanical tautology. The same issues bear upon book illustrations. In fact Dickens's Reading performances were a kind of illustration of his texts. A Dickens Reading was a visual experience as much as it was a recital, and Dickens—the 'little unchanging figure seen from afar off', in a large hall of people, for two hours—needed to maintain consistent gestural illustration. He would not only embody the characters in his stories, but also 'makes pictures of inanimate objects rise before the imagination'. As narrator, he communicated his own delight with his story and characters, and with the help of gestures invited the audience to share that delight. At his first public Reading of the 'Carol', in Birmingham, 'How Mr. Dickens twirled his moustache, or played with his paper-knife, or laid down his book, and leant forward confidentially, or twinkled his eyes as if he enjoyed the whole affair immensely!' These are, as it were, rhetorical gestures to enhance rapport, rather than dramatically illustrative gestures. The latter are exemplified in his Reading copy of 'Sikes and Nancy', which was littered with marginal stage directions as well as underlinings. The underlinings signal special emphasis for the voice, and the marginalia (often right beside underlined passages) prompt a kind of illustrative gestural underscoring. Thus, for example, when Sikes has heard from Noah, under Fagin's sly prompting, about Nancy's betrayal, and is rushing from the house in a fury, the text runs as follows:

'Hear me speak a word,' rejoined Fagin, <u>laying his hand upon the lock</u>. 'You won't be—you won't be—<u>too</u>—<u>violent</u>, Bill?'

Against this speech, and particularly applying to the hand on the lock, Dickens wrote 'Action' in the margin, doubly underlined. The 'Action' prompt occurs again during the narrative of Sikes's return home, when, on entering his own room to find the drowsy Nancy, he '<u>double-locked the door, and drew back the curtain of the bed</u>'. Dickens was evidently performing the actions he narrated fairly consistently in this lead-up to the murder. According to Charles Kent, who had the prompt-copy in front of him as he wrote his account of the 'Sikes and Nancy' Reading, Dickens's marginal stage directions to himself were prompts to him not to give gestural emphasis to the spoken description, but actually to substitute action for narration:

'Fagin raised his right hand, and shook his trembling forefinger in the air,' is there on p. 101, in print. Beside it, on the margin in MS., is the word 'Action.' Not a word of it was said. It was simply *done*.

The examples just cited are transitional moments, when the character has not wholly usurped the narrator, but the narrator is partly animated by the character. This half-acting and half-narrating (a histrionic version, perhaps, of free indirect discourse) fuses the two together at certain points: the combination gives extra dramatic energy to the narrative, while the words pinpoint the detailed direction of the gestures. In this way the audience is drawn more intensively into the suspense and horror of the episode. Dickens needs to build momentum, and the four or five pages of the 'Sikes and Nancy' prompt-copy are ravaged with underscorings and directions to action, from the point where the marginal 'XX <u>Murder coming</u> XX' signals to Dickens the start of the rapid build-up to the terrible event. When the murder did come, the halls resounded with the savage beating of Dickens's fist on the Reading desk as Sikes clubbed Nancy to death. He would beat the desk so hard in his passion that on at least one occasion he dented his gold cuff-links.

These examples of the use of gesture selectively to intensify the narration mark moments when Dickens is fleetingly playing the character whose actions he is describing—Fagin's hand on the lock, Sikes drawing the curtain back. They are brief touches of impersonation to give visual effect to trivial actions that carry ominous significance. However, once Dickens fully entered into the characters, gesture and voice coalesced in a radical transformation from the narrator mode. To get a strong flavour of Dickens the narrator's lighter touches of impersonation as various characters come forward for mention, we can draw on some of Kate Field's descriptions. She was especially alert to his mimic performances and indeed rather more biased towards the dramatic actions than to the words: 'What Dickens *does* is frequently infinitely better than anything he says or the way he says it.' She observed the following moments from Readings of the 'Carol' and 'David Copperfield'. Dickens as Scrooge rubbed his eyes and stared at the door-knocker; a little later he would bite his fingers nervously as he peered at the ghost of Marley. At the Cratchit dinner, Dickens stirred the gravy, mashed the potatoes, dusted the hot plates, and (as Belinda) tasted the apple-sauce and smacked his lips loudly. His 'sniffing and smelling of that pudding would make a starving family believe that they had swallowed it, holly and all'. As Mr Peggotty, he chucks little Em'ly under his arm, 'just as if she were there *to* be chucked'; and as Ham he stands there rubbing his hands with emotion. In another of his Readings sinister Jonas Chuzzlewit in 'Mrs Gamp' was represented by Dickens as incessantly biting his thumbnail. These actions are not particularly striking in themselves, but none of them appears in the original story nor in the prompt-copies. They were invented for the Reading performances only, as Dickens recreated his scenes for the platform. Each instance, although it belongs mainly in the narrative, is a momentary impersonation as Dickens slips briefly in and out of character, with the narrator still in the foreground. I have not found any commentary on the potential technical difficulty of Dickens's projecting himself as David, a character, and then representing *David*'s representation of Ham or Micawber: perhaps the 'I' in 'Copperfield' was neutral enough to be easily dissolved into the 'I' of Dickens-the-Reader. It was more tricky when he had to assume a distinct accent for his narrator, as he did for 'Dr Marigold', and then represent Marigold's (not *Dickens's*) impersonation of the giant or the doctor; but he managed that, apparently: 'he never seemed to forget, when he was personating the doctor, or the giant, or any other characters, that it was Marigold and not Mr. Dickens who was relating the story.'

Dickens's most famous mimic action as narrator came when he was describing the Fezziwig Ball. His hands performed on the desk top, with the fingers dancing as though they were the legs of the party folk. He could not quite allow himself at the desk to break into the 'Sir Roger de Coverley', much as he might have wanted, though he evidently did take some liberties with leg movements: 'He even defies propriety time and again by making gestures with his legs', commented one offended reviewer from the *New York Tribune* at one of the first American Readings.

CHARACTERIZATION

The full, sustained entry into character—and the vanishing of the narrator—was a tour de force. Dickens's commitment to impersonation of the full cast of characters developed over the years of the Readings. Some accounts suggest he was initially sparing in his mimicry. *The Times* reported of his London Readings of the 'Carol' in 1857 that the only character he gave a special voice to was Scrooge, 'whose words he speaks in senile accents'. This is contradicted by a report of the first public Reading of the 'Carol' in Birmingham in 1853, when he 'personated with remarkable force the various characters of the story'. However, through the 1860s he seems to have multiplied and intensified character impersonations as a leading feature of the Readings. The transformations from narrator to character could be spellbinding, and are best caught in some extended descriptions by eyewitnesses. I shall take three famous examples, Fagin, the little judge in the Pickwick Trial, and Mr Micawber. First Fagin, according to two eyewitnesses, Charles Kent and Edmund Yates:

Looking at the Author as he himself embodies these creations—Fagin, the Jew, was there completely, audibly, visibly before us, by a sort of transformation[. . .] the impersonator's very stature, each time Fagin opened his lips, seemed to be changed instantaneously. Whenever he spoke, there started before us—high-shouldered, with contracted chest, with birdlike claws, eagerly anticipating by their every movement the passionate words fiercely struggling for utterance at his lips—that most villainous old tutor of young thieves[. . .] his features distorted with rage, his penthouse eyebrows (those wonderful eyebrows!) working like the antennae of some deadly reptile, his whole aspect, half-vulpine, half-vulture-like, in its hungry wickedness.

You read [his character] in his rounded shoulders, in his sunken chin, in his puckered cheeks and hanging brow, in his gleaming eyes, and quivering hands, in the lithe shiftiness of his movements, and in the intense earnestness of his attitudes.

In all the other Readings Dickens had begun by reading from the prompt-copy, and then eventually (certainly by 1867) learned them all by heart. 'Sikes and Nancy' was the only item in the repertoire to have been devised from the start as a dramatic performance without the aid of the book. Dickens rehearsed it as a piece of theatre, aiming to make the most powerful impression with its sequence of short, violent scenes. Charles Kent, after attending that private trial Reading before an invited audience on 14 November 1868, called it 'as splendid a piece of tragic acting as any one of that select audience has had the privilege of witnessing within the interval of the present generation'. Fagin, like Bolter, Sikes, and Nancy, had been fully developed as a dramatic role before Dickens was ready to give trial performances. This seems clear from the terrible intensity of concentration in his impersonation, as described above: this Fagin is ferociously malicious. The claws, the reptilian and vulpine expression in the features and bodily distortion—these are much the same analogical terms that Dickens used in the original novel to mark Fagin's moral degeneration; and the image of the scrawny, ravenous bird of prey was also famously caught in the Cruikshank illustration of Fagin in the condemned cell. Dickens embodied all these features of his arch-villain in a grotesque impersonation involving the contortion of his whole frame. This was no standard caricature stage Jew, with false nose and pronounced nasal tone.

The scale and rapidity of the transformations from narrator to Fagin, and from character to character during dialogue, must have been very taxing for the performer. It was no longer a matter of the narrator's shifting like a ventriloquist into mimicked speech accompanied by a few characteristic gestures. In order to get the right voice, in a concentrated way, Dickens had to move his full being into that of the character. This was 'assumption' in the fullest sense. The appropriate voice, Fagin's distinctive speech rhythm and accent, was then produced by the way in which the character's whole distorted body posture and mannerisms functioned. The degree of commitment to transforming himself is indicated in this 1868 remark: 'he seems to try and swell into Tony Weller, to shrivel into the Marchioness, or to wriggle into Jingle'. (Oddly, the latter two never featured in the repertoire.)

There were two other particularly celebrated character parts into which Dickens seems to have thrown not only his voice but his whole physique. The first was the little judge in 'Bardell and Pickwick'. Here is one member of the audience at one of the late Readings, which he attended as a child and recalled later with a vividness that testifies to the miracle of transformation:

I shall never forget my amazement when he assumed the character of Mr. Justice Stareleigh. The face and figure that I knew, that I had seen on the stage a moment before, seemed to vanish as if by magic, and there appeared instead a fat, pompous, pursy little man, with a plump imbecile face, from which every vestige of good temper and cheerfulness—everything, in fact, except an expression of self-sufficient stupidity—had been removed. The upper lip had become long, the corners of the mouth drooped, the nose was short and podgy, all the angles of the chin had gone, the chin itself had receded into the throat, and the eyes, lately so humorous and human, had become as malicious and obstinate as those of a pig.

Dickens's apparent ability here so completely to alter his features as well as his voice was matched in his representation of Mr Micawber. Here he reversed the changes made for Fagin: instead of shrinking down into the hunched form of the old villain, he inflated himself and heightened his colour, to the fascination of Kate Field:

I see him 'swelling wisibly before my wery eyes', as he tips backward and forward, first on his heels and then on his toes. Before he stops swelling, he becomes just about the size of our ideal Micawber; his face, quite apoplectic in hue, is fenced in by a wall of shirt-collar; he twirls his eye-glass with peculiar grace; and when he exclaims, 'My dear Copperfield, this is *lux-u-rious*; this is a way of life which reminds me of the period when I was myself in a state of celibacy'—nearly choking himself to death before he arrives at 'a state of celibacy',—the picture is complete[. . .] [Micawber's] all-pervading cough [is] as inseparable from his speech as oxygen from air. Dickens could no more be Micawber without that cough than Micawber could have ever been at all without Dickens[. . .]. None but a great man misunderstood ever had such a propensity to choke. And when Mr. Micawber *does* cough, the two lapels of hair brushed above Dickens's ears, appear to be drawn by capillary attraction towards the sentiments spoken, and, waxing rampant, nod approvingly, as if to say, 'Just so.' Neither cough nor lapel are to be found in the text, but when did finite words ever express a man's soul?

Micawber's obtrusive cough was indeed a new feature of the character whom all knew so well. It incidentally aligns him a little more closely with that other shabby-genteel figure evidently modelled on Dickens's father, William Dorrit. Both characters affect a dignified style of speech that is sometimes hard for them to sustain. Dorrit's magniloquence is as punctuated by hesitations—'hem's and 'ha's—as Micawber's speech (in the Reading version) is broken by coughs. These entries into character involved Dickens in a kind of grafting, so that the hybrid result partook of the physique of both the impersonator and the impersonated. Fagin in performance evidently exploited his author's 'penthouse' eyebrows to increase his grotesque menace; and *Dickens*'s distinctive hair 'lapels' were shaken into action by *Micawber*'s coughing (Micawber had no hair at all, let alone 'lapels'). What weird chimerical creature was this up on the platform? It is as if Dickens were voluntarily possessed by the characters. Where did Dickens's being end and Micawber's begin in this symbiosis? We—that is, our surrogate viewer Kate Field—become aware in this instance of both the character and the man impersonating that character.

The question of how fully the Reader should inhabit the characters he presents in his Reading was one that attracted considerable discussion at the time and we have touched upon it earlier in this book. The problems for the soloist come not so much from managing either the narration or the impersonation of the character parts, but in controlling the transition between them, and judging the appropriate level of immersion in the character part. It is easier to do a straightforward comic cockney monologue, unframed by a narrator, than it is to have the narrator describing, introducing, and then making way for the character whose voice and physical demeanour he then must assume. There is a tension between the narration and the dramatization. Two interesting contemporary witnesses of Dickens's Readings developed distinct ideas, of a prescriptive kind, about the art of Reading and characterization. The first is from the anonymous reviewer for the New York paper, *The Nation* (quoted earlier, in Chapter 2); the second is from a reviewer for one of the Manchester newspapers, A. W. Ward, whose book *Charles Dickens*, from which these comments come, was published in 1882:

The true theory of the performance is not that it is acting in which the actor, as much as possible, forgets himself into the very likeness of what he personates, but is rather that a gentleman dramatically tells a story among friends, indicating rather than perfectly assuming the characters of the personages brought before us; never wholly, indeed, never nearly, losing sight of his hearers and himself; never wholly, never, at any rate, for very long, getting away from the gentlemanly drawing-room, with its limiting conventionalities, into the wider and freer atmosphere of the stage.

Now the art of reading, even in the case of dramatic works, has its own laws, which even the most brilliant readers cannot neglect except at their peril. A proper pitch has to be found in the first instance, before the exceptional passages can be, as it were, marked off from it; and the absence of this groundtone sometimes interfered with the total effect of a reading by Dickens.

The 'true theory' and the 'laws' of Reading indicate that there were conventions governing this kind of performance. It is time to measure Dickens's own practices in this respect. According to A. W. Ward, the prerequisite for any Reader is to develop a 'proper pitch', a 'groundtone'. By this he presumably means a stable narrative style, one that would establish the Reader's particular identity (with whatever idiosyncrasies) as a storyteller and calibrate his primary relationship as narrator to both his audience and his text. That primary relationship turns on the single narrator's responsibility to tell a story, and the audience's willingness to hear the story out. The groundtone is the narrator's signature. A firm, familiar, and consistent groundtone is a guarantee of the controlling presence of the narrator as he unfolds the story. Characters introduced into the story should be 'indicated' only: some flavour of their speech may be demonstrated, but the narrator is always to be the dominant presence as conductor, orchestrating cast, and actions. The disappearance of the narrator into his characters destabilizes that contractual relationship.

This kind of advice on the decorum of a Reading in Victorian England was fairly unexceptionable. However, as far as Ward was concerned, it did not sit easily with Dickens's narratorial style as a Reader. There are two points to be made about the Reader as narrator in the light of Ward's stipulations and those of the *Nation* reviewer, and I want to develop them in the light of reports about Dickens's reading performances. The first point has to do with the relationship between the narration and the characterizations. The second concerns the relationship the narrator develops with his audience—that rapport that Dickens cultivated so strenuously.

NARRATIVE AND CHARACTER

Ward's remarks are made in his book and he would have been recalling particular performances that, as reviewer for the *Manchester Guardian*, he would have attended in the 1860s. One such review appeared in the *Guardian* on 12 October 1868, when Dickens had read 'Dr Marigold' and 'Bardell and Pickwick' at the Free Trade Hall in Manchester. It was one of the first Readings to be given since he had returned from the American tour in April, and Ward was not the only one who sensed that his Reading style had become more flamboyant—even cruder—as a result of the demands of that tour. Some of these remarks from the *Manchester Guardian* have already been cited:

Unless we are mistaken, Mr. Dickens makes his points a little more markedly than was formerly his custom; and more than once passes the bounds which even a dramatic reader should observe. His gesticulations, always admirable in their rapidity and naturalness, have become almost the full gesticulations of the stage. Surely a reader ought never to go beyond indication; in other words, never more than suggest what it is the actor's business thoroughly to express.

If Dickens saw this criticism he must have had mixed feelings about its recommendations, since he was already designing, learning by heart, and rehearsing 'Sikes and Nancy', the most fully theatrical of all his Readings. The 'bounds' indicated by Ward were perhaps by now too constraining. John Oxenford, the critic on *The Times*, remarked of one of the early trial performances of 'Sikes and Nancy' (in November 1868): 'He has always trembled on the boundary line that separates the reader from the actor; in this case he clears it by a leap.' Edmund Yates reported later on this Reading: 'gradually warming with excitement, he flung aside his book and acted the scene of the murder'.

I mentioned earlier that for Dickens to have wandered out in performance from behind the desk would have been tantamount to trespassing into theatre. His remaining at his desk was a symbolic

confirmation that he was a Reader, not an Actor, however cap-
tivating the virtuosity of his impersonations. However, when the
Reader, albeit still at his desk, disappears into the fully developed
impersonation, the boundaries of the occasion risk being breached:

In the first pages of the Carol, which are merely descriptive, his 'reading'
was simply that and nothing more—distinguished only by utterance and
enunciation, and a most discriminating and effective emphasis. There was
not the slightest affectation or effort at effect—very little gesticulation,
and nothing to distinguish the performance from the ordinary reading of a
gentleman in his parlor. But when he came to the introduction of characters
and to dialogue, the reading changed to acting.

That recommendation quoted earlier (from the New York *Nation*)
about 'never wholly, indeed, never nearly, losing sight of [. . .]
himself' is a telling caution. But how appropriately is it applied to
Dickens either as a writer or as a platform performer?

Dickens's narrative voice as a novelist is often polyphonic, slipping
in and out of various discursive modes with an energy and panache
that sometimes upstage the effervescent characters he summons into
life. This is especially so in *A Christmas Carol*, where narration on its
own becomes a highly coloured performance. It is not easy in Dickens's novels and stories to draw a line between what Ward classified as
'proper pitch' and 'exceptional passages' when so much of the *narrative* (let alone the dialogue) is 'exceptional'. Dickens's 'proper pitch'
as narrator is dynamically mercurial and extravagant. The heightened
energy, the unabashed verbal playfulness and hyperbole, the rhetorical gear-changes as comedy or pathos are engaged, the sudden
irruptions into satire and parody—the reader has a bumpy narrative
ride with Dickens the novelist. This characteristic style is naturally
reproduced by Dickens the Reader: 'he can in a minute command
the wrapt attention of an audience that he has just been provoking
to uncontrollable laughter, by an earnest sternness, or a quiet lapsing
into gentleness or pathos.' The rapidity of the transitions is just what
is distinctive in Dickens's narration, and Ward's criticism seems
not to take that into account. If one accepts the characterization

of Dickens as the heteroglot narrator (in the novels and stories), then two things follow. Firstly, the convention of a homogeneous groundtone seems an inappropriate imposition. It may suit other writers and other public Readers, but it is too constraining for Dickens, whose performed narratives, like their written counterparts, are *sui generis*. Secondly, there is the point about the need for an established groundtone in order more clearly to mark off the 'exceptional passages'. However, if one accepts Dickens's narratorial groundtone as inherently multivocal and tonally volatile, then the 'exceptional passages' (especially the character impersonations) to be 'marked off' from that groundtone actually seem less 'exceptional'—more a case of modulation. To shift into a sculptural analogy, one might say that his narratorial style is typically high-relief from the start, so that it takes little additional projection to extend that into the near full relief of the great character impersonations. It is (in sculptural terms) simply a matter of more enhanced volume and three-dimensionality.

My queryings of Ward's criticism by extrapolation from experience of the fiction to its performance in Readings might seem a bit impertinent. After all, Ward saw and heard several of the Readings, and Andrews has not. My point, however, has to do not with a challenge to Ward's reported experience of Dickens's Readings, but with his establishing a yardstick for Readings generally, and taking the measure of Dickens according to that. Dickens was resetting the agenda. For one thing, he was reading Charles Dickens, he was transmitting texts that make singular demands on any reader; for another, he *was* Charles Dickens, someone whose lifelong instinct and impulse for theatre, for bravura performance and highly developed mimicry, made not only the Readings but the whole body of his fiction a thing apart.

Ward's critique continues to dwell on Dickens's handling of the transitions between his narratorial mode and his character-playing, and he registers a jarring quality in these transitions:

There was noticeable in these readings a certain hardness[. . .]. The truth is that he isolated his parts too sharply—a frequent fault of English acting, and one more detrimental to the total effect of a reading than even to that of an acted play.

The complaint, following on from Ward's more general outline of the proprieties of Reading, is that Dickens jumped too abruptly, too completely, from narration and description to impersonation. His characterizations were suddenly fully developed roles, wholly detached from the narrator, whereas, according to the conventions of a Reading, those characters should have been 'indicated' only. A similar sense of Dickens's histrionic forcing of a radical independence of characterization from its narrative matrix is expressed in a broadly favourable review in 1868, by an American newspaper:

It is not reading exactly, the book is there, but not often used. It is simply telling the story, with all the variations in face and voice, with the rigid putting himself into one character and then another, which give it dramatic life and interest.

That term 'rigid' corresponds to Ward's detection of 'a certain hardness'. As Philip Collins has observed, such descriptions are also similar to Henry James's caustic criticism of Dickens's 'hard charmless readings'. Clearly, as the Readings developed over the years, Dickens prized the virtuoso integrity of characterization as one of the most powerful illusions in his performances. Memories of Charles Mathews's brilliantly complete impersonations were no doubt his model. He wanted not simply to suggest a character in action with a little mimicry, but to become that character. 'Each character that is introduced is as completely assumed and individualized by Mr Dickens as though he were personating it in costume on the stage', reported an Edinburgh reviewer; and an American observer remarked, 'Scrooge was himself, and not Scrooge filtered through Dickens'. That he could achieve this is evident from the responses already discussed, in relation to his Fagin, Micawber, and Justice Stareleigh. The Duke of Argyll, whose remarks comparing Dickens the Reader with Dickens the speech-maker we have already heard, said that Dickens 'had the faculty, which many great actors have had, of somehow getting rid of their own physical identity, and appearing with a wholly different face and wholly different voice'. He wanted to people the platform with more than just the figure of the gentlemanly narrator.

However, what some felt to be an inappropriately exaggerated individualizing of characters in a Reading seems not to have troubled audiences generally: indeed many reports commented positively on the skill with which Dickens integrated and harmonized characterization with narrative. These complimentary remarks on the Reading of 'Dr Marigold' from the *Manchester Guardian* may have been by Ward himself, as he reviewed Dickens's performance in 1867 (i.e., before the American tour):

The excellent taste of the reader never allowed him to outstep the limits of a <u>reading</u>. Everything is shaded off into a part of a connected and consistent whole; the vulgarities are not too vulgar, the laughs which are raised are not too loud, the emotions which are stirred are not too intense.

Ward's more stringent criticism (from his 1882 book) suggested that the primary mode in Readings should be that established by the controlling narrator—that is, the groundtone from which the 'exceptional passages' (such as some character representation) are temporary excursions. For Dickens, as the Readings evolved, that hierarchy becomes almost inverted: the essence of the performance became the display of multiple characterization. This is implied in a review of one of the early public Readings: 'With a characteristic voice and a distinct expression of countenance for every character, the now and then recurring natural tones and looks of Mr. Dickens, in the merely descriptive passages, were the links tying together a series of transformations and mimetic simulations which together formed a real dramatic entertainment.' The impersonations were the jewels, the real exhibition pieces, strung together on relatively unobtrusive narrative. Much of Dickens's preparation of the Reading texts, and his constant reworking of them through the 1860s, involved paring away the narrative, as we have seen. The narrative itself was sometimes dramatically enhanced in performance. This is suggested by one report in 1869, which recalls earlier versions of the Readings:

That it is the player's rather than the author's art which elicits much of the approbation of the audience and draws such crowds to hear him read, is we think evident from the manner in which the applause is bestowed. It follows the points made by the reader, far more than the most skillfully arranged phrases or the most carefully expressed sentiments of the writer. We suspect Mr. Dickens thinks so too, for since his earlier readings these entertainments have gradually taken more and more the form of dramatic recitations.

On this whole question of the performer's 'isolating his parts too sharply', and straining the link between narration and characterization (and thereby for some tainting the drawing-room milieu with something too theatrical), Dickens himself had some technical points to make. In a letter of March 1868 he writes to James Osgood, a partner in the American publishing firm of Ticknor and Fields. He is responding to a number of queries raised by Kate Field in connection with her record of the Readings in *Pen Photographs*. From this letter one infers that Kate had asked why Dickens subdued his Reading style in the narrative passages. Here is his answer:

As I have to make the characters stand out prominently and separately, and as *they are not* before the audience, and as *I am*, what I have to do in the level reading is to suppress myself as much as possible. If I were to express myself with the force and individuality I should throw into a speech, does she not see that I must subtract so much from the characters?

Dickens recognized that he needed to maintain as far as possible a lower-key (or bas-relief) narrative style in order to throw into sharper relief the full-bodied character impersonations. However jarring some felt the transitions to be, it was a strategy Dickens very consciously worked. He relied on contrasts, and the play of these contrasts animated the performance. As he reduced the narrative element in the Readings, and relied more and more on dramatic dialogue, the contrasts he had developed between subdued narrator and high-relief characterizations were often transferred to the dialogues between characters. Each would throw the other into relief. This can be seen in three examples, 'Mrs Gamp', the exchange between the Judge and Winkle in the 'Trial', and Scrooge's conversation with his nephew near the start of the 'Carol'.

Kate Field describes the voice and manner of Mrs Gamp:

Take a comb, cover it with tissue paper, and attempt to sing through it, and you have an admirable idea of the quality of Mrs. Gamp's vocal organ, provided you make the proper allowance for an inordinate use of snuff [. . .]. There is an intellectual ponderosity about her that renders an exclamation impossible [. . .]. She holds all notions of light and shade in contempt, and with monotonous cadence produces effects on her hearers undreamed of by her readers [and she sententiously parades her humanity and her modest needs to Mrs Harris] with a pendulum wag to her head in the *tempo* of a funeral march.

This Reading was essentially a portrait piece: the narrative was simply and perfunctorily a frame for a collage of Gampisms gathered from various chapters in the novel. Other characters—Pecksniff, Chuffey, Jonas, Mould, and Mrs Prig—subside into minor roles. Pecksniff, who might well have upstaged Mrs Gamp, is given only about 130 words, and none of his speeches blossoms in his characteristic style. Mrs. Gamp is centre-stage throughout, and the other characters are little more than supernumeraries or little cameos, even though Dickens gave them distinctive vocal characteristics. Mrs.Gamp sails through the Reading like a mighty galleon, hardly jostled from her majestic monotony by the lesser craft, and given extra scale and substance by their fretful, busy comings and goings. The Reading is a good example both of Dickens's radical retailoring of his texts in order to promote what were originally colourful but rather marginal characters into platform stars, and his performance strategy of selective amplification. He intensified the dramatic chiaroscuro.

'Bardell and Pickwick' by its very nature was a rich opportunity to exploit adversarial contrasts, to oppose different styles so that each would accentuate the distinctiveness of the other. One of the highlights, according to Kate Field, was the exchange between the little judge and Mr Winkle as the latter is sworn in as prosecution witness. She reproduces the pacing of their dialogue:

Court. 'Have—you—any—Christian—name, sir?'
'Nathaniel, sir?'
Court. '*Dan*-iel. Have—you—any—other—name?'
'Na*thaniel*, sir,—my lord, I mean.'
Court. 'Na-*thaniel Dan*-iel, - or *Dan*-iel Na*thani*el?'
'No, my lord, only Na*thani*el; not *Dan*-iel at all, my lord. Na*thani*el.'
Court. 'What—did—you—tell—me—it—was—*Dani*el for, then sir?'
'I *did n't*, my lord.'
Court. '*You—did—sir.* How—could—I—possibly—have—got—*Dani*el—on—my—notes—unless—you—*told* me so, sir?'

Kate Field then comments, 'the contrast between the flustered stammering of poor Winkle and the impenetrable infallibility of Justice Stareleigh, delivered in a slow, authoritative tone, as if founded on the Rock of Ages, is remarkable'. 'Bardell and Pickwick' worked its contrasts elsewhere: in the cross-examinations of the baffled Winkle by the wily Skimpin, and of the sharp Sam Weller by the pompous, blustering Serjeant Buzfuz. Each of these paired contrasts offered the dramatic Reader two very distinct and different impersonations, vocally and gesturally, and it made the transitions between them clear, and made it easier to simulate an animated dialogue.

The first dialogue in the 'Carol' happens between Scrooge and his nephew, each the antithesis of the other: Scrooge is the miserable old refrigerator, and his nephew—'all in a glow [. . .] his eyes sparkled, and his breath smoked'—is the radiator. Dickens 'constantly omitted phrases describing who spoke and how they spoke, by making marvelous changes of tone and changes of his facial expression': the nephew's lines were 'so cheerfully spoken, and so crabbily replied to'. The more Dickens could sharpen the contrasts between distinctive characters in a dialogue, the less need there was for narratorial identification, cues, and commentary.

RAPPORT

As narrator, Dickens focused his energy on recreating the fictional world in which his stories and characters live. It was not a matter simply of bringing characters to life: their whole ambience had to be realized and the audience brought into that ambience. It was a process of refraction, whereby what happened on the platform drew the materials of ordinary life from their familiar medium into one of a different density. 'He throws himself into the atmosphere in which they [the characters] all move, and compels his audience to live in it likewise.' The forcefulness of those verbs has a Dickensian ring: 'throws himself into', 'compels his audience'. They are a measure of the energy released and deployed in these Readings, not just in the flamboyant display of histrionic power, but in the concentration on conjuring, detail by detail, that dense, palpable, imaginary world. 'His power of reproducing a scene and bringing to the very eyes of his audience its exact features and the relative bearings of its composing parts has never been equalled.' The effect noticed by this reviewer could equally well apply to Dickens's writings. The density and intensity of physical and social detailing in the novels perform just this task of engulfing the reader in the imaginary world of the novel. Dickens was explicit about this aim. In introducing 'The Story of Little Dombey' he announced that he hoped 'his audience would speedily forget the cold light of day and lose themselves with him amidst those childish footsteps'. This impulse to lure an audience away from the real world into the world specially created by Dickens entailed a narrative dynamic that must have tugged hard at his determination to subdue his narratorial self in the interests of throwing the characters into sharper relief. As we have seen, he had entered whole-heartedly into the spirit of the 'Carol', and described the scenes of Christmas festivity with an energetic—even frenetic—joviality that was quite contagious.

However, while narrative joviality worked well, Dickens's narrative pathos had a more mixed reception. R. H. Hutton recalled the mode in which he used to read the death of Little Dombey: 'It was precisely the pathos of the Adelphi Theatre, and made the most painful impression of pathos feeding upon itself.' He was also accused now and again of resorting to rather puerile theatrical tricks. *The Saturday Review* took him to task for melodramatized sentimentality in his Reading of 'The Poor Traveller', where he developed 'a series of little turns or tricks [. . .] by which an idea is continually brought round and round, and forced upon the attention of the reader or hearer':

Stated in simple language, these melodramatic tricks sound rather simple. They principally consist in perpetually bringing in the name 'Richard Doubledick,' and speaking of the 'dark eyes' of an officer. Entering the service as a dissipated private, Doubledick cuts his way up to the rank of captain. This gives occasion to the writer to read a series of paragraphs with Sergeant Richard Doubledick, Sergeant-Major Richard Doubledick, Ensign Richard Doubledick, and so on [. . .]. He dwelt on the separate syllables, and rolled out the r's as if this little art of repeating the man's name with variations was sure to be gratifying to every one. Richard is reclaimed by the man with the eyes, and Mr. Dickens took every pains to make us feel that the eyes were coming, and that they ought to go through us as they did through Doubledick.

These manoeuvres are very familiar in Dickens's writing, and tailor-made for public storytelling, where the Reader can reinforce the ingratiating archness of the narrative with facial expressions. However, the success or failure of the comic joviality and the pathos, as well as the credibility of the imaginary world conjured up on the platform all depend on the chemistry of the relationship established between performer and audience. This was absolutely the key to Dickens's Readings. A Reader has a choice of Reading roles to assume, before he or she ever gets to the impersonation of the story's characters. The choice will be determined by the nature of what is being read, by the nature of the audience, and by the kind and degree of rapport he or she seeks to develop with that audience. I shall have a little more to say in the last chapter on some of the implications of this rapport; here I want to describe what we know of it from accounts of Dickens's performances.

Dickens's platform naturalness and confidentiality are role-playing strategies, the calculated projection of a particular kind of Readerly persona, designed to engage an audience in a particular way. Nonetheless, it would be a mistake to assume it was wholly artifice; such a relationship, as we have seen in earlier chapters, was an almost instinctive driving force behind the whole of Dickens's career as a writer and journalist, and then as a public Reader. Dickens the Reader was not Dickens the man, au naturel, but an amplified facet of that man. After all, the man who could give the illusion of a boisterous kind of intimacy with a couple of thousand strangers was the same man who then secluded himself in his hotel room and refused invitations to dine with close friends. The tone of address adopted by the Reader to his audience was therefore a barometer of the relationship Dickens wanted to develop with his listeners. Tactical decisions made about that tone raise again the question of the generic status of these occasions: were they Readings, recitations, solo dramatics, or what? Let me briefly rehearse some of the points made earlier, in Chapter 1, as a means of approaching the question of rapport in the Readings.

The putting aside of the book, once he had learned the texts by heart, was an important step in this. The author, the publisher, the book, the readership: these four components established the coordinates in the production and consumption of Dickens's work. Their relationship to each other was thrown into flux by Dickens's Reading career. Book and publisher were sidelined, author was foregrounded. Greeting Dickens's first public Readings at Birmingham in 1853, *The Times* reporter remarked how unprecedented it was at that period to hear authors reading their own works in public: 'The appearance of Mr. Dickens at Birmingham is a return to the practice of the olden [bardic] time.' Modern tastes, it seemed, felt there was something egotistical in a writer's appearing before his public to recite his work. In bardic times, the reporter might have added, the author was in direct contact with his 'readership', in relations unmediated by a commercial publisher: the bard was his own publisher. Mass literacy and the publishing industry eroded that relationship, increased the alienation of the author: 'The multiplication of books seems to remove [the author of genius] further and further from personal observation.' The author disappeared behind his books. They became his public surrogate as he retreated into private life, and the more books there were, the less visible the author became.

Dickens changed this, as we have seen. He did so early on by preferring to publish his fiction in monthly pamphlet form, rather than in books, thereby arranging relationships so that he became a frequent and regular presence in the lives of thousands of readers. He changed it again twenty years later when he became a professional public Reader and a very visible celebrity; and at a certain point in that later phase he even abandoned the book. He abandoned the surrogate, paper-clad 'Dickens' that had first introduced him to all these people. As the author became the visible performer, so the readership became his devoted listening audience. Those complex relationships (public versus private, author–book–readership, recitalist versus actor) are rewritten once Dickens marches onto the platform with his book, opens it, and starts to read aloud from it to a couple of thousand people. They are further re-written when he abandons the book, leans across his desk, and dramatically tells, rather than reads, the story to his listeners, as is clear from this medley of witnesses:

He does not 'read' <u>from</u> his book but <u>to</u> his audience.

He reads as if he were not reading, but telling his story [the 'Carol'] plainly, and without apparent effort, to a circle of friends.

He spoke, rather than read, the entire narrative, glancing at the page only at rare intervals, and more as a fashion than anything else.

Addressing his hearers across the table as if relating an agreeable after-dinner anecdote.

The Times had associated the multiplication of books with the alienation of author from 'personal observation' by his public. Just the opposite began to happen in the municipal halls up and down the country once Dickens went on tour. In preparing to retell his stories orally, he had literally taken his books to pieces, cut-and-pasted new books from them, gradually committed those new books to memory, and eventually laid them aside altogether. He reassimilated his fiction for a new mode of delivery. In place of his books he offered himself, the original source, and, with the book laid aside as a mere accessory furnishing, it seemed as if the stories and the characters were gushing straight from that source. He 'tells' or 'speaks' his stories to his listeners, directly.

Dickens worked hard to increase the relaxed intimacy and apparent spontaneity he practised with his listeners. As we saw earlier, before the Reading he would explicitly encourage them to laugh and cry during the Readings. During the Reading his tone as narrator and his body language implicitly encouraged intimacy. This made a strong impression during the American tour, as the reviewer for the *Hartford Daily Courant* makes clear:

We soon perceive that he is not reading but *talking*, in a manner simply natural, as a gentleman would talk in a parlor. The manner of what he says, the tone in which he says it, are only in confidential explanation to the audience of the characters and scenes he is about to introduce. In this explanation the who[le] body of the talker assists, in gestures, attitudes, significant nods and glances. He is not reading a piece, but displaying a situation, putting us in possession of the surroundings of his story. The extreme naturalness of this high art disarms criticism. It is the perfection of story-telling.

The low-key, confidential tone and the naturalism are a part of that technique of suppressing himself in the narrative portions so as to throw into higher relief the character impersonations. However, it is also designed to engage the audience in particular ways, so that Dickens becomes almost a part of that listening community. He gives the illusion of both shaping and sharing their responses to the characters about to be introduced.

There have been several discussions of Dickens's narratorial persona in the Readings. Alison Byerly has argued that he projected quite strongly, as narrator, the sense that he was the controlling author of the story being told, and that this was in the interests of ensuring both that 'his stories, dramatic as they were, would not be perceived as inappropriately theatrical', and also 'to signify the presence of a stable, sincere self behind the theatrical roles'. Others, notably Susan Ferguson, have argued that the Readings were, in a sense, 'anti-authorial—resisting the presumption that the narrator is the author and directing attention to the characters'. Ferguson adduces as some evidence for this Dickens's preparation of the 'Carol' prompt-copy, in which he deliberately and systematically cut all of the thirty-seven instances from the published version where the narrator refers to himself with the personal pronouns 'I', 'me', or 'my'. These apparently conflicting interpretations of the evidence are not incompatible: Dickens managed to do both. Dickens's prompt-copy may have deleted traces of the authorial/narratorial 'I', but, as the report of the Hartford Reading suggests, the singular, emphatic narratorial presence expressed in body and tonal language amply compensated for the missing textual 'I'. There were also specific points made about the authorial presence in contemporary reviews of the Readings, such as this in 1861 from *The Ipswich Journal* as it praised the Reading for being 'quite without mannerism or artificial effect': 'the egotism of the author never intrudes to embarrass the reader in the delicate position in which he stands as the exponent of his own creations'. *The Times* congratulated him in 1854 on having the good taste not to overindulge dramatic effects 'nor in the actor to sink the individuality of the author'. The difficulty in determining any one view of Dickens's authorial persona on the platform is that, as I have already mentioned, contemporary reports over the 1860s are often conflicting in their responses. Dickens sank his individuality as author-narrator—as 'Dickens'—into his characterizations, but sustained it in the personal relationship he cultivated in description and narration: yet, that last statement needs qualifying, because he also gave the impression that he was sharing his audience's surprised delight at the material being presented as if it were fresh to *him*. Dolby remarked that Dickens had a curious habit of 'referring to his own works as the productions of some one else, and would refer to them as such'.

So where does he belong in relation to the story and to his audience? There is no doubt that he cultivated on the platform a lively, companionable persona along much the same lines as he projected in some of his writings: 'He comes in much as some familiar friend might do—a friend who is perfectly at home and always welcome, a ready-tongued, imitative sort of man, who always has some comical thing to relate—and in a perfectly easy, unaffected and thoroughly colloquial tone, *tells* you the story.' Compare this with *The Illustrated London News*'s obituary characterization of Dickens's serialized fiction (quoted earlier, in Chapter 1): 'It was just as if we received a letter or a visit, at regular intervals, from a kindly observant gossip, who was in the habit of watching the domestic life of the Nicklebys or Chuzzlewits, and who would let us know from time to time how they were going on.' The tone of friendly, informal confidentiality carries through from the writings to the Readings. One of Dickens's most popular fellow-soloists, Albert Smith, the presenter of the 'Mont Blanc' spectaculars, was described by a contemporary as having developed something of the same informal manner with his audience: 'the whole tone of the performance was good, pleasantly and conversationally given as a kind of one-sided chat'. That is the relationship characteristically established by Dickens the narrator in the Readings, his delivery 'rendered additionally pleasing by the fact of his addressing his hearers across the table as if relating an agreeable after-dinner anecdote'. At the very first New York Reading, after sensing the warmth of the audience's welcome, 'he at once repays the heart-homage by putting himself *en rapport* with his hearers and becoming one of them—while occupying his own position as story-teller'. He seems to have done this within the first paragraph of his opening Reading of the 'Carol', which was purpose-built for developing this kind of rapport. Charles Kent remarked on Dickens's evident 'exhilaration' at the start of a Reading, and especially at the start of the 'Carol': 'The opening sentences were always given in those cheery, comfortable tones, indicative of a double relish on the part of a narrator—to wit, his own enjoyment of the tale he is going to relate, and his anticipation of the enjoyment of it by those who are giving him their attention.' *The Times* remarked on how he 'infuses life and warmth into the narrative, as though he were a spectator watching with interest the progress of a scene, and vividly revealing the impression made by it on his mind'. As long as Dickens *did* enjoy the occasion, he could revel in this friendship between performer and audience. When he failed to find this warmth, or when his audience was not what he described as 'magnetic', his performances could suffer severely. He told one acquaintance that at his London season's Readings he had been hardly able to continue his reading because of the ' "genteel" frigidity' of his audience. Kate Field attended several Readings of 'David Copperfield', and was relieved that she had done so, since the first occasion had been very disappointing: 'his tragedy needed force, and [. . .] his description of the shipwreck at Yarmouth [traditionally the *tour de force* in this particular Reading] lacked vividness and intensity.' Subsequent Readings, to audiences who were warmly responsive, proved to her how heavily Dickens depended on the sympathy and support of his audiences.

One detailed account, by the playwright Herman Charles Merivale, suggests how little it took—a mere crumb of comforting responsiveness—to enable Dickens to warm to his storytelling:

Dickens's audience that night was dull, and he became so, too. I was disappointed. His characters were not life-like, and his acting was not good, and got worse as he went on. It was the inevitable law of reaction. His audience bored him, and he began to bore me, amongst the rest. He was not 'in touch' with us, that is all; and his eyes wandered as hopelessly in search of some sympathetic eye to catch them, as the gladiator's of old for mercy in the circus. Then, suddenly, at one point of his reading, he had to introduce the passing character of a nameless individual in a London crowd, a choleric old gentleman who has only one short sentence to fire off. This he gave so spontaneously, so inimitably, that the puppet became an absolute reality in a second. I saw him, crowd, street, man, temper, and all [. . .]. Dickens's electric flash bowled me over so completely and instantly that I broke into a peal of laughter, and, as we sometimes do when hard hit, kept on laughing internally, which is half tears, and half hiccough, for some time afterwards [. . .]. The audience of course glared at me [. . .]. But Dickens's eye—I wasn't much more than a boy, and he didn't know

me from Adam—went at once straight for mine [. . .]. For the next few
minutes he read 'at me', if ever man did. The sympathetic unit is everything
to us. And on my word the result was that he so warmed to his work that
he got the whole audience in his hand, and dispensed with me.

This was not gratuitous ingratiation. The vitality of his performances
depended on establishing this rapport, a rapport achieved by his
ability to identify with his audience.

None of this will surprise seasoned performers, especially those
who know the loneliness of the soloist. The isolation is intimidating
and potentially disabling, even for a celebrity whose popularity is
otherwise wholly secure. The concept of the 'sympathetic unit', the
foundation for a good Reading, is linked to that term 'magnetic' that
Dickens used. Some of the implications of these ideas in relation to
mesmerism will be discussed in Chapter 6. This exercise of sympathy
enabled the Reader to position himself somewhere between the
audience and the characters he was impersonating. He engaged his
audience as if they were familiar acquaintances, and he introduced
them to his (and their) other familiar acquaintances, his characters.
He could assume the identity of his listeners ('becoming one of
them'). With a thoroughly sympathetic audience, observed Dolby,
'he could so identify himself as to be powerless to do other than laugh
when they laughed, and cry when they cried'. This happened very
often. Dickens reported on a Dover Reading of 'Nicholas Nickleby
at the Yorkshire School': 'they really laughed when Squeers read
the boys' letters, with such cordial enjoyment, that the contagion
extended to me. For one couldn't hear them without laughing too.'
Reading 'Bardell and Pickwick' and the 'Carol' in Boston, Dickens
was seen at times to be 'so carried away by his intense appreciation
of the ludicrous character he was representing, that he was nearly
caught joining in the general laughter. The laugh would irresistibly
spread itself over his face and an evident effort was required to restore
his countenance to a dignified composure.'

It was a strange dynamic. The projected text hit the audience,
detonated different responses, ricochetted back at him as a new

experience, and caught him quite off guard. The composed, gentlemanly narrator came across sometimes as an indulgent, amused spectator of his own creations as they exercised their independent life; at other times he became the helpless victim of laughter at what that gentlemanly narrator was describing; and then again, in quick succession, he could become the character that was the object of the gentlemanly narrator's amused scrutiny. Just as he could move with miraculous dexterity between different assumed identities in his impersonations, so he seemed to be able to float his own identity in his audience and retrieve it sufficiently to maintain his principal identity as narrator. He had the ability simultaneously to alienate and appropriate these several roles undertaken in these performances. This degree of rapport struck some as endearing but perhaps a little unprofessional. Comparing him with another well-known soloist, the *Syracuse Daily Standard* felt Dickens's performance was not as 'artistic' as it might be, but it was 'more genuine' inasmuch as 'The author laughs with the hearer all the time'. This was one of the strategies useful in distinguishing a Reading from an actor's stage performance: 'A consummate actor, in a play, would [unlike Dickens] seem to be oblivious of auditors in front of the stage.'

The terms used here to describe Dickens's shared delight in his own entertainments imply a spasmodically helpless passivity on the part of the person who ought to be firmly directing the occasion: he is prey to a 'contagion' of laughter, 'lifted out of myself', 'carried away'. Carried away from *what*? Presumably from the control he ought to be exercising over the audience, the delivery of his text, and himself—most particularly the latter. However, for Dickens the experience of being lifted out of himself was exhilarating: his self-immersion in his audience was, after all, the same kind of experience as his full-blooded impersonations ('assumption has charms for me'). The surrender of control at such moments, the suspension of immunity to contagious laughter or tears—these are the sensations that so excited Dickens. It is precisely at such moments, absorbing himself in his characters or in his audience, that he fulfils his dream of companionship and community of feeling with his listeners. At those same moments his fiction detaches itself from his authorship—as something he invented—and becomes a sequence of actual events and characters that all are witness to, Reader and audience: 'so real are my fictions to myself, that, after hundreds of nights, I come with a feeling of perfect freshness to that little red table, and laugh and cry with my hearers, as if I had never stood there before.' Dickens projected this surprised freshness of response just as robustly and effectively as he projected his character impersonations: (at the Fezziwig ball) 'Mr. DICKENS seems to enjoy their humour as if he had never heard of it before,—and as if it took him quite as much by surprise as it could take anybody else.'

However, for all this sense of shared enjoyment, Dickens was acutely aware of his audience *as* auditors. He gave to his Readings 'a most fascinating air of spontaneity', said a Belfast newspaper; in voice, gesture, and facial expression 'he always suggests the idea that it is the insensible result of genuine emotions, and not a trick to counterfeit these emotions.' That 'air of spontaneity' was a part of the performance. There is no doubt that he did very often surprise himself emotionally during the Readings, but the apparently effortless freshness of response to the text on his part was also a technical accomplishment. This became evident to those who attended repeat performances of certain Readings, as did the eagle-eyed New York reviewers. The first of these observations is from the *New York Times* and the second from the *New York Tribune*:

There was little variety in Mr. DICKENS' style of reading. He read the *Christmas Carol* last night almost precisely as he read it a week ago, with the same tones, the same expressions of face, the same gestures, and so on.

we had the opportunity of observing how carefully studied is every part of these performances. The tone is the same, the gestures are the same; little things that were so carelessly done they looked like accidents the first night, were as careful-carelessly repeated the second.

But it worked! And those remarks on Dickens's highly developed technique take no account of the fluctuating rapport that was a prime ingredient of those performances, and something Dickens could never rely on. When technique and rapport came together there was nothing else quite like a Dickens Reading. Robert Patten has suggested acutely that in the text of the 'Carol' there is an analogy between the narrator's voice and the Christmas Ghosts, to the extent that 'our senses respond to his [the narrator's] voice as Scrooge does to the Ghosts'. In this construction, Dickens as narrator was making as sensational an intervention in the lives of his readers as the four ghosts were doing in Scrooge's life. How much more sensational would it have been in a dramatic Reading? In mid-Victorian towns and cities he arrived in person to conduct people nightly into a world where the great blaze of Christmas celebration issuing from the red hearth of the Reading platform threw giant shadows around the hall of listeners, and where, as for Scrooge, Past and Present, reality and illusion became therapeutically confused.

'Sikes and Nancy':
A Reading

The figure in evening dress sways to and fro behind his desk, the heat from the gaslamps bringing a light dew onto his forehead. He is Boots and he speaks in a soft cockney murmur, mouthing as if he were chewing a straw, and when he comes to a point needing to be emphasized he half-closes his eyelids and tilts his head forward. He is sunk deep in character, but every now and again pulls himself out to let Charles Dickens intervene briefly. 'That's about it . . .', says Boots laconically: his story is ambling towards its end. Dickens interrupts: 'In conclusion, Boots puts it to me whether I hold with him in two opinions'—and Boots resumes in his drawling way, with a touch or two of that eyelidded emphasis:

Firstly, that there are not many couples on their way to be married, who are half as innocent as them two children; secondly, that it would be a jolly good thing for a great many couples on their way to be married, if they could only be stopped in time and brought back separate.

Finish. Dickens pulls himself upright, chuckling as the applause and laughter bring the Reading to a close. Boots fades somewhere into the background, and now the maroon chamber is empty.

While Dickens is backstage, an uneasy murmuring ripples for a while in the auditorium. The mood is changing from the genial companionship generated by Boots. Everyone knows what is coming. Dickens, backstage and in solitude, is bracing himself to come out and murder Nancy in public once more. 'I shall tear myself to pieces,' he mutters.

To pieces.... Night after night of the Readings for over a decade he had been detaching pieces of himself to generate the medley of separate characters and make them live brightly in the gas-light. The dance of his performing selves had become the miracle of these occasions. But 'Sikes and Nancy' was always to be different, ever since he first conceived and tested it privately in the spring of 1863: 'I have been trying, alone by myself, the Oliver Twist murder, but I have got something so horrible out of it that I am afraid to try it out in public.' So he put it aside. Five years later the idea seized him again, this time with a new urgency: the wish to leave behind him 'the recollection of something very passionate and dramatic, done with simple means'. By the autumn of 1868 he was embarking on his Farewell Tour, knowing that his Readings days were now limited (he was to give his Final Farewell Reading just 15 months later). Worth tearing himself to pieces if he could crown his Readings with an unforgettable sensation.

Dolby comes to signal to him the start of the next Reading. Seconds later the audience sees Dickens back again behind his red desk. He announces 'Sikes and Nancy', and suddenly the narrative has begun.

Fagin the receiver of stolen goods was up, betimes, one morning, and waited impatiently for the appearance of his new associate, Noah Claypole, otherwise Morris Bolter...

'Here I am. What's the matter? Don't yer ask me to do anything till I have done eating. That's a great fault in this place. Yer never get time enough over yer meals.'

Bolter stands dozily at Dickens's desk, a half-knowing, half-stupid clod—a mix you might not quite have gathered from the novel. He gets some surprised laughs from those watching: they hadn't been prepared for touches of comedy. But little by little, as Bolter insolently chaffs away to Fagin, the shadow of the old villain grows, damps the comedy, and slowly darkens the stage. In Fagin's longer speeches Dickens seems to disappear. His whole stature, not just his face and voice, changes radically. Shoulders hunched high, chest contracted, his hands become bird claws, hooking and kneading the air in anticipation of the words passionately struggling for expression. The voice is husky and with a slight lisp, but otherwise

*unremarkable except for its ferocious controlled intensity. His features
are distorted with rage, his eyebrows work like the antennae of some
deadly reptile. His whole aspect is wolf-like, vulture-like, in its hungry
wickedness. This is no stage Jew; it is a living person with a terrifying
vitality burning in that shrunken body. Fagin hisses his final directions
to Bolter to follow Nancy to her rendezvous with Brownlow and Rose
Maylie: 'After her!! To the left. Take the left hand, and keep on the other
side. After her!!'*

*Now the Reader embarks on a section of steady, highly concentrated
narrative as Bolter tracks the girl and her associates to their midnight
meeting down by London Bridge's landing stairs. Dickens traces every
twist and turn in the route, voice and gestures working together to
recreate the setting so vividly that dank, dark riverside London becomes
a ghostly superimposition on the little red platform area. Step by step,
several hundred men and women in evening dress find themselves stealing
down those slimy river stairs to hear the fatal rendezvous. 'This is far
enough', says a new voice, peremptorily (Mr Brownlow): 'for what
purpose can you have brought us to this strange place?' Dickens at his
desk is now shuddering. Out of the shudder comes yet another voice,
plaintive, raised now and then to a treble and sometimes a rushed
whisper (Nancy): 'I have such a fear and dread upon me to-night that I
can hardly stand . . . horrible thoughts of death.' As this furtive midnight
conversation develops, the contrasts stretch wide: Brownlow stern and
still, Nancy trembling and looking wildly around her as she draws
close to the moment of betrayal, and now and again the softer voice of
Rose trying to temper Brownlow's gruffness and soothe Nancy's terror.
Each character is produced with complete distinctness, even in the rapid
transitions from speaker to speaker: Dickens has left the stage to them.
When patches of narrative intervene in these fevered conversations, it is
as though a new character and voice come into play.*

*The betrayal is over. Nancy has done what she came to do, has seized
Rose's offered handkerchief as a keepsake, and fled the scene. An odd
hollowness and stillness follow as the voices cease. One can almost hear
the hall echoing to the sound of Nancy's retreating footsteps. Bolter then
steals from his hiding place, cranes his neck to left and right over the*

Reading desk, 'to make sure that he was unobserved, darted away, and made for Fagin's house as fast as his legs would carry him'. End of Chapter II. Dickens takes a slight pause. His listeners feel the auditorium returning around them. Some coughing and shuffling, and then silence again. The voice now has a kind of solemn music:

It was nearly two hours before daybreak; that time which in the autumn of the year, may be truly called the dead of night; when the streets are silent and deserted; when even sound appears to slumber, and profligacy and riot have staggered home to dream; it was at this still and silent hour, that Fagin sat in his old lair. Stretched upon a mattress on the floor, lay Noah Claypole, otherwise _Morris Bolter_, fast asleep. Towards him the old man sometimes directed his eyes for an instant, and then brought them back again to the wasting candle.

The audience has been waiting for Bill Sikes, and here he comes, heavy, brutish. His voice is a dull growl, but explodes into a powerful roar as now and again he loses patience with Fagin. Fagin bit by bit prompts the yawning Bolter to tell what he heard at London Bridge. Sikes is a silent, smouldering presence: one dreads the outcome. All one can hear now are these voices—none of them Dickens's—the wheedling Fagin, the careless sleepy Bolter, and occasionally the bark or growl of Sikes. All one can see now are these three figures, one melting into the other as the fierce talking reaches its crescendo. 'Bill, _Bill!_' cries Fagin, as Sikes rushes from the room: 'Hear me . . . . You won't be—you won't be—_too—violent_, Bill?' It's extraordinary—just one man on that stage, but two characters are now looking into each other's eyes. '. . . Bill? I mean, not too—_violent—for—for— safety._'
    Narrative is now headlong, and the audience has started to hold its breath as Sikes reaches his house door, and every action of opening, closing, and locking doors is seen, and felt with a terrible fear. Dickens's hand goes up and draws back the curtain of Nancy's bed. 'Get up!!!' he roars, twice. Sikes's chest is heaving and nostrils flared as he reaches to grasp her by the throat. Dickens's hands close around thin air, which then materializes into the terrified kneeling girl who is looking upwards, arm raised and pleading for her life: 'I have been _true_ to

you, <u>*upon my guilty soul I have!!!*</u>' *Many in the audience cannot bear the sight and cover their face with their hands, as if they are about to see a live atrocity happen on that stage. One hand clutches Nancy's neck, the other frees itself, reaches for the pistol, smashes it down—and again down—on the upturned face. He sees the girl struggle back on to her knees, in a prayer. He staggers backwards, puts his own hand up to his face in horror, gropes for his heavy club, and smashes it on the upturned face. Dickens, in evening dress, sweat pouring down, is battering the air and the desk with ferocious energy. Again and again and again. It is over.*

There is an appalled silence and stillness in the hall. Slowly faces begin to steal out from behind hands, eyes towards the platform, half-expecting to see a bloodbath. What they see is a man behind the red desk, leaning on it, head bent and breathing heavily. And what Dickens has just seen in his audience is a fixed expression of horror of himself, as if he had done something truly atrocious. A great wave of giddiness followed his withdrawal from Sikes and sent the gas-lamps into a swirl for a moment or two. Now he steadies himself, and plunges back into the turbulent story. In just ten minutes he will have reached the shore.

Dawn breaks and stirs the paralysed murderer into action. He lights a fire and thrusts the club into it, holding it until it breaks up. He washes himself, tries to rub his clothes clean but has to cut away the indelible stains: '<u>*such*</u> *flesh,* <u>*and so much blood!!!*</u> *....* <u>*The very feet of his dog were bloody!!!*</u>' *The Reader hisses out the horror and the terrible details lodge themselves throughout the audience. A narrative crescendo now begins to build. Sikes takes flight, haunted by the ghastly figure of his victim, and plunges into the country. A day and a night and another day, and he is still in flight, his dog at his heels, the spectral figure and the eyes—those haunting eyes—of the girl before him at every turn. He circles back to London, to his gang's old house in Jacob's Island, for safety. Safety? A great crowd is swarming towards the hide-out. Seizing a rope, his dog following, Sikes is driven out onto the rooftop, aiming to lower himself to the ground at the back of the house. He fastens one end of the rope around the chimney stack and makes a noose to tie round his own body:*

At the instant he brought the loop over his head before slipping it beneath his arm-pits, <u>looking behind him</u> on the <u>roof he threw up his arms, and yelled, 'The <u>eyes</u> again!'</u> Staggering as if struck by lightning, he lost his balance and tumbled over the parapet. The noose was at his neck; it ran up with his weight; tight as a bowstring, and swift as the arrow it speeds. He fell five-and-thirty feet, and hung with his open <u>knife clenched in his stiffening hand!!!</u>

The <u>dog</u> which had lain concealed 'till now, ran backwards and forwards on the parapet with a dismal howl, and, collecting himself for a spring, jumped for the <u>dead man's shoulders</u>. Missing his aim, he fell into the ditch, turning over as he went, and striking against a stone, <u>dashed out his brains!!</u>

He finishes to silence. The last words reverberate around the hall, and die away. He slowly takes up the book from the desk. Unsteadily, with great deliberation, he moves away towards the wings. Applause comes late, crashing out in pursuit of the departing figure. Now the scene of the murder is empty. The audience continues to gaze at the small red chamber.

Dickens reaches the dressing room, watched anxiously by Dolby and Scott, and eases himself full-length onto the couch. Head thrown back and eyes closed, he breathes heavily, his face drained of colour. He starts to say something, but the voice blurs and fades. After a few more minutes he still cannot complete a sentence. Scott gently strokes a towel over the sweat-streaked face. Dolby tries to coax him into taking a glass of iced brandy and water. Nearly ten minutes go by before he can lift himself up to take a drink. His eyes are lustreless, and take time to focus on anyone who speaks to him. 'Yes—yes,' he murmurs abstractedly, as Dolby asks if he's ready; and he nods as he receives the book. Very slowly he pulls himself off the couch, takes a sip of champagne, goes to the mirror and gazes impassively at the face in it. Now he can hear the audience. He checks the book in his hand—yes, 'Mrs Gamp'. Colour slowly seeps back into the haggard face in the mirror, and now a comb is passing through thin hair and beard, in short deft strokes. Dickens hands the comb to Scott, turns and nods to Dolby. Yes—ready. He follows Dolby out to the wings. They pause in the darkness just as George Allison the gas man is coming off stage towards them. Allison's frightened smile is caught by Dickens, and he strides out into the light.

17. Harry Furniss, 'Charles Dickens Exhausted.' Dickens is imagined in a state of collapse after a Reading of 'Sikes and Nancy' (the murder scene is shadowed just above him). In Harry Furniss, *Some Victorian Men* (1924), facing page 194.

6

A 'New Expression of the Meaning of my Books'

When I first entered on this interpretation of myself (then quite strange in the public ear), I was sustained by the hope that I could drop into some hearts, some new expression of the meaning of my books, that would touch them in a new way.

To Robert Lytton, 17 April 1867: *Letters* XI, 353–4

The trial of 'Bardell vs Pickwick' we venture to say was perfectly familiar to the entire audience, and yet it seemed like a new thing as interpreted by its creator.

Syracuse Daily Standard, 3 October 1868

Dickens's 'interpretation' of himself and his books through his public Readings was the major new project of his life in his last decade. He invested heavily in it. Did it work as he had hoped? Did those who attended the Readings experience him and his imaginary worlds 'in a new way'? It is time to take stock of what was new about this venture, in terms of insight into the man, his works, and the ways in which he and his audiences saw those works.

AUTHENTICATION

'Interpretation' implies a distinctive, individualized variation on a familiar text, like a modern soloist bringing a new dynamic meaning to Beethoven's 'Moonlight Sonata'. However, in the case of the Dickens Readings the more appropriate analogy would be Beethoven's return to give his own performance of the 'Moonlight Sonata', both idiosyncratic and authoritative. The musical analogy is a useful one and is implied in one newspaper description of how Dickens 'plays [his works] to the public in evening dress', as an instrumentalist might do. Turgenev, in great admiration, once remarked, 'One could say that he *performs his novels*'. The idea of 'interpretation' is glossed in this review of a Reading of the 'Carol':

Mr. Dickens is a delightful interpreter of the productions of his own genius, and those who had previously read and admired his Christmas Carol could not fail to have discovered new beauties and fresh attractions in that remarkable story from the effective manner in which it was delivered.

The revelation of new beauties and fresh attractions was something any intelligent and skilful actor could have achieved with the 'Carol'. The special attraction of a Reading of Dickens by Dickens lay in having familiar material not only enlivened by some inventive 'fresh attractions' but also interpreted by the novelist as the authoritative rendering of the text. 'It is not every day', wrote the *Manchester Guardian*, 'that men have an opportunity of listening to a great writer's adequate interpretation of his own creations.' On 22 January 1867 Dickens read 'Bardell and Pickwick' at Chester Music Hall. The *Chester Chronicle*, reporting on the occasion, suggested that his audience 'wished not merely to verify or correct their impressions, but to enjoy the treat of having Charles Dickens the novelist interpreted by himself'. Those listening could 'descend into his brain [...] and see how Mr. Pickwick and Mr. Weller, Mrs. Bardell and Sergeant Buzfuz existed there'. One can imagine the Chester citizens in the audience thinking to themselves: 'So *this* is how Sam Weller should behave and sound', while they watched and heard the author's Sam holding forth nonchalantly in the witness box. The original *Pickwick* Trial scene had been published in 1837: this Reading of the Trial was in 1867. Dickens had come to Chester to 'verify or correct' thirty-year-old impressions of the speech and behaviour of one of his most famous characters, one of those 'creations which have become so real to us that their very names have passed into national proverbs'. This 'new expression' was the authentically original 'interpretation' of Sam's character, 'as the author intended it to be understood'.

It is difficult to register fully the tension between a reader's ingrained impression of a fictional character, construed from the literary portrait, and the disturbance to that impression caused by someone else's impersonation of the character. Each version has its own authenticity, often jealously preserved against invasive rivals: 'If I choose to conceive my Sam Weller as two inches taller than yours, he is just that taller in reality to me,' insisted one American witness to Dickens's Reading of the Trial scene. However, it is one thing to adjust to, or resist, a television or film version of a Dickens character, testing it against one's own sense of how that character ought to be: it is another to confront the author's own acted version. His 'interpretation', after all, must have unique authority, since he was that character's author—or so the deferential feeling ran. As the *Daily Telegraph* observed, 'It is an inestimable privilege to see the author [. . .] exhibit in public the very originals of the people whose comparatively pale counterfeits have long since had more interest for us than our own kith and kin.' In retrospect, the importance of the Readings, as far as G. K. Chesterton was concerned, was 'that they fixed as if by some public and pontifical pronouncement, what was Dickens's interpretation of Dickens's work'. Thus, for example, when Kate Field attended the Reading of 'The Story of Little Dombey', in which Dickens rendered little Paul's speech as a treble monotone throughout, she came to the conclusion that 'having once heard his Little Dombey, it is difficult to conceive how else the child could be successfully treated'. But what if one strongly disagreed with such interpretations? The reviewer for the *New York Times* disliked Dickens's rendering of Paul and coupled it with his impersonation of Smike: both 'whine there in simple monotony [. . .] on the platform of Steinway Hall'.

For quite a number of people, surprisingly, Dickens's interpretations of his own characters were a disappointment and permanently damaged their cherished impressions formed from reading the books. This happened to the actor Laurence Hutton when he heard Dickens read in New York:

I had devoured his stories; his people were mine own people; his characters were my intimate friends. I knew them, of course, by sight and by sound [. . .] every turn of their thoughts, every expression of their faces, every tone of their voices. [. . .] And, lo! when Dickens himself presented them to me they were not my Toots, not my Ham Peggotty, not my Tiny Tim at all! Yet Dickens must have known them better than I did. But, thanks to Dickens, they were all lost in the crowds at Steinway Hall. And they have never altogether been recovered.

There is not, actually, much evidence from the many reviews of the Readings that people did feel Dickens had definitively established these characterizations in such a way as fully to dislodge their own impressions; but they certainly registered and reflected on his interpretations. Their own impressions, of course, had mixed provenance. It would have been hard for them to say just how much their own sense of Sam or Fagin or Scrooge had been influenced or even formed over the years by these characters' typological evolution through various stage 'interpretations', or recitations, or other forms of representation, including the original Phiz or Cruikshank engravings. It is the same for readers of Dickens today: for how many has Fagin become some composite of those landmark twentieth-century interpretations of the character by Alec Guinness and Ron Moody?

Dickens's Readings, then, were seen by many as authorial correctives, or verifiers, of thousands of individual interpretations of his novels. This mid-career benchmarking of his earlier works raises interesting questions about the novelist's continuing relation to his fictional offspring. What Dickens said of his feelings about *David Copperfield* in his 1867 Preface to the Charles Dickens edition of that novel has some bearing on this: ' [the] Author feels as if he were dismissing some portion of himself into the shadowy world, when a crowd of the creatures of his brain are going from him for ever.' The creatures had finally left their creator. The situation brings to mind W. H. Auden's elegy 'In Memory of W. B. Yeats', in which he reflects on the helplessness of the dead poet to exercise any further control over the way his poetry is read, appreciated, and understood: from being a private man ('it was his last afternoon as himself') Yeats became, in death, a kind of public property:

> Now he is scattered among a hundred cities
> And wholly given over to unfamiliar affections;
>   .   .   .   .
> The words of a dead man
> Are modified in the guts of the living.

Dickens's characters and stories had been rendered in a thousand different inflections, across two decades or more, silently or aloud, in drawing room, study, railway carriage, Penny Readings, subscription reading circles, theatrical adaptations, amateur recitations. From the mid-1830s through to the 1860s, Dickens had been watching the careers of his fictional progeny as they left him to become adopted into many forms of popular culture. They drifted away from him and bit by bit became what others wanted them to be—'modified in the guts of the living'. However, Dickens in the 1860s was still very much one of 'the living', and he now systematically intervened to offer his public 'a new expression of the meaning of [his] books'. It was not only a form of interpretation: it was an act of recuperation in the face of diaspora. Night after night, all around the country, for two hours up there on his Reading platform, the author himself came to retrieve his texts from their dispersal among thousands of readers.

This, then, was one sense in which his public Readings of his own works 'touched [his readers] in a new way'. They did something else. For most of his listeners the Readings transformed familiar texts not just by offering to 'correct' the plurality of interpretations of particular characters, but more generally by raising the question of whether his present listeners, who were also his past and present readers, might have misread or under-read Dickens more comprehensively. A hint of this appears in a reflective review by *The Times* of a Reading of

'Christmas Carol' given at St Martin's Hall, London, on 15th April 1858. It was Dickens's last charity Reading before he launched his career as a professional Reader, at the same venue, two weeks later, so it was a good point at which to take stock of the project. The reviewer observed that 'the author gives additional colouring to his already highly elaborated work, and astonishes the auditor by revelations of meaning that had escaped the solitary student'. That remark pinpoints one striking achievement in that 'new expression of the meaning of my books' that Dickens had hoped for. His Readings reopened his texts and produced startling results: without apparently any undue distortion, these same texts—so very familiar—became broader, brighter, with higher resolution, and at the same time more *realistic*, than his readers had expected, based on their own experience of the writings. *The Times*'s 'solitary student', the private reader, had evidently not only missed certain meanings in the story, but perhaps also had not the imaginative resources to give it that 'additional colouring' demonstrated in Dickens's Reading of it. The reviewer in a Leamington newspaper expressed vividly the surprising ways in which the Reading of the 'Carol' heightened its colour, tone and realism:

Everybody has read the 'Christmas Carol'; and yet on Tuesday afternoon the 'Christmas Carol' was something new. What had before seemed but a rich outline became a full, deeply-toned, picture—vivid, bursting with animation, and startlingly real in its most delicate developments.

In exploring this response I want to separate the accolades about additional colouring and deeper toning from the specific issue of the enhanced realism given to these familiar texts as Dickens performed them in his Readings.

COLOUR AND DEFINITION

The Readings gave to Dickens's writings a disconcerting brilliance and sharpness of definition. When Dickens read, he 'described scenes with pre-Raphaelistic distinctness'. But surely these scenes had that degree of distinctness in the original text? Dickens had not significantly changed his text, so what exactly was happening to make this striking difference? He had abridged his stories, certainly, but he had not introduced new material except in a few, very minor, light touches, and yet in his performance it was no longer the same text that had embedded itself for years in the minds of his readership, even allowing for the latitude of shapes it might have assumed as it settled into each reader's memory.

We can identify certain techniques that contributed to this: one of the ways he could surprise the reader was by dramatic accentuation, by working up a small detail into new eccentric form. Here are three examples. In the Reading of 'Mr. Bob Sawyer's Party' he made the character of Jack Hopkins more sharply idiosyncratic than was apparent from the text. Hopkins, in Dickens's impersonation, was stiff-necked, with drooping eyelids, hands in pockets, and spoke through clenched teeth 'from a mouth apparently full of mush', and he delivered his story about the child swallowing the beads with highly eccentric inflections. The word 'necklace', repeated in staccato fashion, came out as 'neck-*luss*' with the last syllable pitched absurdly high. It was this particular interpretation that the *Providence Daily Journal* seized on to illustrate a more general point about the Readings: 'There are little jets of illumination [. . .] slight touches and momentary glimpses of character, some sentences, some character flashing in for a minute, and lighting up the picture just as a painter will with one dash of odd color, which cannot be readily caught and described.' Another example of the surprise moment and its analogy made with the painter's art came in a review of a certain passage (often remarked on) in the Reading of 'Boots at the Holly-Tree Inn':

If we were asked to say at what point Mr Dickens focussed the light of this beautiful, tender child-pastoral, we should say it was in the way he brought out the single word 'jam.' 'We should like some cakes after dinner,' answers Master Harry, 'and two apples—and jam.' A little point, but take it out, and there is a fatal loss; a little speck of white, but all the color is worked up to that as Turner works up all his color in a drawing to the high light on a gleaming sail, or the sunlight on a tower; put your hand over it and the picture is nothing but a blot.

The third example comes from the 'Carol'—a striking moment that was still fresh in one listener's memory thirty years after Dickens's death:

There is so little that is subtle about his work as a writer that it was surprising to find what an illumination he sometimes cast over passages in his work. For example, in his reading of the *Christmas Carol*, there was one astonishing little episode where the ghost of Jacob Marley first appears to Scrooge. 'The dying fire leapt up as if it cried: I know him—Marley's ghost.' The unexpected wild vehemence and weirdness of it were striking in the extreme.

What Dickens is doing in these instances is not enhancing realism, in the sense of perfecting the mirror-image portrayal of scene and character. It is more akin to defamiliarizing disturbance—the introduction of 'one dash of odd color' to put the whole picture in a new light, and that was probably something beyond the powers of the ordinary reader of the 'Carol'. Dickens was a master of these abrupt chromatic tilts.

The enhancement of the stories by such inventive moments was supplemented by something less easily definable and more pervasive—a general energizing of a mysterious kind. The texts became greatly amplified, more brilliant and resonant, fuller of energy. Many of the smaller details dulling in the recesses of the story suddenly scintillated. 'Sly touches of humour are discovered in sentences that before seemed unproductive.' Comments of this kind are made again and again in reviews of the Readings. Here are three, the first from a Birmingham newspaper: 'By a judicious management he imparted strongly-marked light and shade to the story, and brought out points that even in an attentive closet perusal might easily have been overlooked.' *The Times* saw the Readings as Dickens's 'practical commentary' on his works: 'We use the term "practical commentator" because, although he does not utter a syllable of note or comment in the ordinary sense of the words, he gives to the incidents, and more especially to the characters described in his books, a significance which mere readers gifted with only an average power of imagination could never discover.' One of Dickens's first biographers, Friswell, remarked in 1858: 'The *viva voce* expression does to his work what French polish does to an oak plank, it brings out the beauties in the grain.'

What is at issue in these observations is not just the professional Reader's strengths but his readers' inadequacy. To some extent the lustrous renovation of well-known stories can happen in any act of recitation. Reading aloud a familiar text is by its very nature a technique of defamiliarization. The voice is slower than the eye in making its way down a page. The Reading text for 'Sikes and Nancy' takes about ten minutes to read silently to oneself: Dickens took forty minutes to deliver it from the platform. In recitation, words or phrases are lingered over and savoured, language is stirred around the taste buds, accents fall differently, textual pauses are enacted rather than just described, and transitions from narrator's voice to impersonated character voices require distinct breaks. The recitalist's rhythms give new inflections to well-known scenes; the text acquires surprising elasticity, its chiaroscuro alters and its contours change.

There is also the environment of a public Reading to consider, in terms of its effect upon the listener. The intense concentration on the Reader and his story is of a kind different from privately reading to oneself. The imagination has few if any distractions and is trapped in the world conjured by the Reader for the duration of the performance. In private reading one can break off at any point and reflect on what's going on in the story, or simply break off as concentration wanes. In private reading one is also testing (albeit unconsciously) the authenticity of characters, dialogue, events, locations against one's own experience; there is nothing else to bounce the story off. Silent, solitary reading is a mix of information gathering and creative reverie. What I mean is something like Yves Bonnefoy's contention in his 1990 essay, 'Lifting Our Eyes From the Page', where he explores the productive rupture of the attention on a text during the process of reading. He argues that 'poetry is what attaches itself [...] to what cannot be designated by a word of language': 'what a poet hopes for from words is that they might open to that plenitude that descriptions and formulations cannot reach.' True reading is what happens when one lifts one's eyes from the page. This was not possible in a Dickens Reading. His audience was both captivated and captive. He ensured the minimizing of all distractions: there were no opportunities to relax concentration for the duration of the story, to let particular moments resonate for a while in silence. We have seen how carefully he devised his staging to narrow the focus onto his performance, at the desk, in that small brightly glowing red chamber. We know how very particular he was to prevent interruptions from latecomers or early leavers. We know how he wanted to draw to himself the emotional energies of his audience by inviting them to be like friends sitting round a fire together, and to respond audibly to him, with laughter or crying. The intensity of the concentration achieved by these means together with the slowing down of the transmission of the text (compared with private reading) would have meant each detail in the narrative stood out in higher relief for the listener, regardless of the narrator's varying emphases. Dickens wrested the orchestration of the reading experience away from the reader and back to the author-narrator.

The way in which he read his stories reflected the way in which he wrote them, testing the characters out by acts of impersonation. According to him he was effectively re-creating his stories each night as he got up on his platform: they seemed as familiar and yet fresh to him in this 'new expression' as they were to his audiences. Let us take the case of the 'Christmas Carol', the most enduringly popular of the Readings. How Dickens conceived and wrote the story is well known. In his own words, he 'wept, and laughed, and wept again, and excited himself in a most extraordinary manner, in the composition; and thinking whereof, he walked about the black streets of London, fifteen and twenty miles, many a night when all the sober folk had gone to bed.' This extraordinary and sustained near-delirious state of mind issued in what Hillis Miller has registered as the story's 'wonderful verbal and behavioural excess [where everything] is in the superlative', and the reader is drawn into 'a marvellous but somewhat dizzying country where everything changes shape constantly'. Miller's article (celebrating the sesquicentenary of the story's composition) responds very strongly to the 'Carol''s powerful but elusive energy, its disconcerting surrealism, and its linguistic exuberance: on first approach he suggests 'perhaps all that can be done is to put "Wow!" in the margin of the text'. He goes on to argue that the 'Carol' spectacularly, joyously breaks down generic boundaries (when does Dickens *not* trample across generic boundaries?) by the force of its sustained hyperbole, and he recognizes with a zestful eloquence the extent to which the text is, from the start, a performance piece. Miller's essay is the closest (as far as I know) that any modern sophisticated response has got to what contemporary witnesses felt to be the extraordinary impact not just of their private reading of the story but of a Dickens Reading of the story. Wow! Some of that near-delirious state in which he composed the story returned to energize the Reading and, in turn, the effect of *that* could be intoxicating on the listeners. As Dickens gleefully reported after a 'Carol' Reading in Darlington: 'the town was drunk with the Carol far into the night.'

Most of us are what *The Times* called 'mere readers gifted with only an average power of imagination'. Dickens has habitually demanded more from his reader; indeed his fiction seems often to be a passionate campaign to educate and revitalize the reader's imagination. Few of his contemporaries realized quite how much more he expected from them until they heard him read in ways that transformed their reception of the texts, and made them question their own adequacy as readers. Certain demands that Dickens makes on the reader have often been recognized. Susan Horton, for example, has clearly demonstrated in *The Reader in the Dickens World* the kind and scale of interpretative and moral-judgemental work that the reader is called upon to do. She describes, for instance, how the reader must draw his or her own independent moral conclusions when Dickens sometimes provides loudly directive rhetorical judgements and at other times provides no moral guidance at all in narrating scenes that rouse the reader's strong emotions. 'The energy of the novels', Horton concludes, is 'partly that of the reader.' That, however, is largely an *interpretative* energy of engagement, an intellectual exercise; it is not affective in quite the way I am questioning.

The elaborated emphasis on the experience of reading (however silently and privately) as 'active' or 'creative' is familiar enough these days: the reader is 'no longer a consumer, but a producer of the text', in Roland Barthes's famous remark. Barthes also insisted that 'Reading is not a parasitical act [. . .]. To read, in fact, is a labor of language.' Such theory so strenuously reverses the dynamic-book/passive-reader formula that the book becomes the passive, inert parasite waiting for its vigorous host, the reader. The productive energy of the reader in such views of reader relations has also been compared with the relation of actor to script. 'Active' reading is but a short step from 'acting', and some have argued that imaginative literature necessarily calls out the actor in the reader. Here, for example, is Reuben Brower in an essay speculating on the implications of 'Reading in Slow Motion': 'Many if not most of the writers from the past, from Homer to novelists like Jane Austen and Dickens, have assumed reading aloud and a relatively slow rate of intellectual digestion. Literature of the first order calls for lively reading; we must almost act it out as if we were taking parts in a play.' In *Acting as Reading* (1992) David Cole argues that 'Texts are only realized in the performance of them by active readers' and he is convinced that there is a lost physical dimension to reading. Some research has detected minute tremors in the musculature of the throat in studies of the activity of silent reading—so-called subvocalization of the text being read. Cole suggests that there are eroded or suppressed physical (neurovocal) impulses triggered in the silent reader that are properly realized in the actor's engaging a script. 'Readers are like actors because what an actor does to a script is what any reader must do to any text—"realize" it, "actualise it," make it happen as an event.' All silent readers are, in effect, repressed actors. So are some authors. As we have seen, there was a strong physical and vocalized dimension to Dickens's composing of his stories, let alone his Readings of their slightly re-scripted forms. A script is a text clear about its state of dependency on the actor-reader, with stage directions for gesture and vocal tone.

Dickens's prompt-copies, adapting 'silent' text for oral performance, go a long way towards converting his novels into scripts. This was indeed a 'new expression of the meaning' of his books.

We must, of course, recognize that we are not dealing here with any old adroit recitalist, well able to tailor his material and bring the texts to life. There was evidently something exceptional in Dickens's personality, a force that he was able to amplify and focus powerfully during these Readings. Many of those who came into personal contact with Dickens were struck by the aura of energy that played about him. Thackeray's daughter Anne Ritchie first met Dickens at the house of one of her father's friends: 'my sister and I first realised Mr. Dickens himself, though only as a sort of brilliance in the room, mysteriously dominant and formless. I remember how everybody lighted up when he entered.' Dickens's very presence in company was like that 'one dash of odd color' that suddenly, mysteriously, illuminated a whole scene. Blanchard Jerrold recalled that 'the air about him vibrated with his activity, and his surprising vitality'. Percy Fitzgerald had much the same experience:

As he entered a room, sat or stood before you, you felt you were in the presence of amazing vitality. He spoke always with warmth and ardour. When he came to write, he brought all this with him; it overflowed into every sentence. Hence it is impossible to look on him as a conventional narrator.

Readers unable or unwilling to raise their imaginative game in confronting a Dickens text miss the full force of that energy in 'every sentence', but the Readings, where the man himself animated his own texts, made the level of imaginative energy so very evident, so sustained and pervasive throughout the read text, that those familiar stories, episodes, and characters were apocalyptically transfigured.

Dickens, as we have seen, used to preface performances by emphasizing not so much the fact that he was reading *to* the audience, as reading *with* them, that he was *accompanying* them through the story of Scrooge or Little Dombey. Many in the audience were following the text in their own copies, many more were running through their memories of the story as Dickens read it anew. In this light Dickens was both re-orchestrating the text and also reenergizing it, goading his listeners to raise the intensity of the story. He habitually spurred people into raising their energy levels. He saw it almost as his mission. His daughter Mamie recalled parties where Dickens, even when he was not dancing, was intent on maintaining the party spirit and festive energy:

He would insist upon the sides keeping up a kind of jig step, and clapping his hands to add to the fun, and dancing at the backs of those whose enthusiasm he thought needed rousing, was himself never still for a moment until the dance was over.

This is how one might imagine Dickens the writer, from his study, silently but ebulliently performing his narrative and his impersonations so as to galvanize his readers, wherever they might be, into intense levels of responsiveness. The story itself is not enough, just as the party dancing is not enough if people just go through the paces. There must also be a continuous current of high energy connecting narrator to reader, so that readers participate with full imaginative and emotional vitality in the reading—indeed, perhaps, feel that they are involuntarily *performing* the texts, and that, in David Cole's words, they are making the text 'happen as an event'.

What exactly was Dickens doing to so transform these well-known characters and stories? We have taken account of some of the factors involved—the novel accentuation techniques ('neck-*luss*'), the high-energy performance of high-energy scripts, the charismatic personality of the Reader—but there is still an elusive and pervasive sense of something more. Was he somehow adding extravagant new layers of colour, histrionically applied, to the original? Or was he restoring colour that had been lost to the textual fabric as it had faded with years of overexposure? Or was he simply disclosing the full radiance and colour that had always been there but that his readers had been or become too colour-blind to appreciate?

Dickens himself suspected we might suffer from a perceptual dullness, despite all his efforts:

What is exaggeration to one class of minds and perceptions, is plain truth to another. That which is commonly called a long-sight, perceives in a prospect innumerable features and bearings non-existent to a short-sighted person. I sometimes ask myself whether there may occasionally be a difference of this kind between some writers and some readers; whether it is *always* the writer who colours highly, or whether it is now and then the reader whose eye for colour is a little dull.

Partly responding to this, Geoffrey Tillotson long ago asked a key question: 'Are Dickens's descriptions no more than a silent criticism of the inadequacy of the seeing and observing done by most of us, and no more than an indication that Dickens's bodily apparatus was a more efficient one than our own? Or did his superiority lie in what the mind added to the report supplied to it by the bodily apparatus?' Both, perhaps. Dickens combined an extraordinarily sharp and retentive eye for detail with a compulsion to heighten the descriptive record of such detail. As to the latter, stylistic flamboyance was second nature to Dickens in his writing and performing. It was part of his editorial policy, as Percy Fitzgerald recalled in connection with his work on *Household Words*:

The writers were compelled, owing to the necessity of producing effect, to adopt a tone of exaggeration. Everything, even trivial, had to be made more comic than it really was [. . .]. I often think with some compunction of . . . the bad habit one gradually acquired of colouring up for effect, and of magnifying the smallest trifles.

'Brighten it, brighten it, brighten it!' Dickens urged his sub-editor in relation to a clutch of articles submitted to *Household Words*. The odd thing is that in his Readings Dickens seems to have been able to intensify effect without artificial heightening of the kind described by Fitzgerald: and yet 'Brighten it' is just what he did in giving 'new expression to the meaning' of his books in those Readings. In turn, the reviewers, as we have already seen, reached for the same kind of language of colour and radiance in trying to explain how Dickens had enhanced these familiar texts. 'Illustrate' means literally to 'make lustrous'. Dickens became, in his own person through his Readings,

a much better illustrator of his own works than any he had enlisted
to provide engravings and woodcuts for his novels. This overall effect
of intensified colour and light is conveyed very eloquently in an 1866
review by *The Scotsman*:

> If to read a story of Dickens's may be said to remind one of looking on a
> painted window, crowded with characters and full of cunning devices, to
> hear the story read by Dickens himself is to look on the same window with
> the sun shining behind it; when the figures glow afresh, and the quaint
> devices come forth with a grace and force before unappreciated, if not
> altogether unnoted.

It may indeed be that the boisterousness and brightness of Dickens's
earlier idiom was a shock to sensibilities that had become used to the
comparative gloom of the cultural environment in the 1860s. Colour
had indeed drained from national life in the 1850s and 1860s—in
dress as in other aspects of the environment (and that may partially
answer Tillotson's questions)—and the national eye had perhaps
adjusted to a more muted normality. In 1856 Ruskin was drawing
attention to the 'eminently sombre' nature of colour in contemporary
painting as he marked out the exceptional brilliance of colour in
Turner and the Pre-Raphaelites: 'whereas a mediaeval paints his sky
bright blue and foreground bright green, gilds the towers of his
castles, and clothes his figures with purple and white, we paint our
sky grey, our foreground black, and our foliage brown.' In the same
year, Dickens was asked to advise on appropriate dress for the girls
under care at Urania Cottage, his 'Home for Homeless Women',
and reacted strongly against the recommended drab material—'a
mortal dull color'. 'Color these people always want,' he insisted, 'and
color (as allied to fancy), I would always give them. In these cast-iron
and mechanical days, I think even such a garnish to the dish of their
monotonous and hard lives, of unspeakable importance.'

This is one of Dickens's most passionate missions, just as important
as his better known reformist campaigns against social deprivation,
poor educational provision, and legal and political obfuscation.
He is a great cultural activist. We talk now about greening the

environment—curbing, varying, and adorning our over-urbanized, over-industrialized *physical* habitat. Dickens was doing something like this with the *cultural* habitat of his fellow Victorians. He did not plant trees and flowers and parks; however, he certainly intervened in the cultural landscape: wherever he went he planted exotic metaphors and analogies. He purposely dwelt on the romantic side of familiar things. As a literary eco-warrior, he believed, as he said, that what was vital to the welfare of any community was 'the fusion of the graces of the imagination with the realities of life'; and then, nearly a generation after his first appearance as a writer, he returned in person to revivify his own works.

Were Dickens's readers, indeed are *we* as 'mere readers' of Dickens, imaginatively up to the task? We may well have become more sophisticated analysts of his works—recognizing in them more complexity than did his contemporaries. But are we adequate readers in the sense I am pursuing here? Dickens's contemporaries certainly doubted their capacities. Here are two newspaper reviews: 'Many expressed their surprise that they had not seen in the works, which some had read more than once, the wonderful ability, truth to life, humour and pathos, which they now had learned to discover.' ' "I never knew how to read a book before", was the exclamation of a friend of ours at the close of the "Christmas Carol." [...] He only expressed what the whole audience felt on each occasion.' Perhaps that applies to us today, bereft of any chance to hear those Readings. Without Dickens the Reader, are we habitually under-reading Dickens the writer?

REALISM

The Leamington newspaper quoted earlier, in praising the 'Carol' Reading for its 'full, deeply-toned, picture' of the story, also emphasized another revelation. 'He imparts to his works a reality which is not to be obtained by a simple reading of them.' Dickens's Reading had made it 'startlingly real in its most delicate developments'.

Many witnesses drew specific attention to the realism or naturalism of Dickens's characters as evident in his performance of
them—'*startlingly* real' because Dickens's stories and characters
were commonly judged as somewhat fanciful, exaggerated, and caricatured, especially by the realist criteria of the 1860s. Even those
who already granted a degree of realism to the text versions were
struck by this new dimension in the Readings impersonations:

His writings have been compared to photographs, but his readings make
of them what photographs are made by the stereoscope. The realism of his
creations and of his style is made more real.

We have seen earlier in this book how Dickens impersonated
his characters into life and then prepared them for their roles in
the novels. They had a life before they were inserted into the story
(maybe that is why so many carry on an independent life long after
their story is over). Dickens's utter conviction of the reality of even
his most highly coloured fictional characters evidently empowered
his performances as a Reader. One who watched him on several
occasions in New York remarked that 'His characters were real to
us, because they were so real to him. As he wrote of them or read
of them, they were not so much creations of his brain as persons
whom he knew.' Dickens had no reservations about this: 'So real
are my fictions to myself that, after hundreds of nights, I come with
a feeling of perfect freshness to that little red table, and laugh and
cry with my hearers, as if I had never stood there before.' Why
does this conviction not consistently carry through to the private
reader, as consistently as evidently his listeners experienced each time
they heard him read the characters aloud? As a novelist Dickens
habitually 'expands traits into people', observed Walter Bagehot in
1858: 'we have exaggerations pretending to comport themselves as
ordinary beings, caricatures acting as if they were real characters'.
This disparaging criticism seems to have been contradicted by the
Readings. Here is one witness to a performance of 'Sikes and Nancy':

Where the temptation to caricature was great, it is [. . .] remarkable that
Mr. Dickens should have kept so entirely clear of it as he has done in

his presentment of the jew [...]. This freedom from exaggeration and caricature is the more noticeable, because it will hardly be doubted by any one who is familiar with Mr. Dickens's writings [...] that his characters are all more or less thus distorted and unnatural.

What happened at the Readings was a realization by the listeners that as readers they had under-estimated the naturalism of these characters. How had this come about? One suggestion was that Dickens's early illustrators had done him a disservice:

The great value of Dickens's readings was the proof they afforded that his leading characters were not caricatures. His illustrators, especially Cruikshank, made them often appear to be caricatures, by exaggerating their external oddities of feature or eccentricities of costume, rather than by seeking to represent their internal life; and the reader became accustomed to turn to the rough picture of the person as though the author's deep humorous conception of the character was embodied in the artist's hasty and superficial sketch [...]—when [the audience] saw him visibly transform himself into Scrooge or Squeers [these] characters then seemed, not only all alive, but full of individual life; and, however odd, eccentric, unpleasing, or strange, they always appeared to be natural, always appeared to be personal natures rooted in human nature.

One must remember that the original illustrations were the only authorized visual aid to the texts for years, until Dickens arrived on the platform to represent the characters he had created. To the visual imagination trained by the illustrations they were grotesques in fixed postures. But when Dickens brought them from his study to the Reading platform they were living, breathing persons. The reviewer for the *Chester Chronicle* watched Dickens read 'Bardell and Pickwick' in January 1867:

Sergeant Buzfuz himself [...] was not the fat pluffy lawyer he is sometimes represented, who utters five words and stops like a hippopotamus to blow, but a grave and keenly suasive advocate, who, while he has acquired the usual pauses and swings of the head common to old practitioners, utters his words with an apparent conviction of their truth, and with an evident grasp of the plaintiff's view of the whole subject. So Sam Weller, as Dickens thought of him, is not the slangy dried-up cockney, who jerks out his drolleries with a consciousness of their force, and gives a self-satisfied smirk when he sees how they sting, but rather a pleasant, smart young fellow, shrewd as he is quick of motion, ready with his flooring joke as he is amusing with his comical smile, but doing it all with a perfectly natural and almost artless air.

Dickens seems to have been lowering the key here. Was this how he originally saw Buzfuz in 1836? Had he re-thought his character? It is just possible (though I have not come across any direct evidence of this) that Dickens in the 1860s was deliberately, though not consist-ently, rehabilitating his old caricatures to meet tastes that were chan-ging in favour of a more subdued naturalism. His Sam Weller, one of the more controversial impersonations, does seem generally to have been played in a more low-key manner than expected. One reviewer speculated that perhaps Dickens 'had intended that [Sam] should not be externally distinguished from the general run of persons in his station, and should be, like his sayings, not pointed either by voice or manner'. Dickens by and large managed to reconcile idiosyncrasy with naturalism in presenting his famous characters. For example, his rendition of the slow-witted and eccentric Tilly Slowboys, in the Reading of 'Cricket on the Hearth', 'while losing none of the oddity of the character, had the rare merit of being entirely free of caricature'.

These speculations about changing tastes and Dickens's adapta-tion to the changes need some context. T. W. Robertson's plays in the 1860s introduced a new school of realistic domestic drama, nicknamed 'Teacup and Saucer Drama', and this encouraged a new style of naturalistic acting that was established during the later period of Dickens's Reading tours. Dickens would have been fully aware of such trends. He also knew, and much admired, the French actor Charles Fechter. Fechter's London performances of Ruy Blas in 1860 and Hamlet in 1861 brought a new, concentrated realism to acting technique, a highly intelligent observation of small details of behaviour and speech in building character, rather than the tradi-tional, stylized rhetorical gestures. The older school of acting—the 'strutting, strident, "bow wow" school' as The Times critic called it—seemed increasingly artificial to audiences in the 1860s: 'the younger generation wanted new blood, less declamation, more art, more taste, more nature'. Dickens, ever acutely sensitive to theatrical styles, may well have contrived on the platform to tone down some of the high colouring in his famous characters (while maintaining it elsewhere in his presentations, as suggested a little earlier in this chapter), without wholly sacrificing their idiosyncrasies. He had faced, and challenged, accusations of extravagance in plot and characterization throughout his career. However, there were increased pressures for realism in the later 1850s and 1860s—just when Dickens took to the Reading platform—and some of these, notably by Walter Bagehot and G. H. Lewes, were targeted specifically on Dickens's work, and especially on his characterization. Ruskin, who in many respects was an admirer of Dickens, acknowledged in 1870 that 'Dickens's delight in grotesque and rich exaggeration [...] has made him, I think, nearly useless in the present day'. Conscious of this reputation, Dickens may well have wanted to adjust the platform reproductions of his work. This, anyway, was the effect: 'Mr. Dickens as a writer is somewhat of a caricaturist; as a reader or actor he appears to aim at a more faithful imitation of nature.'

It may well have been the case that he came to pitch his Readings not only against his hostile literary critics but also against other Readings from his work by other recitalists, or against dramatic adaptations, in which many of his characters had indeed been caricatured for performance. Amy Sedgwick, the distinguished actress, visited Bath in the mid-1860s and gave a recital of Serjeant Buzfuz's address to the jury at the Trial and, according to the *Bath Chronicle*, not surprisingly 'made a farce' of what the reviewer felt to have been 'an outrageous caricature [...] as originally written'. When Dickens arrived two years later to read the Trial, he did something strikingly new: 'He has omitted, added, and altered, and has in this way succeeded in giving the scene an air of probability which in the original version it does not wear [...]. The humour is still exaggerated but it no longer runs riot with excess of caricature.'

Dickens began his Readings career at a time when there were indications of weariness not only with highly mannered stage acting but also with conventional styles of elocution on public platforms—'drum and trumpet declamation' in the words of *The Aberdeen Journal,* in a very complimentary review of Dickens's tonal subtlety. There were some who thought 'his manner was undeniably "stagey"' and that he 'over-acted his part', but the great majority judged him to be 'utterly void of mannerism, and entirely natural', and that, 'without any attempt at acting, he succeeds in producing a dramatic effect'. He was 'simply a good reader, with scarcely a trace of the "manner" which spoils the readings of some celebrated actors of the stage'. The 1860s, in fact, was a period when controversy about acting styles altogether produced some stimulating debates, when both the old-fashioned 'drum and trumpet' and the modern, muted styles were targeted for criticism. In a series of essays in *Fortnightly Review* in 1865 G. H. Lewes referred to the new low-key naturalism as 'coat-and-waistcoat realism', which, he said, brought about 'a creeping timidity of invention [. . .] with all the reticences and petti-nesses of drawing-room conventions.' The 'impassioned movements of life' seemed to have ebbed out of literature and painting, and 'Artists have become photographers.' The stylistic antithesis to this would be the melodramatic actor, who, according to Lewes in 1875, 'is required to be impressive, to paint in broad, coarse outlines, to give relief to an exaggerated situation; he is not required to be poetic, subtle, true to human emotion.' In some ways these debates provided the perfect climate for Dickens's enterprise and his distinctive gifts. In his Readings, as in his novels, he was a master of the surface minutiae of daily life, of the tumid melodramatic intensification of that naturalism, and of the poetic transfiguration of material reality ('the romantic side of familiar things').

As in the theatre, so in the publishing world: there were comparable changes in favour of greater naturalism in the style of illustrations to Dickens's own novels. The start of his career as a professional Reader coincided with the end of Phiz's career as his illustrator. Phiz's style was indelibly associated with early Dickens even though he adapted his mode somewhat for the novels of the 1850s (notably in the 'dark plates'). The sober realism of the illustrations by Marcus

Stone and Luke Fildes for the last novels were analogous in some respects to the new naturalism then marking London theatre. There was a suggestion that Dickens was consciously favouring a more naturalistic pictorial style when, in 1867, he approved Sol Eytinge's illustrations to the American edition of *Our Mutual Friend*: 'They are remarkable for a most agreeable absence of exaggeration [. . .] and a general modesty and propriety which I greatly like.'

If Dickens aimed consciously for a greater naturalism in this 'new expression of the meaning' of his work, it is perhaps odd that his repertoire consisted mainly of scenes and characters from his earlier, humorous work, the work more closely associated with his caricaturing mode. He knew this material would be the most popular and that he was indelibly associated with it, so that is natural. It may also be that he knew he could throw these figures into sharper relief as characters than he might have been able to do with characters from his later, post-*Copperfield* work. There is an interesting hint of the diminished performance potential of some of his subtler writing in an 1858 review of his Reading of 'The Story of Little Dombey':

Charles Dickens has to contend against the difficulty of enlisting the unwearied attention of his audience, while reading a composition so conversational as 'Dombey and Son'. The striking and dramatic passages to be found in such a work as Scott's 'Talisman' affords [sic] a wider scope for illustration and histrionic portraiture than this light and rapid dialogue, the photographs of ordinary life, and the every-day chit-chat of this common-place world.

'Conversational' here is associated with 'every-day chit-chat', where speech and speakers are not given the kind of sharp idiosyncratic distinctiveness typical of earlier Dickens dialogue. Dickens himself had used the term 'conversational' in a similarly disparaging manner when describing his boredom or inability to focus speech and character in a book he was reading: 'I have been trying other books; but so infernally conversational, that I forget who the people are before they have done talking, and don't in the least remember what they talked about before when they begin talking again!' Kate Field remarked of the 'Dombey' Reading that every chapter was 'written in a minor key'. 'Dombey' joined the repertoire in 1858 but had quite a short run: twenty-nine performances in 1858–9, but thereafter only thirteen in Britain through the 1860s and five during the American tour. Citing two shrewd witnesses, Philip Collins suggests a couple of explanations for the item's relative unpopularity: Dolby remarked that Dickens found 'Little Dombey' painful to read and therefore performed it only under pressure (though that does not seem to have been the case in 1858–9), and Kate Field said 'people dislike to be made miserable'. However, it may also have been the case that the sustained minor key of the Reading, over about an hour and a half, overtaxed the audience's sympathetic attention. Too much subdued realism could be as demanding as too much caricature and exaggeration.

The very qualities that made his later style so distinctive, the tonal suppleness, the reflectiveness (so finely tuned in the Uncommercial Traveller's essays), the more sustained gravity in mounting his social criticism, the subdued ironic mode, would have been more difficult to project in a solo two-hour Reading. Conversely the Readings gave Dickens the chance to supply to his readers/audiences what many felt had become lacking in his later work: high-spirited comedy and highly coloured characterization. Dickens was acutely aware of such criticism: 'you will not have to complain of the want of humour as in *The Tale of Two Cities*', he assured Forster as he approached the opening chapters of *Great Expectations*. On finishing *Great Expectations* in August 1861, he went straight into preparation of three new Readings: 'David Copperfield', 'Nicholas Nickleby at the Yorkshire School', and 'Mr. Bob Sawyer's Party'—all three of them vintage early Dickens for which the reading public had been pining.

'THIS INTERPRETATION OF MYSELF'

We have discussed on several occasions the rapport Dickens cultivated with his readership and his Readings audiences, and we return to it once more, because an assessment of his insistently manipulative presence as both author and Reader is crucial in determining the success of that 'new expression' of his books. The Readings were so much more than a transmission of familiar texts. They were, for a start, a species of translation or adaptation into an auditory medium. The text metamorphosed into a hybrid of sound and spectacle as it emerged from Dickens's voice(s), facial expressions, and gestures up there on the platform; and so different senses were called into play as people absorbed the story.

This defamiliarizing of the text was one step in disconcerting the readership and manoeuvring them into a position for greater emotional leverage. Dickens insinuated his presence into the experience of the story (powerfully so, since he was both narrator and creator of what he was reading), sometimes, as we have seen, sharing their enjoyment as if he were a detached spectator of the characters he paraded, at other times deliberately opening spaces for their responses and then, as it were, assimilating those responses into the ensuing recitation. All the time he was heightening the level of engagement of the audience with both himself and his imaginary worlds. For example, at the very start of the 'Carol' Reading he announced, 'Marley was dead: to begin with', and then paused, 'as if to take in the character of the audience, or to see if there was any possibility of their disputing it'. Thus he opened a kind of one-way dialogue with his audience, a kind of 'interpretation' of himself.

These are techniques familiar to performers, of course, and the 'Carol''s archly pugnacious narrator in those early paragraphs is a rather special case, ideal for directly engaging the listener or private reader. An accumulation of such moments can contribute towards that mysterious 'sympathy' exercised by Dickens, but cannot wholly explain it. It was there from the start of his Reading career. The audience at the first Birmingham Readings in 1853, according to *The Times*, gave 'ready homage to that magic power which, by the bonds of sympathy, "makes the whole world kin"'. Dickens's fiction and journalism over the previous twenty years had laid the ground for this sense of sympathetic kinship between author and reader, but it was at the Readings that they felt the full force of that 'magic power'. We might say today that it amounted to a charismatic presence. Dickens's letter about dropping into some hearts 'some new expression of the meaning of my books' was written in response to Robert Lytton's very warm praise of a Reading of 'Copperfield' in which he had told Dickens, 'You play with the heart, like the Japanese juggler with his paper butterfly, as tho' it were a creature of your own construction, turn it this way and that at a breath, and make it rise or sink just as you will.' Dickens could not have achieved this kind of effect without something that went beyond technique (however consummate that technique), and beyond the extraordinary energy discussed a little while ago. The issue is well expressed by the writer T. C. De Leon in the following response to the Readings in America:

There are some far better readers; there are many more exact mimics; there are thousands of better actors: but the electric genius of the man fuses all these into a magnetic amalgam that once touched cannot be let go until the battery stops working [. . .]. There is something indescribable; a subtle essence of sympathy that can only be felt, not described, that puts him *en rapport* with the most antagonistic spirits and makes them his, while the spell is upon them.

De Leon is using the technical terminology of mesmerism when he talks about 'magnetic amalgam' and 'sympathy'. It was a useful vocabulary for trying to identify the subtle influences brought into play during these performances. 'Sympathy' has now lost this particular sense of engaging almost occult affinities between people, but that is what De Leon is alluding to. Whether or not De Leon knew of Dickens's own interest in 'animal magnetism', he had sensed in Dickens's capacity to hold his audiences a near supernatural power. This idea of 'sympathy' and Dickens's interest in it has been usefully explored in an essay by Arthur Cox, where he seeks to identify in *Edwin Drood* some subtler forces at play than those conventionally ascribed to Dickens's fascination with mesmerism. He argues persuasively that 'sympathy' in this quasi-technical sense—'an electric cord of sympathy [. . .] a fine chain of mutual understanding, sustaining union through a separation of a hundred leagues', as Charlotte Brontë put it—was widely accepted as a given in human psychology. It was '*heart-to-heart communion* and consists largely of the conveyance of *emotion and sensation*' (Cox's italics). Cox quotes Annie Fields's remark (in her *Memories of a Hostess*) about Dickens: 'No one could believe more entirely than he in magnetism and the unfathomed ties between man and man.' There is a passing allusion to this in a letter from Dickens to Georgina Hogarth, reporting on a Reading given before a 'very Lumpish audience' in an uncomfortable hall: ' They were not magnetic, and the great place was out of sorts somehow.'

How far Dickens was consciously adapting his proven mesmeric powers to the Reading performances in order to generate 'sympathy' is not known, however much its influence might be inferred. It was a two-way process, though, with Dickens apparently just as capable of being mesmerized by the emotional energy from his audience as they by him:

Every eye was bent on the reader's expressive face, and the contagion of his mood seemed to pass directly to every individual in the room like a subtle magnetic influence. Mr DICKENS appeared to feel the sympathy of his audience, and to be inspired by it.

Annie Fields's coupling of Dickens's absolute belief in mesmerism with his belief in the 'unfathomed ties between man and man' is particularly striking, given Dickens's commitment to affirming class connections in the face of great divisions. It suggests an occult underpinning to his social creed, and it certainly relates to his ambition to fuse together into one community his Reading audiences. As we have seen, Dickens did not exploit a cult of personality during these tours. What he wanted to be was a kind of power, a force for bonding into a community a wide cross section of people, and himself to be one in that community. The peculiar interaction of these components, complicated even further by Dickens's acts of wholesale impersonation, needs to be focused a little more.

In the letter quoted at the head of this chapter, Dickens initially described the Readings as 'this interpretation of *myself*' (my italics), and then a little later developed that into explaining their function as offering a 'new expression of the meaning of my books'. We probably should not put too much weight on that first phrase as indeed meaning *self*-interpretation in any psychological sense, but it is a useful cue in taking the measure of the Readings and Dickens's commitment to them as a means of understanding Dickens himself in this role.

Carol Hanbery Mackay, in introducing a collection of essays, *Dramatic Dickens* (1989), drew attention to the way all of her contributors 'perceive and respond to a special Dickensian *energy* [proceeding] from the interaction of Dickens's opposing views of the self'. She associates these opposing forces, present as much in the man as in his work, with the Nietzschean antithesis: 'one Apollonian, representing rigid order, and subdued emotions; the other Dionysian, chaotic, emotional, melodramatic, spontaneous, unscripted, and deceptive'. This analysis has some support in several confessional statements made by Dickens in his letters. For example, in 1857 he confided to Forster the internal struggles that continually beset him: 'You are not so tolerant as perhaps you might be of the wayward and unsettled feeling which is part (I suppose) of the tenure on which one holds an imaginative life, and which I have, as you ought to know well, often only kept down by riding over it like a dragoon.' The conflict between Dickens's 'wayward' imaginative impulses and the almost military discipline he exerted over them is well known and has been much pored over. As far as his writings are concerned, Mackay suggests that the Dickens 'canon records how he developed a narrative form which could contain his energy while not suppressing it'. In one of the book's essays, by James Kincaid, this 'energy' is explored and identified with the friction between the 'earnest' and the 'playful' characters:

The earnest performers have plans and proceed as best they can along straight lines; they struggle to constitute what we think of as a plot; the playful performers float free, improvising whatever composition they find to their fancy; they write anti-plots.

John Carey had made an observation of a similar kind about this kind of creative antagonism some years earlier: 'Having stuffed the novels with noble sentiment, he retained a troop of comics to punish and deride it.' Dickens's novels are energized by the friction generated between such contending impulses—earnest/playful, plot/anti-plot—and assume the status of a kind of *discordia concors.* *The Old Curiosity Shop* is a paradigmatic novel in this respect, in the elemental opposition between Nell and Quilp. Terry Eagleton, in an echo of Carey's point, has also observed how Quilp 'symbolises the smouldering, anarchic vengeance which the novel wreaks on its own decorous, sentimental story-line'. These conflicts were sensationally dramatized in the Reading 'Sikes and Nancy', where the pattern of violence-committed-on-virtue was acted out with appalling ferocity as Sikes in a frenzy of savage energy smashes the newly pious Nancy to death. At a subtler level, one might instance the Betsey Trotwood ménage in *David Copperfield* as a domestic analogue for the energizing opposition identified by Kincaid. The Dover household is a model of containment without suppression. Mr Dick represents the principle of waywardness, chaos, spontaneity, playfulness, and 'floating free' (almost literally in his symbiotic relationship to his kite); Betsey represents the controlling principle of order and discipline. Even her eccentric allergy to donkeys is related to her territorial homekeeping. The miracle is the coexistence of the two.

How might this schema apply to the Readings as the project developed? Dickens, as we have seen, devised the platform set with great care so as to afford him the maximum focus, visually and acoustically. It put him at the centre of a bright frame. The set, the strict two-hour allocation of performance time, the establishment of the occasion as 'drawing-room' entertainment and not 'theatre', the command of the narrative, the Reader as impresario, wholly conscious of his responsibilities: all these are instruments and expressions of order and control. Within this securely structured framework, Dickens could intermittently lose himself, or, one might better say, liberate the other self or selves normally held in custody by his dragoon-like discipline. He could during those two hours surrender to that waywardness integral to his imaginative life, indulge to the full in public that 'exquisite foolery' of temporarily 'being someone, in voice &c not at all like myself'.

This relishing of the fluidity of identity both as compositional asset (in Forster's words, 'what he desired to express he became') and performance project was, as we have seen (in the chapter on impersonation), contrary to conventional constructions of the self as unitary. The unitary and multiple self, the self that is both 'playful' and 'earnest', both anarchic, wayward spirit and dragoon disciplinarian, finds its perfect outlet for expressing these contradictions in the public Readings. The Readings enabled Dickens to play out the full variety of selves, each magically dissolving into the others with evident relish. Kate Field observed, for example, that Dickens's impersonation of Squeers 'impresses us with the belief that he enjoys being a brute and is not an actor trying to be brutal'. The implied fissility of self is represented in a curious confession apparently made by Dickens in conversation with Dostoyevsky in 1862. Dostoyevsky reports Dickens as follows:

There were two people in him, he told me: one who feels as he ought to feel and one who feels the opposite. From the one who feels the opposite I try to make my evil characters, from the one who feels as a man ought to feel I try to live my life. Only two people? I asked.

Dickens does not say quite what is covered by the 'opposite' to how one 'ought to feel', but his reported comments seem tailor-made for that line of analytical criticism developed long ago by Edmund Wilson in his 1941 essay 'The Two Scrooges', and extended in subsequent criticism, such as that represented in Carol Mackay's collection of essays and in Harry Stone's *The Night Side of Dickens* (1994). The public Readings constituted a recreation ground for the dynamic coexistence of the contending selves in Dickens's make-up. The internal drama became a public spectacle. The Jekyll-and-Hyde duality latent in Dickens's make-up was alarmingly dramatized in 'Sikes and Nancy', when Dickens both enacted Nancy's murder by the brutal thug Sikes with a gusto that appalled audiences, and also remained the gentlemanly narrator in evening dress, apparently just as appalled as his audience. In Stevenson's story Jekyll concluded that 'man is not truly one, but truly two'. However, he went on to speculate, 'I hazard the guess that man will be ultimately known for a mere polity of multifarious, incongruous, and independent denizens.' Indeed, why limit the potential range of selves? Dickens had more than just 'two Scrooges' in his make-up: it was not just a matter of 'acting out' his other side. 'Only two people?' asked Dostoyevsky as Dickens described his split self. Alas, no reply is recorded.

The manifestly multiform self had peculiar attractions for Dickens. There are two moments in Dickens's fiction that bear upon this dissolution of the unitary identity and that make the multiform self a potentially redemptive force, instead of an anarchic threat or some kind of pathological failure. What I am suggesting about the peculiar value of the Readings for an 'interpretation' of Dickens's self may become more apparent in the light of a brief consideration of these moments. In *Hard Times* the early description of the circus folk delights in the confusions between the folk themselves, the roles they assume professionally, and the animal world that is an integral part of their professional life:

His [Childers's] legs were very robust, but shorter than legs of good proportions should have been. His chest and back were as much too broad, as his legs were too short. He was dressed in a Newmarket coat and tight-fitting trousers; wore a shawl round his neck; smelt of lamp-oil, straw, orange-peel, horses' provender, and sawdust; and looked a most remarkable sort of Centaur, compounded of the stable and the play-house. Where the one began, and the other ended, nobody could have told with any precision. This gentleman was mentioned in the bills of the day as Mr. E. W. B. Childers, so justly celebrated for his daring vaulting act as the Wild Huntsman of the North American Prairies; in which popular performance, a diminutive boy with an old face, who now accompanied him, assisted as his infant son: being carried upside down over his father's shoulder, by one foot, and held by the crown of his head, heels upwards, in the palm of his father's hand, according to the violent paternal manner in which wild huntsmen may be observed to fondle their offspring. Made up with curls, wreaths, wings, white bismuth, and carmine, this hopeful young person soared into so pleasing a Cupid as to constitute the chief delight of the maternal part of the spectators; but in private, where his characteristics were a precocious cutaway coat and an extremely gruff voice, he became of the Turf, turfy.

It is very difficult to keep a steady focus on identities here. The capacity for exotic metamorphosis is the most arresting aspect of these folk. Nothing is quite what it seems—or not for long. Mr Childers is an oddly assembled human being: everything is out of proportion, as if he has been fitted together from the wrong component limbs. And does he belong in the stable or in the play-house? Like a Centaur, there is something indeterminate about his species identity. His stage son is another mass of physical contradictions: a charmingly diminutive, ethereal Cupid, whose off-stage character is forbiddingly gruff and earthy. The fluidity of identity of these circus folk, their polymorphous, carnivalesque being, is their chief attraction, and the most conspicuous symptom of their opposition to the monolithic inflexibility of Gradgrind and Bounderby. The nonchalantly habitual role-playing that is the circus's *raison d' être* will survive the constraints of Gradgrindism, and by a grotesque symbolic irony Gradgrind's son will have to black up into another identity in order to be safely smuggled away by the generous folk so maligned by his father's philosophy.

The circus folk choose to lead, or are obliged to lead, a marginalized, vagrant life. They are permitted to pitch the circus for a period only, and on neutral ground at the outskirts of the town. This is analogous to the situation in which Dickens sometimes felt he belonged—or perhaps one might say it is analogous to the situation to which a part of Dickens felt he permanently belonged. I do not just mean in terms of the lure of the theatre for him, and the conflicts he had with those who feared his association with that bohemian subculture. I mean something more deeply ingrained in his being, the kind of thing he meant when he described his persistent sense (quoted a little earlier) of that 'wayward and unsettled feeling [. . .] which I have [. . .] often only kept down by riding over it like a dragoon'. 'Wayward and unsettled' are terms applicable to the situation of the circus folk. Both they and Dickens are committed to the vagrant life of the imagination. In this construction the life of the imagination, like the multiform identity, which is by definition 'wayward and unsettled', has no secure place in that respectable society policed by the dragoons of self-discipline and uniformity. The same applies to Dickens's sense that he is often one who feels the opposite of how 'he ought to feel'. The imagination under threat is somewhat feral. When Dickens spoke of the strong appeal of impersonating people not at all like him ('Assumption has charms for me') he seemed to shy at the question of why this was so: 'I hardly know for how many wild reasons.' Perhaps he did not want to investigate. The term 'wild', though, suggests this activity belongs to that same 'wayward' modus vivendi that was the natural habitat of the circus folk. In another context, and using terms that amalgamate circus and savagery, Dickens reflected on the predicament he sometimes found himself in: 'I feel like a Wild Beast in a Caravan, describing himself in the keeper's absence.'

The vagabond impulse is reflected in Dickens's taste for 'flânerie', identified so acutely in Michael Hollington's essay of 1981. Hollington associates Dickens's self-confessed love of 'amateur vagrancy', particularly in the obscure quarters of London, with Baudelaire's characterization of the wanderer in his essay *Le Peintre de la Vie Moderne*: 'sa passion et sa profession, c'est épouser la foule'. The flâneur's great joy is 'to live in multitude, in fluctuation, in movement, in the fugitive and the infinite'. This describes perfectly Dickens's delight in one aspect of the Readings, his sense that he can immerse himself in the crowd of people listening to him, as well as in the characters he brings to life through 'assumption'. And it is more than just immersion. The experience of the Readings as 'fluctuating' and 'fugitive' and the passionate engagement with the crowd of listeners ('épouser la foule')—these are what revitalized Dickens.

The other moment of celebration of the redemptive instability of identity is the description of the Ghost of Christmas Past in *A Christmas Carol*.

A strange figure—like a child: yet not so like a child as like an old man viewed through some supernatural medium [. . .] the figure itself fluctuated in its distinctness: being now a thing with one arm, now with one leg, now with twenty legs, now a pair of legs without a head, now a head without a body: of which dissolving parts, no outline would be visible in the dense gloom wherein they melted away. And in the very wonder of this, it would be itself again; distinct and clear as ever.

This protean figure, a kind of supernatural condensation of the circus folk, is the agent of Scrooge's liberation from rigid introspective uniformity. As Childers is a compound of horse and human, and his stage son a compound of child-Cupid and man of the turf, so the Ghost amalgamates all ages in one figure. Itself constantly metamorphosing, the Ghost has come to disturb Scrooge into a recognition—first painful then joyous—of his true multifaceted self: surrogate father, uncle, child, businessman, pledged to live in the Past, the Present, and the Future.

Hybridity and exhibitionist polymorphousness take us back to the 'monopolylogue', the famous virtuoso performance by Charles Mathews, Dickens's model, if not inspiration for the art of imperson-ation, and a prototype for the public Readings. The monopolylogue highlighted the potential diversity of selves of which the single identity might be composed. Dickens's Readings celebrated this. They were far more than displays of virtuoso mimicry; they were demonstrations of the power of the imagination to conjure up people and places that seemed as real as the audience watching. He gave a reading of the 'Carol' at Leamington in November 1858, and the awed reviewer recorded, 'When he reached the end, it was to his audience *as though a real society had suddenly broken up*, and not that a mere narrative had come to a graceful conclusion' (my italics). Impersonation, or 'assumption', of the kind practised by Dickens and Mathews was an act of the sympathetic imagination. Byron praised Mathews as one who was gifted with the rare talent of intuitively identifying himself with the minds of others: in other words an act of 'sympathy' in the sense discussed earlier. 'Impersonation' of this kind is a sympathetic capacity to inhabit the personality of an-*other* and thereby minimize their other-ness: the staunchly unitary self, on the other hand, depends for its supposed integrity on others' being distinctly 'other'. The corollary to making a wide variety of imaginary characters seem wholly real is its converse, Dickens's delight in casting real people as partly fictional dramatis personae: 'he looked at all things and people dramatically', recalled Arthur Helps. 'He assigned to all of us characters; and in his company we could not help playing our parts ... [he] brought all that he saw and felt into a magic circle of dramatic creation.' Such repeated acts of imaginative identification, as a writer, actor, or performing Reader, involved temporary suspensions of the self—the self, that is, constituted by the evening dress.

One admiring account of Mathews expressed this capacity even more strongly: 'The power of self-annihilation possessed by Mr Mathews, gives to all his portraits a separate identity.' Dickens's willingness as an actor or Reader to indulge his 'wayward' and 'wild' impulses amounted to a public experiment in a kind of self-annihilation. This is the Dionysian part of him, the voluntary fissility of the self. The violence of that concept is reflected in the language he used when he prepared for or reported on the theatricals and public Readings. 'I have just come back from Manchester', he writes in 1857, after performances of *The Frozen Deep*, 'where I have been tearing myself to pieces, to the wonderful satisfaction of thousands of people.' He stood in the wings just before going onstage to give a Reading of 'Sikes and Nancy' pledging, 'I shall tear myself to pieces.' He talked of himself as 'the modern embodiment of the old Enchanters, whose Familiars tore them to pieces'. Torn to pieces—this is a revealing phrase. Like the redeeming Ghost of Christmas Past Dickens in performance became an exhilarating medley of floating dismemberment.

These acts of self-morcellation were performed before his Familiars, those he referred to as 'my large miscellaneous following, which is limited to no class'. His very first public Reading, in December 1853 at Birmingham Town Hall, was partly dedicated to this ideal, 'the fusion of different classes, without confusion', as Dickens put it in his speech before the Reading. (Dickens's career-long dislike of matinee performances was partly because they excluded the labouring population who would be at work in the daytime.) *The Times* remarked on the constitution of his audiences: 'The very aspect of that crowd, composed of the most various classes, hanging on the utterance of one man, was in itself an imposing spectacle.' That heterogeneous crowd, tens of thousands of them, had been hanging on the utterance of one man since *Pickwick Papers*. The many dependent on the one: this was a writer whose greatest ambitions were to educate the emotional sympathies, to restore community, to reunite classes, to repair the web of corroded or broken connections, to make others less 'other'. One of his strangest ideas for a story (described in his *Book of Memoranda*) was to create social connections by means of electricity:

Open a story by bringing two strongly contrasted places and strongly contrasted sets of people, into the connexion necessary for the story, by means of an electric message. Describe the message—*be* the message—flashing along through space—over the earth, and under the sea.

'*Be* the message'. Dickens as an electric charge, bringing people into connection: that is not a bad way of identifying his ambition for the Readings. As he insisted, this 'new expression of the meaning of [his] books' was designed to touch the hearts of his readers 'in a new way'.

Dickens's nightly self-annihilation under the gas-lamps ('the platform absorbs my individuality'), generating the extraordinary dance of proliferating selves and parading in one person the full panorama of English society, was an extension of his mission as a novelist. By all accounts he achieved it in auditoria all round the country. Listen to him reporting again on the *Frozen Deep* performances, in the same letter as he mentions the old Enchanters: 'I had a transitory satisfaction in rending the very heart out of my body by doing that Richard Wardour part. It was a good thing to have a couple of thousand people all rigid and frozen together in the palm of one's hand.' Obviously the exercise of power of this kind fascinated Dickens. But notice again the language: personal disintegration is practised so as to produce corporate integration. After a reading of 'Little Dombey' he reported, 'I never saw a crowd so resolved into one creature before.'

Night after night, luxuriating in polymorphousness and mono-polylogue, the Old Enchanter tore himself to pieces, in order to fuse thousands of strangers into one community.

Finale:
London, March 1870

Dickens was in Leeds in mid-April 1869, at the start of his Farewell Reading tour. It was 'Farewell' because he had finally yielded to family and friends and persuaded himself to bring his Reading career to an end before it brought an end to him. His friend Edmund Yates, son of the man who, half a century earlier, had partnered Charles Mathews in some of those bravura shows of impersonation, met Dickens in Leeds on 12th April and was shocked by the change in his appearance and manner: 'He looked desperately aged and worn; the lines in his cheeks and round his eyes, always noticeable, were now deep furrows; and there was a weariness in his gaze, and a general air of fatigue and depression about him.' It was obvious to everyone else and must have been obvious to Dickens that he was slowly collapsing. His extraordinary resilience was supplying him with shorter and shorter bouts of recuperation. He refused to acknowledge that he was ill in any long-term sense, but his body was surrendering to the prolonged strain of the Readings. Dolby had been warning him of this for some time, as tactfully as he could, continuing all the while to support his Chief—quite literally on some occasions in America and Britain. A Mrs Flora Sampson and her party were in the audience one night for a Reading at Boston's Tremont Temple, in seats that had a good view of the entrance from the dressing room:

As Mr. Dickens, leaning heavily on his manager, climbed the steps leading to the stage, he appeared to be very lame and entirely unable to walk alone.

But the moment he passed the screen separating him from the audience and emerged into plain view, lo! what a transformation! He walked erect without assistance, with his accustomed ease and grace of deportment . . . [At intervals he retired] to fall into the arms of his waiting manager, evincing great pain and weariness, when sure he was out of sight of the audience.

Dolby was always his backstage support, assisting him into the gas-lit world where he could rely on that other great support, his listening readership. Dickens could just about disguise his deep physical frailty, less so his mental frailty when that betrayed itself. A stroke, or perhaps several small strokes, now prevented his reading the halves of the letters over the shop-doors on his right, as his son Charley recalled. Charley also listened to him stumbling verbally on the platform one night at St James's Hall: 'He found it impossible to say Pickwick, and called him Picksnick, and Picnic, and Peckwicks and all sorts of names except the right with a comical glance of surprise at the occupants of the front seats which were always reserved for his family and friends.'

The Farewell Tour was abruptly brought to an end when Dickens's health broke down, some days after that April 1869 meeting in Leeds with Yates. He now admitted to 'a certain sense of deadness on the left side' and to the 'difficulty of taking hold of any object with the left hand'. It was just as well he had learned his Readings by heart, if he could no longer rely on being able to hold his book in the left hand. He reported the symptoms to his doctor, Thomas Beard, who hurried up to Preston where the next Reading was due to be given and examined Dickens. Beard then made it clear that if he continued the Readings his health would be damaged beyond repair and he could well collapse. That was the end of the provincial Readings. Some months later, it was agreed that Dickens would wind up this aborted last tour with twelve Readings at St James's Hall, in February and March of 1870. In addition to the usual staging arrangements for the Hall Readings, Dr Beard (who was now always to be in attendance at the performances) had ordered some steps to be put up against the side of the platform. He instructed Charley, 'You must be there [in the front row] every night and if you see your father falter in the least, you must run up and catch him and bring him off with me, or, by Heaven, he'll die before them all.'

'He'll die before them all.' For those twelve nights Dickens took his life in his hands as he went before his audience. The self-confessed 'modern Embodiment of the old Enchanters, whose Familiars tore them to pieces' went on stage for the last time at 8 p.m. on Tuesday 15th March, his manager on watch from the wings, his family and doctor just a few yards away, ready for rescue. Crowds had been turned away that day at the Piccadilly and Regent Street entrances to the Hall, missing their last opportunity to hear Charles Dickens read. Inside the Great Hall, under the radiance of the pendant lamps, two thousand people rose to their feet as Dickens came on stage, and cheered for several minutes. The emotional tension was evident in Dickens's face as he stood receiving the applause. Then he announced 'A Christmas Carol' and launched into the story. For the last time, lame and partly stricken with paralysis, he summoned his characters and together they soared and dipped on the gusts of warmth from that vast company before him, riding the old thermals of public love for the man. The 'Trial' followed. Serjeant Buzfuz, Mrs. Cluppins, Winkle, Sam Weller, the little judge—each was cheered loudly as he or she made their entry, as if they were all taking their final bow. Then it was over. Dickens left the platform, and was recalled several times. On his last return he stopped by the desk, waited for the applause to subside, and spoke to his audience:

Ladies and Gentlemen, it would be worse than idle—for it would be hypocritical and unfeeling—if I were to disguise that I close this episode in my life with feelings of very considerable pain. For some fifteen years, in this hall and in many kindred places, I have had the honour of presenting my own cherished ideas before you for your recognition; and in closely observing your reception of them, have enjoyed an amount of artistic delight and instruction which, perhaps, is given to few men to know. In this task, and in every other which I have ever undertaken, as a faithful servant of the public, always imbued with a sense of duty to them, and always striving to do his best, I have been uniformly cheered by the readiest response, the most generous sympathy, and the most stimulating support. Nevertheless, I have thought it well, at the flood-tide of your favour, to retire upon those older associations between us, which date from much further back than these, and henceforth devote myself exclusively to that art which first brought us together.

Ladies and gentlemen, in but two short weeks from this time I hope that you may enter, in your own homes, on a new series of readings, at which my assistance will be indispensable; but from these garish lights I vanish now for evermore, with a heartfelt, grateful, respectful, and affectionate farewell.

There was a kind of sigh from the audience when Dickens finished. The speech had been delivered with great steadiness and clarity, in the dead stillness of the Hall. There was just one brief tremor, a cadence on the edge of breakdown, when he said 'from these garish lights I vanish now for evermore'. Twelve weeks later those words appeared on the Funeral Card distributed at the doors of Westminster Abbey, on the day Charles Dickens was buried in Poets' Corner.

APPENDIX

Schedule of the Public Readings

The following schedule is based on unpublished notes by Philip Collins and subsequently correlated with information in the Pilgrim edition of *The Letters of Charles Dickens*.

THE REPERTOIRE OF READINGS IN ORDER OF FIRST PUBLIC PERFORMANCE (ABBREVIATED FORM IN BRACKETS)

'A Christmas Carol' (Carol)
'The Cricket on the Hearth' (Cricket)
'The Chimes' (Chimes)
'The Story of Little Dombey' (Dombey)
'The Poor Traveller' (Poor Traveller)
'Boots at the Holly-Tree Inn' (Boots)
'Mrs. Gamp' (Gamp)
'Bardell and Pickwick' (Trial)
'David Copperfield' (Copperfield)
'Nicholas Nickleby at the Yorkshire School' (Nickleby)
'Mr. Bob Sawyer's Party' (Sawyer)
'Doctor Marigold' (Marigold)
'Barbox Brothers' (Barbox)
'The Boy at Mugby' (Boy)
'Mr. Chops, the Dwarf' (Chops)
'Sikes and Nancy' (Sikes)

CHARITY READINGS

Date	Venue	Programme
1853		
December 27 Tuesday	Birmingham, Town Hall	Carol
December 29 Thursday	Birmingham, Town Hall	Cricket
December 30 Friday	Birmingham, Town Hall	Carol
1854		
December 19 Tuesday	Reading, Mechanics' Institution	Carol
December 21 Thursday	Sherborne	Carol
December 28 Thursday	Bradford, St George's Hall	Carol
1855		
March 27 Tuesday	Ashford, Railway Institute	Carol
October 5 Friday	Folkestone, Saw Mill	Carol
December 18 Tuesday	Peterborough, Corn Exchange	Carol
December 22 Saturday	Sheffield, Mechanics' Institute	Carol
1857		
June 30 Tuesday	London, St Martin's Hall	Carol
July 24 Friday	London, St Martin's Hall	Carol
July 31 Friday	Manchester, Free Trade Hall	Carol
December 15 Tuesday	Coventry, Corn Exchange	Carol
December 22 Tuesday	Chatham, Lecture Hall	Carol
1858		
January 19 Tuesday	Bristol, Athenaeum	Carol
March 26 Friday	Edinburgh, Music Hall	Carol
April 15 Thursday	London, St Martin's Hall	Carol
November 8 Monday	Reading, Institute	Dombey, Trial
December 29 Wednesday	Chatham, Lecture Hall	Dombey, Trial
1860		
December 18 Tuesday	Chatham, Lecture Hall	Poor Traveller, Boots, Gamp

Date	Venue	Programme
1862		
January 16 Thursday	Chatham, Lecture Hall	Copperfield
1863		
January 17 Saturday	Paris, British Embassy	Copperfield
January 29 Thursday	Paris, British Embassy	Dombey, Trial
January 30 Friday	Paris, British Embassy	Carol, Trial
December 15 Tuesday	Chatham, Lecture Hall	Nickleby, Sawyer
1865		
December 19 Tuesday	Chatham, Lecture Hall	Carol, Trial
1866		
January 31 Wednesday	London, Islington, Myddelton Hall	Copperfield, Trial

PROFESSIONAL READINGS

'(mat)' = matinee: otherwise all performances are evening ones

Date	Venue	Programme
1858		
April 29 Thursday	London, St Martin's Hall	Cricket
May 6 Thursday	London, St Martin's Hall	Chimes
May 13 Thursday	London, St Martin's Hall	Carol
May 20 Thursday	London, St Martin's Hall	Cricket
May 26 Wednesday	London, St Martin's Hall	Carol
May 27 Thursday	London, St Martin's Hall	Chimes
June 3 Thursday	London, St Martin's Hall	Chimes
June 9 Wednesday	London, St Martin's Hall	Carol
June 10 Thursday	London, St Martin's Hall	Dombey
June 17 Thursday	London, St Martin's Hall	Poor Traveller, Boots, Gamp
June 23 Wednesday	London, St Martin's Hall	Dombey
June 24 Thursday	London, St Martin's Hall	Carol

'Professional Readings (*cont.*)'

Date (1858)	Venue	Programme
July 1 Thursday	London, St Martin's Hall	Poor Traveller, Boots, Gamp
July 8 Thursday	London, St Martin's Hall	Chimes
July 14 Wednesday	London, St Martin's Hall	Carol
July 15 Thursday	London, St Martin's Hall	Poor Traveller, Boots, Gamp
July 22 Thursday	London, St Martin's Hall	Dombey
August 2 Monday	Clifton, Victoria Rooms	Chimes
August 3 Tuesday	Exeter, Royal Public Rooms	Carol
August 4 Wednesday	Plymouth, St George's Hall	Carol
August 5 Thursday (mat)	Stonehouse, Nr Plymouth, St George's Hall	Dombey
August 5 Thursday (evg)	Stonehouse, Nr Plymouth, St George's Hall	Poor Traveller, Boots, Gamp
August 6 Friday	Clifton, Victoria Rooms	Carol
August 10 Tuesday	Worcester, Music Hall	Carol
August 11 Wednesday	Wolverhampton, Corn Exchange	Carol
August 12 Thursday	Shrewsbury, Music Hall	Carol
August 13 Friday	Chester, Music Hall	Carol
August 18 Wednesday	Liverpool, Philharmonic Hall	Carol
August 19 Thursday	Liverpool, Philharmonic Hall	Dombey
August 20 Friday	Liverpool, Philharmonic Hall	Poor Traveller, Boots, Gamp
August 21 Saturday	Liverpool, Philharmonic Hall	Carol
August 23 Monday	Dublin, Rotunda	Carol
August 24 Tuesday	Dublin, Rotunda	Chimes
August 25 Wednesday	Dublin, Rotunda	Dombey
August 26 Thursday	Dublin, Rotunda	Poor Traveller, Boots, Gamp
August 27 Friday	Belfast, Victoria Hall	Carol

Date (1858)	Venue	Programme
August 28 Saturday (mat)	Belfast, Victoria Hall	Dombey
August 28 Saturday	Belfast, Victoria Hall	Poor Traveller, Boots, Gamp
August 30 Monday	Cork, Athenaeum	Carol
August 31 Tuesday (mat)	Cork, Athenaeum	Dombey
August 31 Tuesday	Cork, Athenaeum	Poor Traveller, Boots, Gamp
September 1 Wednesday	Limerick, Theatre Royal	Carol
September 2 Thursday	Limerick, Theatre Royal	Poor Traveller, Boots, Gamp
September 8 Wednesday	Huddersfield, Gymnasium Hall	Carol
September 9 Thursday	Wakefield, Corn Exchange	Carol
September 10 Friday	York, Festival Concert Room	Carol
September 11 Saturday (mat)	Harrogate, Cheltenham Room	Dombey
September 11 Saturday	Harrogate, Cheltenham Room	Carol
September 13 Monday (mat)	Scarborough, Assembly Rooms	Dombey
September 13 Monday	Scarborough, Assembly Rooms	Carol
September 14 Tuesday	Hull, Music Hall	Carol
September 15 Wednesday	Leeds, Music Hall	Carol
September 16 Thursday	Halifax, Oddfellows' Hall	Carol
September 17 Friday	Sheffield, Music Hall	Poor Traveller, Boots, Gamp
September 18 Saturday	Manchester, Free Trade Hall	Poor Traveller, Boots, Gamp
September 21 Tuesday	Darlington, Central Hall	Carol
September 22 Wednesday	Durham, New Town Hall	Carol
September 23 Thursday	Sunderland, Theatre Royal	Carol
September 24 Friday	Newcastle, New Town Hall	Carol

'Professional Readings (*cont.*)'

Date (1858)	Venue	Programme
September 25 Saturday	Newcastle, New Town Hall	Dombey
September 25 Saturday (mat)	Newcastle, New Town Hall	Poor Traveller, Boots, Gamp
September 27 Monday	Edinburgh, Queen Street Hall	Chimes
September 28 Tuesday	Edinburgh, Queen Street Hall	Dombey
September 29 Wednesday (mat)	Edinburgh, Queen Street Hall	Cricket
September 29 Wednesday	Edinburgh, Queen Street Hall	Poor Traveller, Boots, Gamp
September 30 Thursday	Edinburgh, Queen Street Hall	Carol
October 1 Friday	Dundee, Corn Exchange Hall	Carol
October 2 Saturday	Dundee, Corn Exchange Hall	Poor Traveller, Boots, Gamp
October 4 Monday (mat)	Aberdeen, County Rooms	Dombey
October 4 Monday	Aberdeen, County Rooms	Carol
October 5 Tuesday	Perth, City Hall	Carol
October 6 Wednesday	Glasgow, City Hall	Chimes
October 7 Thursday	Glasgow, City Hall	Poor Traveller, Boots, Gamp
October 8 Friday	Glasgow, City Hall	Carol
October 9 Saturday	Glasgow, City Hall	Dombey
October 14 Thursday	Bradford, St George's Hall	Poor Traveller, Boots, Gamp
October 15 Friday (mat)	Liverpool, Philharmonic Hall	Dombey
October 15 Friday	Liverpool, Philharmonic Hall	Poor Traveller, Boots, Gamp
October 16 Saturday	Manchester, Free Trade Hall	Dombey, Boots
October 18 Monday	Birmingham, Music Hall	Poor Traveller, Boots, Gamp

Date (1858)	Venue	Programme
October 19 Tuesday	Birmingham, Music Hall	Dombey, Trial
October 20 Wednesday	Birmingham, Music Hall	Poor Traveller, Boots, Gamp
October 21 Thursday	Nottingham, Mechanics' Hall	Carol
October 22 Friday	Derby, Lecture Hall	Poor Traveller, Boots, Gamp
October 23 Saturday	Manchester, Free Trade Hall	Carol, Trial
October 26 Tuesday	Hull, Music Hall	Poor Traveller, Boots, Gamp
October 27 Wednesday	Hull, Music Hall	Dombey
October 28 Thursday	Leeds, Music Hall	Poor Traveller, Boots, Gamp
October 29 Friday	Sheffield, Music Hall	Dombey, Trial
November 2 Tuesday (mat)	Leamington, Royal Music Hall	Carol
November 2 Tuesday	Leamington, Royal Music Hall	Poor Traveller, Boots, Gamp
November 3 Wednesday	Wolverhampton, Corn Exchange	Poor Traveller, Boots, Gamp
November 4 Thursday	Leicester, New Music Hall	Carol
November 9 Tuesday	Southampton, Victoria Rooms	Poor Traveller, Boots, Gamp
November 10 Wednesday	Southampton, Victoria Rooms	Carol
November 11 Thursday (mat)	Portsea, St George's Hall	Carol
November 11 Thursday	Portsea, St George's Hall	Poor Traveller, Boots, Gamp
November 12 Friday	Brighton, Town Hall	Carol
November 13 Saturday (mat)	Brighton, Town Hall	Dombey
November 13 Saturday	Brighton, Town Hall	Poor Traveller, Boots, Gamp

'Professional Readings (*cont.*)'

Date (1858–1859)	Venue	Programme
December 24 Friday	London, St Martin's Hall	Carol, Trial
December 27 Monday	London, St Martin's Hall	Carol, Trial
1859		
January 6 Thursday	London, St Martin's Hall	Carol, Trial
January 13 Thursday	London, St Martin's Hall	Carol, Trial
January 20 Thursday	London, St Martin's Hall	Dombey, Trial
January 28 Friday	London, St Martin's Hall	Poor Traveller, Gamp, Trial
February 3 Thursday	London, St Martin's Hall	Carol, Trial
February 10 Thursday	London, St Martin's Hall	Carol, Trial
October 10 Monday	Ipswich, Corn Exchange	Carol, Trial
October 11 Tuesday	Norwich, St Andrew's Hall	Carol, Trial
October 12 Wednesday	Norwich, St Andrew's Hall	Dombey, Gamp
October 13 Thursday	Bury St Edmunds, Athenaeum Hall	Carol, Trial
October 17 Monday	Cambridge, Town Hall	Carol, Trial
October 18 Tuesday	Cambridge, Town Hall	Dombey, Gamp
October 19 Wednesday	Peterborough, Corn Exchange	Dombey, Trial
October 20 Thursday	Bradford, St George's Hall	Dombey, Trial
October 21 Friday	Nottingham, Mechanics' Hall	Dombey, Trial
October 24 Monday	Oxford, Town Hall	Carol, Trial
October 25 Tuesday	Oxford, Town Hall	Dombey, Gamp
October 26 Wednesday	Birmingham, Music Hall	Carol, Trial
October 27 Thursday (mat)	Cheltenham, Old Wells Music Hall	Dombey
October 27 Thursday	Cheltenham, Old Wells Music Hall	Carol, Trial
December 24 Saturday	London, St Martin's Hall	Carol[a]
December 26 Monday	London, St Martin's Hall	Carol, Trial

Date (1860–1861)	Venue	Programme
1860		
January 2 Monday	London, St Martin's Hall	Carol, Trial
1861		
March 14 Thursday	London, St James's Hall	Carol, Boots
March 22 Friday	London, St James's Hall	Dombey, Trial
March 28 Thursday	London, St James's Hall	Carol, Trial
April 4 Thursday	London, St James's Hall	Dombey, Trial
April 11 Thursday	London, St James's Hall	Carol, Gamp
April 18 Thursday	London, St James's Hall	Dombey, Trial
October 28 Monday	Norwich, St Andrew's Hall	Copperfield
October 29 Tuesday	Norwich, St Andrew's Hall	Nickleby, Trial
October 30 Wednesday	Bury St Edmunds, Athenaeum Hall	Copperfield
October 31 Thursday	Ipswich, Corn Exchange	Copperfield
November 1 Friday	Colchester, Theatre	Nickleby, Trial
November 4 Monday	Canterbury, Theatre Royal	Copperfield
November 5 Tuesday	Dover, Apollonian Hall	Nickleby, Trial
November 6 Wednesday	Hastings, Music Hall	Carol, Trial
November 7 Thursday	Brighton, Town Hall	Copperfield
November 8 Friday	Brighton, Town Hall	Nickleby, Trial
November 9 Saturday	Brighton, Pavilion	Copperfield
November 21 Thursday	Newcastle-on-Tyne, Music Hall	Copperfield
November 22 Friday	Newcastle-on-Tyne, Music Hall	Nickleby, Trial
November 23 Saturday	Newcastle-on-Tyne, Music Hall	Dombey, Trial
November 25 Monday	Berwick, King's Arms Assembly Hall	Carol, Trial
November 27 Wednesday	Edinburgh, Queen Street Hall	Copperfield
November 28 Thursday	Edinburgh, Queen Street Hall	Nickleby, Trial
November 30 Saturday (mat)	Edinburgh, Queen Street Hall	Dombey

'Professional Readings (*cont.*)'

Date (1861–1862)	Venue	Programme
November 30 Saturday	Edinburgh, Queen Street Hall	Copperfield
December 2 Monday	Edinburgh, Queen Street Hall	Nickleby, Trial
December 3 Tuesday	Glasgow, City Hall	Nickleby, Trial
December 4 Wednesday	Glasgow, City Hall	Copperfield
December 5 Thursday	Glasgow, City Hall	Nickleby, Trial
December 6 Friday	Glasgow, City Hall	Copperfield
December 7 Saturday	Edinburgh, Queen Street Hall	Nickleby, Trial
December 9 Monday	Carlisle, Athenaeum Hall	Carol, Trial
December 10 Tuesday	Carlisle, Athenaeum Hall	Copperfield
December 12 Thursday	Lancaster, Music Hall	Carol, Trial
December 13 Friday	Preston, Corn Exchange	Carol, Trial
December 14 Saturday	Manchester, Free Trade Hall	Copperfield
December 30 Monday	Birmingham, Music Hall	Nickleby, Sawyer
December 31 Tuesday	Birmingham, Music Hall	Copperfield
1862		
January 1 Wednesday (mat)	Leamington, Music Hall	Copperfield
January 1 Wednesday	Leamington, Music Hall	Nickleby, Trial
January 3 Friday	Cheltenham, Assembly Rooms	Nickleby, Boots
January 4 Saturday	Cheltenham, Assembly Rooms	Copperfield
January 6 Monday	Plymouth, St George's Hall	Nickleby, Trial
January 7 Tuesday	Plymouth, St George's Hall	Copperfield
January 8 Wednesday	Torquay, Bath Saloon	Carol, Trial
January 9 Thursday	Torquay, Bath Saloon	Copperfield
January 10 Friday	Exeter, Royal Public Rooms	Nickleby, Trial
January 11 Saturday	Exeter, Royal Public Rooms	Copperfield
January 25 Saturday	Manchester, Free Trade hall	Nickleby, Trial

'Professional Readings (*cont.*)'

Date (1862–1863)	Venue	Programme
January 27 Monday	Liverpool, St George's Hall	Nickleby, Sawyer
January 28 Tuesday	Liverpool, St George's Hall	Copperfield, Sawyer
January 29 Wednesday	Liverpool, St George's Hall	Nickleby, Trial
January 30 Thursday	Chester, Music Hall	Nickleby, Trial
March 13 Thursday	London, St James's Hall	Copperfield, Sawyer
March 20 Thursday	London, St James's Hall	Copperfield, Sawyer
March 27 Thursday	London, St James's Hall	Copperfield, Sawyer
April 3 Thursday	London, St James's Hall	Copperfield, Sawyer
April 10 Thursday	London, St James's Hall	Copperfield, Trial
April 24 Thursday	London, St James's Hall	Nickleby, Trial
May 7 Wednesday	London, St James's Hall	Copperfield
May 17 Saturday	London, St James's Hall	Nickleby, Boots, Sawyer
May 21 Wednesday (mat)	London, St James's Hall	Copperfield
June 6 Friday	London, St James's Hall	Copperfield, Sawyer
June 19 Thursday	London, St James's Hall	Carol, Trial
1863		
March 6 Friday	London, Hanover Square Rooms	Copperfield, Sawyer
March 11 Wednesday	London, Hanover Square Rooms	Nickleby, Boots
March 13 Friday	London, Hanover Square Rooms	Dombey, Trial
April 21 Tuesday	London, Hanover Square Rooms	Copperfield, Sawyer

'Professional Readings (*cont.*)'

Date (1863, 1866)	Venue	Programme
April 23 Thursday	London, Hanover Square Rooms	Nickleby, Boots
April 28 Tuesday	London, Hanover Square Rooms	Carol, Trial
April 30 Thursday	London, Hanover Square Rooms	—[b]
May 5 Tuesday	London, Hanover Square Rooms	Nickleby, Boots
May 8 Friday	London, Hanover Square Rooms	—[b]
May 15 Friday	London, Hanover Square Rooms	Dombey, Trial
May 22 Friday	London, Hanover Square Rooms	Carol, Trial
May 29 Friday	London, Hanover Square Rooms	Copperfield, Sawyer
June 5 Friday	London, Hanover Square Rooms	Nickleby, Boots
June 12 Friday	London, Hanover Square Rooms	Poor Traveller, Gamp, Trial
June 27	London, St James's Hall	Nickleby, Boots, Gamp
1866		
March 23 Friday	Cheltenham, Assembly Rooms	Copperfield, Trial
March 24 Saturday	Cheltenham, Assembly Rooms	Dombey
April 10 Tuesday	London, St James's Hall	Marigold, Sawyer
April 11 Wednesday	Liverpool, St George's Hall	Marigold, Nickleby
April 12 Thursday	Manchester, Free Trade Hall	Marigold, Nickleby
April 13 Friday	Liverpool, St George's Hall	Copperfield, Trial

Date (1866)	Venue	Programme
April 14 Saturday	Liverpool, St George's Hall	Dombey
April 17 Tuesday	Glasgow, City Hall	Marigold, Sawyer
April 18 Wednesday	Edinburgh, Music Hall	Marigold, Nickleby
April 19 Thursday	Glasgow, City Hall	Carol, Trial
April 20 Friday	Edinburgh, Queen Street Hall	Boots, Sawyer, Trial
April 21 Saturday	Edinburgh, Queen Street Hall	Copperfield
April 24 Tuesday	London, St James's Hall	Marigold, Trial
April 26 Thursday	Manchester, Free Trade Hall	Boots, Sawyer, Trial
April 27 Friday	Liverpool, St George's Hall	Marigold, Nickleby
April 28 Saturday (mat)	Liverpool, St George's Hall	Copperfield, Trial
May 1 Tuesday	London, St James's Hall	Copperfield, Boots
May 2 Wednesday	London, Crystal Palace	Dombey
May 4 Friday	Greenwich, Literary Institution	Marigold, Trial
May 9 Wednesday	Clifton, Victoria Rooms	Marigold, Nickleby
May 10 Thursday	Birmingham, Town Hall	Marigold, Nickleby, Trial
May 11 Friday	Clifton, Victoria Rooms	Copperfield, Trial
May 14 Monday	London, St James's Hall	Marigold, Sawyer
May 16 Wednesday	Aberdeen, Music Hall	Copperfield, Trial
May 18 Friday	Glasgow, City Hall	Marigold, Trial
May 19 Saturday	Edinburgh, Music Hall	Marigold, Trial
May 22 Tuesday	London, St James's Hall	Carol, Trial

'Professional Readings (*cont.*)'

Date (1866–1867)	Venue	Programme
May 24 Thursday	Portsmouth, St George's Hall	Marigold, Sawyer
May 25 Friday	Portsmouth, St George's Hall	Copperfield, Trial
May 29 Tuesday	London, St James's Hall	Marigold, Nickleby
June 5 Tuesday	London, St James's Hall	Copperfield, Boots
June 12 Tuesday	London, St James's Hall	Marigold, Trial
1867		
January 15 Tuesday	London, St James's Hall	Barbox, Boy
January 17 Thursday	Liverpool, St George's Hall	Barbox, Boy
January 18 Friday	Liverpool, St George's Hall	Marigold, Trial
January 19 Saturday	Liverpool, St George's Hall	Carol
January 22 Tuesday	Chester, Music Hall	Marigold, Trial
January 23 Wednesday	Wolverhampton, Exchange	Barbox, Boy
January 25 Friday	Leicester, Temperance Hall	Marigold, Trial
January 29 Tuesday	London, St James's Hall	Barbox, Boy
January 31 Thursday	Leeds, Music Hall	Barbox, Boy
February 1 Friday	Leeds, Music Hall	Marigold, Trial
February 2 Saturday	Manchester, Free Trade Hall	Marigold, Trial
February 8 Friday	Bath, Assembly Rooms	Marigold, Trial
February 9 Saturday	Bath, Assembly Rooms	Copperfield
February 12 Tuesday	London, St James's Hall	Marigold, Trial
February 13 Wednesday	Birmingham, Town Hall	Carol, Boy
February 14 Thursday	Liverpool, St George's Hall	Marigold, Trial
February 15 Friday	Liverpool, St George's Hall	Copperfield, Boy
February 16 Saturday	Manchester, Free Trade Hall	Carol, Boy
February 18 Monday	Glasgow, City Hall	Copperfield, Boy
February 21 Thursday	Glasgow, City Hall	Marigold, Trial
February 22 Friday	Edinburgh, Music Hall	Marigold, Trial

Date (1867)	Venue	Programme
February 23 Saturday	Edinburgh, Queen Street Hall	Barbox, Boy
February 26 Tuesday	London, St James's Hall	Copperfield, Sawyer
February 28 Thursday	York, Festival Concert Room	Marigold, Trial
March 1 Friday	Bradford, St George's Hall	Marigold, Trial
March 4 Monday	Newcastle-on-Tyne, Music Hall	Marigold, Trial
March 5 Tuesday	Newcastle-on-Tyne, Music Hall	Carol, Sawyer
March 7 Thursday	Wakefield, Corn Exchange	Marigold, Trial
March 12 Tuesday	London, St James's Hall	Carol, Boots
March 15 Friday	Dublin, Rotunda	Marigold, Trial
March 18 Monday	Dublin, Rotunda	Copperfield, Sawyer
March 20 Wednesday	Belfast, Ulster Hall	Marigold, Trial
March 22 Friday	Dublin, Rotunda	Carol, Trial
March 26 Tuesday	London, St James's Hall	Marigold, Trial
March 28 Thursday	Cambridge, Guildhall	Marigold, Trial
March 29 Friday	Norwich, St Andrew's Hall	Marigold, Trial
April 3 Wednesday	Gloucester, Theatre Royal	Marigold, Trial
April 4 Thursday	Swansea, Music Hall	Marigold, Trial
April 5 Friday	Cheltenham, Assembly Rooms	Marigold, Trial
April 6 Saturday	Cheltenham, Assembly Rooms	Carol
April 8 Monday	London, St James's Hall	Copperfield, Sawyer
April 10 Wednesday	Worcester, Music Hall	Marigold, Trial
April 11 Thursday	Hereford, Shire Hall	Marigold, Trial
April 12 Friday	Clifton, Victoria Rooms	Marigold, Trial
April 25 Thursday	Preston, Theatre Royal	Marigold, Trial
April 26 Friday	Blackburn, Town Hall	Marigold, Trial
April 29 Monday	London, St James's Hall	Nickleby, Trial

'Professional Readings (*cont.*)'

Date (1867)	Venue	Programme
April 30 Tuesday	Stoke	__ *c*
May 1 Wednesday	Hanley, Mechanics' Hall	Marigold, Trial
May 2 Thursday	Warrington, Public Hall	Marigold, Trial
May 8 Wednesday	Croydon, Public Hall	Copperfield, Trial
May 13 Monday	London, St James's Hall	Dombey, Sawyer

a+Trial? No further record.
*b*Programme undiscovered.
*c*Advertised in *All The Year Round*, but no performance record found.

USA TOUR

Date	Venue	Programme
1867		
December 2 Monday	Boston, Tremont Temple	Carol, Trial
December 3 Tuesday	Boston, Tremont Temple	Copperfield, Sawyer
December 5 Thursday	Boston, Tremont Temple	Nickleby, Boots
December 6 Friday	Boston, Tremont Temple	Dombey, Trial
December 9 Monday	New York, Steinway Hall	Carol, Trial
December 10 Tuesday	New York, Steinway Hall	Copperfield, Sawyer
December 12 Thursday	New York, Steinway Hall	Nickleby, Boots
December 13 Friday	New York, Steinway Hall	Dombey, Trial
December 16 Monday	New York, Steinway Hall	Carol, Trial
December 17 Tuesday	New York, Steinway Hall	Copperfield, Sawyer
December 19 Thursday	New York, Steinway Hall	Nickleby, Boots

Date (1867–1868)	Venue	Programme
December 20 Friday	New York, Steinway Hall	Dombey, Trial
December 23 Monday	Boston, Tremont Temple	Copperfield, Sawyer
December 24 Tuesday	Boston, Tremont Temple	Carol, Trial
December 26 Thursday	New York, Steinway Hall	Carol, Trial
December 27 Friday	New York, Steinway Hall	Nickleby, Sawyer
December 28 Saturday	New York, Steinway Hall	Copperfield, Boots
December 30 Monday	New York, Steinway Hall	Nickleby, Boots
December 31 Tuesday	New York, Steinway Hall	Copperfield, Sawyer
1868		
January 2 Thursday	New York, Steinway Hall	Marigold, Trial
January 3 Friday	New York, Steinway Hall	Carol, Boots
January 6 Monday	Boston, Tremont Temple	Carol, Trial
January 7 Tuesday	Boston, Tremont Temple	Nickleby, Sawyer
January 9 Thursday	New York, Steinway Hall	Marigold, Trial
January 10 Friday	New York, Steinway Hall	Nickleby, Boots
January 13 Monday	Philadelphia, Concert Hall	Carol, Trial
January 14 Tuesday	Philadelphia, Concert Hall	Copperfield, Sawyer
January 16 Thursday	Brooklyn, Plymouth Church	Carol, Trial
January 17 Friday	Brooklyn, Plymouth Church	Copperfield, Sawyer
January 20 Monday	Brooklyn, Plymouth Church	Marigold, Trial
January 21 Tuesday	Brooklyn, Plymouth Church	Nickleby, Boots
January 23 Thursday	Philadelphia, Concert Hall	Nickleby, Boots

'USA Tour (*cont.*)'

Date (1868)	Venue	Programme
January 24 Friday	Philadelphia, Concert Hall	Dombey, Trial
January 27 Monday	Baltimore, Concordia Opera House	Carol, Trial
January 28 Tuesday	Baltimore, Concordia Opera House	Copperfield, Sawyer
January 30 Thursday	Philadelphia, Concert Hall	Marigold, Sawyer
January 31 Friday	Philadelphia, Concert Hall	Copperfield, Boots
February 3 Monday	Washington, D. C., Carroll Hall	Carol, Trial
February 4 Tuesday	Washington, D. C., Carroll Hall	Copperfield, Sawyer
February 6 Thursday	Washington, D. C., Carroll Hall	Marigold, Trial
February 7 Friday	Washington, D. C., Carroll Hall	Nickleby, Boots
February 10 Monday	Baltimore, Concordia, Opera House	Marigold, Trial
February 11 Tuesday	Baltimore, Concordia Opera House	Nickleby, Boots
February 13 Thursday	Philadelphia, Concert Hall	Carol, Boots
February 14 Friday	Philadelphia, Concert Hall	Marigold, Trial
February 18 Tuesday	Hartford, Allyn Hall	Carol, Trial
February 20 Thursday	Providence, City Hall	Carol, Trial
February 21 Friday	Providence, City Hall	Marigold, Sawyer
February 24 Monday	Boston, Tremont Temple	Marigold, Trial
February 25 Tuesday	Boston, Tremont Temple	Copperfield, Sawyer
February 27 Thursday	Boston, Tremont Temple	Carol, Boots
February 28 Friday	Boston, Tremont Temple	Nickleby, Trial
March 9 Monday	Syracuse, Wieting Hall	Carol, Trial
March 10 Tuesday	Rochester, Corinthian Hall	Carol, Trial
March 12 Thursday	Buffalo, St James's Hall	Carol, Trial

Date (1868)	Venue	Programme
March 13 Friday	Buffalo, St James's Hall	Marigold, Sawyer
March 16 Monday	Rochester, Corinthian Hall	Marigold, Sawyer
March 18 Wednesday	Albany, Twiddle Hall	Carol, Trial
March 19 Thursday	Albany, Twiddle Hall	Marigold, Sawyer
March 20 Friday	Springfield (Mass.), Music Hall	Carol, Trial
March 23 Monday	Worcester, Mechanics Hall	Carol, Trial
March 24 Tuesday	New Haven, Music Hall	Marigold, Sawyer
March 25 Wednesday	Hartford , Allyn Hall	Marigold, Sawyer
March 27 Friday	New Bedford, Liberty Hall	Carol, Trial
March 30 Monday	Portland, City Hall	Carol, Trial
April 1 Wednesday	Boston, Tremont Temple	Carol, Trial
April 2 Thursday	Boston, Tremont Temple	Nickleby, Boots
April 3 Friday	Boston, Tremont Temple	Marigold, Gamp
April 6 Monday	Boston, Tremont Temple	Copperfield, Sawyer
April 7 Tuesday	Boston, Tremont Temple	Dombey, Trial
April 8 Wednesday	Boston, Tremont Temple	Marigold, Gamp
April 13 Monday	New York, Steinway Hall	Marigold, Gamp
April 14 Tuesday	New York, Steinway Hall	Nickleby, Boots
April 16 Thursday	New York, Steinway Hall	Copperfield, Sawyer
April 17 Friday	New York, Steinway Hall	Marigold, Gamp
April 20 Monday	New York, Steinway Hall	Carol, Trial

FAREWELL TOUR

Date (1868)	Venue	Programme
October 6 Tuesday	London, St James's Hall	Marigold, Trial
October 10 Saturday	Manchester, Free Trade Hall	Marigold, Trial
October 12 Monday	Liverpool, St George's Hall	Marigold, Trial
October 13 Tuesday	Liverpool, St George's Hall	Copperfield, Sawyer
October 14 Wednesday	Liverpool, St George's Hall	Nickleby, Boots
October 17 Saturday	Manchester, Free Trade Hall	Copperfield, Gamp
October 19 Monday	Brighton, Grand Concert Hall	Marigold, Trial
October 20 Tuesday	London, St James's Hall	Copperfield, Gamp
October 22 Thursday	Brighton, Grand Concert Hall	Copperfield, Gamp
October 24 Saturday	Manchester, Free Trade Hall	Nickleby, Sawyer
October 26 Monday	Liverpool, St George's Hall	Carol, Gamp
October 27 Tuesday	Liverpool, St George's Hall	Dombey, Sawyer
October 28 Wednesday	Liverpool, St George's Hall	Copperfield, Chops
October 31 Saturday	Manchester, Free Trade Hall	Carol, Trial
November 2 Monday	Brighton, Grand Concert Hall	Nickleby, Sawyer
November 3 Tuesday	London, St James's Hall	Nickleby, Boots
November 7 Saturday	Brighton, Grand Concert Hall	Carol, Boots
November 17 Tuesday	London, St James's Hall	Dombey, Sawyer

Date (1868–1869)	Venue	Programme
December 1 Tuesday	London, St James's Hall	Carol, Chops
December 7 Monday	Edinburgh, Music Hall	Marigold, Trial
December 9 Wednesday	Glasgow, City Hall	Carol, Trial
December 11 Friday	Edinburgh, Music Hall	Copperfield, Gamp
December 14 Monday	Edinburgh, Music Hall	Nickleby, Sawyer
December 15 Tuesday	Glasgow, City Hall	Copperfield, Sawyer
December 16 Wednesday	Glasgow, City Hall	Marigold, Gamp
December 17 Thursday	Glasgow, City Hall	Nickleby, Trial
December 19 Saturday	Edinburgh, Music Hall	Carol, Boots
December 22 Tuesday	London, St James's Hall	Carol, Trial
1869		
January 5 Tuesday	London, James's Hall	Boots, Sikes, Gamp
January 8 Friday	Belfast, Ulster Hall	Carol, Trial
January 11 Monday	Dublin, Rotunda	Carol, Trial
January 12 Tuesday	Dublin, Rotunda	Copperfield, Sawyer
January 13 Wednesday	Dublin, Rotunda	Boots, Sikes, Gamp
January 15 Friday	Belfast, Ulster Hall	Copperfield, Sawyer
January 19 Tuesday	London, St James's Hall	Chimes, Trial
January 20 Wednesday	Clifton, Victoria Rooms	Boots, Sikes, Sawyer
January 21 Thursday	Newport, Victoria Assembly Rooms	Carol, Trial
January 22 Friday	Cheltenham, Assembly Rooms	Boots, Sikes, Gamp
January 25 Monday	Clifton, Victoria Rooms	Copperfield, Trial
January 27 Wednesday	Torquay, Royal Assembly Rooms	Marigold, Trial

'Farewell Tour *(cont.)*'

Date (1869)	Venue	Programme
January 29 Friday	Bath, Assembly Rooms	Boots, Sikes, Sawyer
January 30 Saturday	Bath, Assembly Rooms	Carol, Gamp
February 2 Tuesday	London, St James's Hall	Copperfield, Chops
February 4 Thursday	Nottingham, Mechanics' Hall	Marigold, Trial
February 5 Friday	Leicester, Temperance Hall	Boots, Sikes, Sawyer
February 22 Monday	Glasgow, City Hall	Boots, Sikes, Gamp
February 24 Wednesday	Edinburgh, Music Hall	Boots, Sikes, Gamp
February 25 Thursday	Glasgow, City Hall	Poor Traveller, Sikes, Sawyer
February 26 Friday	Edinburgh, Music Hall	Sikes, Carol
March 2 Tuesday	London, St James's Hall	Boots, Sikes, Gamp
March 4 Thursday	Wolverhampton, Exchange Hall	Marigold, Trial
March 6 Saturday	Manchester, Free Trade Hall	Boots, Sikes, Gamp
March 8 Monday	Manchester Free Trade Hall	Nickleby, Chops
March 10 Wednesday	Hull, Music Hall	Boots, Sikes, Gamp
March 11 Thursday	York, Festival Concert Room	Boots, Sikes, Gamp
March 16 Tuesday	London, St James's Hall	Boots, Sikes, Gamp
March 17 Wednesday	Ipswich, Public Hall	Marigold, Trial
March 18 Thursday	Cambridge, Guildhall	Boots, Sikes, Gamp

Date (1869–1870)	Venue	Programme
March 20 Saturday	Manchester, Free Trade Hall	Marigold, Trial
March 22 Monday	Manchester, Free Trade Hall	Sikes, Carol
March 30 Tuesday	London, St James's Hall	Dombey, Sawyer
March 31 Wednesday	Sheffield, Music Hall	Boots, Sikes, Gamp
April 1 Thursday	Birmingham, Town Hall	Boots, Sikes, Sawyer
April 2 Friday	Birmingham, Town Hall	Nickleby, Trial
April 5 Monday	Liverpool, Theatre Royal	Boots, Sikes, Sawyer
April 6 Tuesday	Liverpool, Theatre Royal	Marigold, Trial
April 8 Thursday	Liverpool, Theatre Royal	Boots, Sikes, Gamp
April 9 Friday	Liverpool, Theatre Royal	Carol, Sikes
April 13 Tuesday	London, St James's Hall	Boots, Sikes, Gamp
April 16 Friday	Leeds, Mechanics' Institution	Boots, Sikes, Sawyer
April 19 Monday	Blackburn, Exchange Assembly Rooms	Carol, Sawyer
April 20 Tuesday	Bolton, Temperance Hall	Marigold, Trial
1870		
January 11 Tuesday	London, St James's Hall	Copperfield, Trial
January 14 Friday	London, St James's Hall	Carol
January 18 Tuesday	London, St James's Hall	Marigold, Sawyer
January 21 Friday	London, St James's Hall	Boots, Sikes
January 25 Tuesday	London, St James's Hall	Nickleby, Chops
February 1 Tuesday	London, St James's Hall	Boots, Sikes, Gamp

'Farewell Tour (*cont.*)'

Date (1870)	Venue	Programme
February 8 Tuesday	London, St James's Hall	Dombey, Sawyer
February 15 Tuesday	London, St James's Hall	Boots, Sikes, Gamp
February 22 Tuesday	London, St James's Hall	Nickleby, Chops
March 1 Tuesday	London, St James's Hall	Copperfield, Trial
March 8 Tuesday	London, St James's Hall	Boots, Sikes, Sawyer
March 15 Tuesday	London, St James's Hall	Carol, Trial

Abbreviations

The place of publication is London, unless indicated otherwise.

Collins, *Readings*	Philip Collins (ed.), *Charles Dickens: The Public Readings* (Oxford, 1975).
Collins, *I&R*	Philip Collins (ed.), *Dickens: Interviews and Recollections* (2 vols., Houndmills, 1981).
Dolby	George Dolby, *Charles Dickens as I Knew Him: The Story of the Reading Tours 1866-1870* (1885).
Field	Kate Field, *Pen Photographs of Charles Dickens's Readings* (Boston, 1868; ed. Carolyn Moss, New York, 1998).
Forster	John Forster, *The Life of Charles Dickens*, ed. J. W. T. Ley (1928).
Kent	Charles Kent, *Charles Dickens as a Reader* (1872).
Letters	*The Letters of Charles Dickens*, ed. Madeline House, Graham Storey et al. (12 vols., Oxford, 1965–2002).
Speeches	K. J. Fielding (ed.), *The Speeches of Charles Dickens: A Complete Edition* (Hemel Hempstead, 1988).

Notes

The place of publication is London, unless indicated otherwise.

PREFACE AND ACKNOWLEDGEMENTS

p. vii **Henry Dickens reading the *Carol*:** David Dickens, 'Dickens was Dead: To Begin With', *Dickensian* 89(1993), 207–13.

p. viii **'Gently, slowly the book...':** 'Dick Donovan', *Pages from an Adventurous Life* (1907), 53.

A PREMIERE: NEW YORK, DECEMBER 1867

p. 1 **'A little, trim-looking gentleman...':** H. H. Boone, Review of a Reading, *Albany Evening Journal*, 21 March 1868: *Letters* XII, 80, n. 4.

'Like a comet... *in* it': R. Shelton MacKenzie, *Life of Charles Dickens* (Philadelphia, 1870), 298.

'The Europiăn...': To W. H. Wills, 10 & 11 December 1867: *Letters* XI, 507.

'An admirable mixture...': To Mary Dickens, 11 December 1867: *Letters* XI, 508.

'One might be living...': To Forster, 15 December 1867: *Letters* XI, 511.

p. 2 **'The platform absorbs...':** To W. H. Wills, 10 and 11 December 1867: *Letters* XI, 507.

'New York is grown...': Ibid.

'The brightest chapter...': Dolby, 155.

New York queue sizes: see [Walter Dexter] 'Dickens as a Reader', *Dickensian* 23(1927), 276.

The ticket speculators: see *New York Post*, 11 December 1867.

$20 dollar place in the queue: George William Curtis (political editor, *Harper's Weekly*), 'Dickens Reading' [1867], *From the Easy Chair* (1892), 49.

Singing and dancing in the queues: see Dolby, 164–6.

p. 3 **'Taking the bearings':** Kent, 266.

'My hardest hall': To Georgina Hogarth, 12 January 1868: *Letters* XI, 9.

p. 4 **'If you were to behold...':** To Mary Dickens, 11 December 1867: *Letters* XI, 508.

Scott and Dickens arriving at Steinway: E. F. Payne, *Dickens Days in Boston*, (Boston and New York, 1927), 214: Payne is actually describing Dickens's arrival at his Boston Reading venue, but the routine would have been similar for New York.

Quarter of an hour tuning up: Dolby, 346.

'Five dollars downstairs . . . ': *New York Herald*, 10 December 1867.

Speculators and police quiet: George William Curtis, op. cit., 44.

p. 5 *Long climb to auditorium . . . 'Where . . . ticket?'*: Field, 11.

Brooklyn friends and storm: Edwin Coggleshall, 'Some Evenings with Dickens in New York', *Dickensian* 16 (1920), 202.

Human sea: *New York Tribune*, 10 December 1867.

Gas-burners turned up: Curtis, op. cit., 46.

Dickens's gliding entry: *Portland Transcript*, 4 February 1868.

Head partly down: *New York Post*, 10 December 1867.

p. 6 *Hair brushed . . . gale behind*: Mark Twain, 'Charles Dickens', *Alta California*, 5 February 1868: Twain heard Dickens read 'Copperfield' at Steinway Hall on 31 December 1867.

Lively eyes and 'juicy' nose: *Worcester Evening Gazette*, 24 March 1868.

Eyes like diamonds . . . taking all in: C. J. Hamilton, 'How I heard Charles Dickens Read,' *Chambers's Journal*, October 1926, 683.

Glinting shirt-studs: *Limerick Reporter & Tipperary Vindicator*, 3 September 1858.

Dickens's glance, 'taking stock': R. Shelton MacKenzie, op. cit., 272.

Rolling eyes: *New York Evening Post*, 10 December 1867.

Dickens's introduction: Edwin Coggleshall, op. cit., 201.

p. 7 *Husky voice*: Field, 17.

Lisp; and as if telling story for first time: *New York Times*, 10 December 1867.

Rising inflection: Coggleshall, op. cit., 201.

Right hand moving: Curtis, op. cit., 201.

Like a parlour reading: *New York Times*, 10 December 1867.

Reading becomes acting: Ibid.

Magnetic current: Field, 17.

Like a great turtle:: Henry M. Field, *Summer Pictures: From Copenhagen to Venice* (New York, 1860), 32.

Lisping Bob Cratchit: Field, 18.

A blind man could see . . .: *New York Herald*, 10 December 1867.

Rubs and pats his fingers . . .: *Portland Transcript*, 4 February 1868.

Stirs the gravy . . . sniffs the pudding: *New York Times*, 10 December 1867.

The smell of the feast: *New York Post*, 10 December 1867.

p. 8 *The 'wonderful' smile*: *Springfield Semi-Weekly Republican*, 21 March 1868.

CHAPTER 1: A COMMUNITY OF READERS

p. 9 'To commune with you...': Dickens's announcement that he is discontinuing *Master Humphrey's Clock*, October 1841. Reprinted in full in J. Butt and K. Tillotson, *Dickens at Work* (1968), 88–9.

p. 10 'Will you try...': To Forster [30 March 1858]: *Letters* VIII, 539.
'I have long held...': *Speeches*, 264, 29 April 1858.
'Ladies and gentlemen...': *Speeches*, 413.

p. 11 'A literary form attuned...': Linda Hughes and Michael Lund, *The Victorian Serial* (1991), 8. Hughes and Lund also see in serialization a structure attuned to actual female experience in an era when women were major consumers of literature—menstrual cycles and the rhythmical patterns of feminine rather than masculine sexual pleasure: See their 'Textual/Sexual Pleasure and Serial Publication,' in J. O. Jordan and R. L. Patten (eds.), *Literature in the Marketplace* (Cambridge, 1995), 143–64.
'The assumption...evolutionary time)': Hughes and Lund, op. cit., 4–5.

p. 12 'Perpetually defers desire...': Roger Hagendorn, 'Technology and Economic Exploitation: the Serial as a Form of Narrative Presentation', *Wide Angle*, 10 (4) (1988), 5: cited in Jennifer Hayward, *Consuming Pleasures: Active Audiences and Serial Fictions from Dickens to Soap Opera* (Kentucky, 1997), 2.
'Reading did not occur...': Hughes and Lund, op. cit., 8–9.

p. 13 'Reading and living...': Robert Darnton, *The Kiss of Lamourette: Reflections in Cultural History* (1990), 157.

p. 14 'It tended to deflect...critical confrontation...of modern life': Christopher A. Kent, 'Victorian Periodicals and the Constructing of Victorian Reality', in J. Don Vann and Rosemary T. Van Arsdel (eds.), *Victorian Periodicals: A Guide to Research,* vol. 2 (New York, 1989), 1–2.
'To shew people coming together...': To Forster, 19 August 1857: *Letters* VII, 692–3.

p. 15 'The characters and scenes...': *National Magazine* (December 1837), 83: quoted in Jennifer Hayward, op. cit., 37.
'The literary and the social...': Laman Blanchard, 'Charles Dickens', *Ainsworth's Magazine* (January 1844), 84.
'Reading one instalment...': Hughes and Lund, op. cit., 11.

'It is not a mere healthy . . . ': *The North British Review*, 3 May 1845, 85: quoted in Jennifer Hayward, 26: 'Warren' refers to Samuel Warren, author of the hugely popular serialized novel *Ten Thousand a Year* (1839–41).

p. 16 'We had sometimes . . . ': To the Editor of *Daily News*, 11 July 1849: *Letters* V, 570.

'His method of composing . . . ': *Illustrated London News*, 18 June 1870.

p. 17 'Very few things . . . ': To Arthur Helps, 30 November 1868: *Letters* XII, 228.

p. 18 'The author of a periodical . . . contributed to their amusement': 'Preface to the Original Edition', *Nicholas Nickleby*, ed. Michael Slater (Harmondsworth, 1978), 46–7.

p. 19 'The complex temporal involutions . . . ': Jennifer Hayward, op. cit., 2.

p. 20 'In the case of *Middlemarch* . . . ': quoted in Hughes and Lund, op. cit., 11.

Half a million was the estimate of Dickens's regular readership: *Bentley's Monthly Review,* October 1853.

'Imagined community . . . popular newspaper': Benedict Anderson, *Imagined Communities: Reflections on the Origin and Spread of Nationalism* (1983), 39 & n. 60.

'What a thing it is to have Power': To Mrs Charles Dickens, 2 December 1844: *Letters* IV, 235.

p. 21 'To assist in the Discussion . . . ': Advert for *All The Year Round* in *Illustrated London News*, 17 September 1859, 273.

'We get on now . . . ': Anthony Trollope, *The Warden* (1962), 147.

'I believe that . . . ': Speech to Administrative Reform Association, 27 June 1855: *Speeches*, 202–3.

'Dickens's readings were not . . . ': Helen Small, 'Dickens and a Pathology of the Mid-Victorian Reading Public', in J. Raven, H. Small and N. Tadmor (eds.), *The Practice and Representation of Reading in England* (Cambridge, 1966), 266.

p. 22 **John Sutherland:** see *Victorian Fiction: Writers, Publishers, Readers* (1995), 87–8.

'Spoilt the novel sale' . . . standard three-volume form: To Thomas Mitton, 23 August 1841: *Letters* II, 365–6.

p. 23 'In monthly parts . . . ': To Thomas Mitton, 30 August 1841: *Letters* II, 372.

'Labour of love . . . Weekly Numbers': The announcement, published in October 1841, was composed the previous month. See Butt and Tillotson, op. cit., 87–9.

'Sense of intimacy . . . ': S. Connor, *Charles Dickens* (Oxford, 1985), 167.

'The interest of such a character...': To Maclise, 8 July 1857: *Letters* VIII, 367.

p. 24 'To read a new...': To F. M. Evans, 16 March 1858: *Letters* VIII, 533.

'The wish to have...': *Speeches*, 166.

'Passengers' altered to 'travellers': *A Christmas Carol: The Public Reading Version*, Intro and Notes by Philip Collins (New York, 1971), 9.

'My countrymen...house-hold gods': See *Letters* II, 389 n: the paragraph containing this sentence was cancelled in proof.

p. 25 'Writers could gauge...greater unity of his text': Bradley Deane, *The Making of the Victorian Novelist: Anxieties of Authorship in the Mass Market* (2003), 51–4: the *Prospective Review* quotation is from the July 1851 issue.

p. 26 'Mr Pickwick's Stage Manager': 'Address' to the Reader, in the January 1837 monthly number of *Pickwick*: reprt. in the Everyman Dickens edition, ed. Malcolm Andrews (1998), 818–9.

'To settle down...my command': Charles Kent anecdote: in T. E. Pemberton, *Charles Dickens and the Stage* (1888), 100.

p. 27 'Always a leader...': Forster, 44.

'I had regular plots...': To Forster, 26 May [1842]: *Letters* II, 246.

'Almost ubiquitous...': Pemberton, op. cit., 121.

p. 28 'I have often thought...': To Forster, ?30–31 December 1844 and 1 January 1845: *Letters* IV, 244.

'Charley, you carry...': Amy Woolner, *Thomas Woolner, R. A.: His Life in Letters* (1917), 232–3.

p. 29 'The Shadow...at everybody's elbow': To Forster, [7 October 1849]: *Letters* V, 622–3.

'Showed once more...': Arthur Waugh, *A Hundred Years of Publishing: Being the Story of Chapman and Hall Ltd* (1930), 121.

'We just surrender...': Vladimir Nabokov, '*Bleak House* (1852–1853)': reprt. in Michael Hollington (ed.), *Charles Dickens: Critical Assessments* (Mountfield, 1995), III, 145, 147.

p. 30 'The loudness of Dickens's voice...': Robert Garis, *The Dickens Theatre* (Oxford, 1965), 14.

'The obvious effect...': *Illustrated London News*, 18 June 1870.

p. 31 'We aspire to live...': 'A Preliminary Word', *The Amusements of the People and Other Papers*, ed. Michael Slater, Vol. 2 of the Dent Uniform Edition of *Dickens' Journalism* (1996), 177. Hereafter cited as *Journalism*.

'No one thinks first...': Charles Eliot Norton, 'Charles Dickens', *North American Review*, 106 (April 1868), 671.

'A friend of mine...': Henry Fielding Dickens, 'The Social Influence of Dickens', *Dickensian* 1 (1905), 63.

p. 32 'A personal affection...': To Miss Burdett Coutts, 27 October 1858: *Letters* VIII, 689.

p. 33 'I was thinking the other day...': To Forster, [11 October 1846]: *Letters* IV, 631.

'It was a substitution of lower for higher aims...': Forster, 641.

'My experience has taught me...': *The Journal of William Charles Macready*, ed. J. C. Trewin (1967), xv–xvi.

Actors first classed as professional men in 1861: See Michael Baker, *The Rise of the Victorian Actor* (1978), 140.

Mimicry, spectacle and ostentation...targets for puritanical distrust: See Jonas Baring, *The Anti-Theatrical Prejudice* (Berkeley, California, 1981), 299.

p. 34 'The Victorian fascination with the theatre...suggest artifice': Alison Byerly, 'From Schoolroom to Stage: Reading Aloud and the Domestication of Victorian Theatre', in P. Scott and P. Fletcher (eds.), *Culture and Education in Victorian England* (Lewisberg, 1990), 125–6.

'I think it...bad character': *Report of Select Committee on Dramatic Literature* 1832, 27: quoted in E. Halevy, *England in 1815* (1961), 504 n.

p. 35 'MATHEWS: Formerly...it is now': 'Minutes of Evidence' from *Select Committee*, 2 July 1832: in *Memoirs of Charles Mathews, Comedian*, by Mrs Mathews (1839), IV, 488.

'A truly...solecism': *Christian Observer*, 24 (1824), 200.

p. 36 'A dangerous elevation of the fancy': *Christian Observer*, 7 (1808); see pp. 326–34 for the *Observer*'s review of Thomas Bowdler's expurgated *Family Shakespeare*.

'By feeding...dissipation': *Christian Observer*, 14 (1815), 512–17.

'To shew...of the stage...with a good grace': William Hazlitt, 'On Actors and Acting', *Examiner*, 5 January 1817: *Selected Essays of William Hazlitt, 1778–1830*, ed. Geoffrey Keynes (1948), 687.

'An essentially theatrical...': Deborah Vlock, *Dickens, Novel Reading, and the Victorian Popular Theatre* (Cambridge, 1998), 59–60.

p. 37 'Reverent Victorians...': Nina Auerbach, *Private Theatricals: The Lives of the Victorians* (Harvard, 1990), 4.

'As opposed to the official feast...': M. Bakhtin, *Rabelais and His World*, tran. H. Islowsky (Indiana, 1984), 10.

p. 38 'A set of shifting...theatrical roles': Joseph Litvak, *Caught in the Act: Theatricality in the Nineteenth-Century English Novel* (California, 1992), p. xii.

'The only honest hypocrites': Hazlitt, op. cit., 686.

p. 39 'One of our most remarkable Insularities...': 'Insularities', *Household Worlds* 19 January 1856: *Journalism* 3, 342–3.

p. 40 'He paints the outside . . . ': *Bath Chronicle*, 4 February 1869.

'Very miserable . . . ': To Mrs Cowden Clarke, 22 July 1848: *Letters* V, 374.

p. 41 'I have a turning notion . . . ': To Wilkie Collins, 21 March 1858: *Letters* VIII, 536.

' . . . experience of Houselessness': 'Night Walks', *Journalism* 4, 150.

'The descendant . . . ': 'Shy Neighbourhoods', *Journalism* 4, 119.

' . . . hearth-manqué . . . ': John Glavin, *After Dickens: Reading, Adaptation and Performance* (Cambridge, 1999), 212.

'It might be a wild . . . ': Forster, 641–2.

p. 42 'If it had any influence . . . ': To F. M. Evans, 16 March 58: *Letters* VIII, 533.

'The benevolent "reader" . . . ': *The Times*, 16 April 1858: *Letters* VIII, 542 n.

'Merchandise of himself . . . ': *Derby Mercury*, 27 October 1858.

'However people may cavil . . . ': *Shrewsbury Chronicle*, 13 August 1858.

'It has been objected . . . ': *Plymouth, Devonport, and Stonehouse Herald*, 7 August 1858.

p. 43 'Mr. Dickens, always fond . . . ': [J. Friswell], *Dickens: A Critical Biography*, (1858), 80.

p. 44 'Mr. Dickens has not hidden . . . none of us doubt': *Liverpool Daily Post*, 17 August 1858.

p. 45 **London labourer earnings:** see 'Wages and Cost of Living in the Victorian Era', J. Skipper and G. Landow, *The Victorian Web*, http://www.victorianweb.org/economics/wages2.html.

Dickens's income from his writings: R. L. Patten, 'The Sales of Dickens's Works', in Philip Collins (ed.), *Charles Dickens: The Critical Heritage* (1971), 620.

American earnings from Readings: See Dolby, 331–2.

Estate value: See Collins, *Readings*, p. xxix.

p. 46 'Worldly circumstances . . . consideration': To W. H. Wills, 6 June 1867: *Letters* XI, 377.

'There was nothing wrong . . . ': *Liverpool Daily Post*, 17 August 1858.

p. 47 'The audience was highly respectable . . . ': *Preston Guardian*, 14 December 1861.

'Mr Dickens has ever used . . . ': *Wolverhampton Chronicle*, 10 November 1858.

'To conceive . . . ': *The Constitution or Cork Advertiser*, 2 September 1858.

p. 48 **Huddersfield papers and Dickens's marriage:** *Huddersfield Weekly Chronicle*, 4 September 1858.

'**Mr. Dickens is performing . . .** ': Cutting from a Leeds newspaper ?September/October 1858, source untraced.

'**A widespread assumption . . .** ': Michael Baker, op. cit., 32.

p. 49 '**Certain fantastic notions . . .** ': Kent, 20 – 1.

'**Not only in this country . . .** ': *Leeds Mercury*, 17 April 1869.

'**His reading was not . . .** ': *Freeman's Journal* (Dublin), 14 January 1869.

'**I shall never recall . . .** ': *Speeches*, 384.

CHAPTER 2: READING, RECITING, ACTING

p. 50 '**[People] don't quite understand . . .** ': To Wilkie Collins, 11 August 1858: *Letters* VIII, 623.

'**As if . . . not reading . . .** ': *Belfast News-Letter*, 28 August 1858.

p. 52 **The most popular Penny-Readings authors:** See Thomas Wright, *Some Habits and Customs of the Working Classes* (1867), 168 – 83.

Chamberlain's Sam Weller: See Amy Cruse, *The Victorians and Their Books* (1935), 160.

'**Readers are abundant . . .** ': *The Times*, 7 October 1868.

p. 53 '**As the century wore on . . .** ': Martha L. Brunson, 'Novelists as Platform Readers: Dickens, Clemens, and Stowe', in David Thompson (ed.), *Performance of Literature in Historical Perspectives* (Maryland, 1983), 652.

' **. . . "useful knowledge"** ': H. P. Smith, *Literature and Adult Education a Century Ago* (Oxford, 1960), 35.

'**A great Educational Institution . . .** ': *Speeches*, 167.

'**I fancied I detected . . . creatures like themselves**': *Journalism*, 4, 144 – 5.

p. 54 '**Mr. Dickens scarce knows the force . . .** ': John Hollingshead, 'Mr.Charles Dickens As A Reader', *The Critic*, 4 September 1858.

'**For the use of members . . .** ': H. P. Smith, op. cit., 35.

p. 55 '**The formation of a working . . .** ': Ibid., 37.

' **. . . mothers . . . free admittance**': *Charles Kingsley: His Letters and Memories of his Life*, ed. by his Wife (1881), II, 190 – 1.

p. 56 '**Done almost to the death**': *The Suffolk Chronicle*, 20 March 1869.

Locksmith's shop reading circle: See Edgar Johnson, *Charles Dickens: His Tragedy and Triumph* (1953) I, 155.

p. 57 '**It turned out that she lodged . . .** ': Forster, 454.

Interviews with working classes: See Jonathan Rose, *The Intellectual Life of the British Working Classes* (Yale, 2001), 84.

'**What a pity . . .** ': James Staples, Letter to John Forster, 19 March 1872: Miscellaneous Manuscripts Collection (Collection No. 100), University of California, Los Angeles.

'It would have given me...': To J. V. Staples, 13 April 1844: *Letters* IV, 95.

p. 58 'My grandfather's whole family...': Herman Merivale, quoted in Percy Fitzgerald, *The History of Pickwick* (1891), 26.

'Many people met...': Philip Collins, 'Reading Aloud: A Victorian Metier', *Tennyson Society Monographs*, No. 5, (Lincoln, 1972), 27.

p. 59 'The tropes of the theatre...': Deborah Vlock, *Dickens, Novel Reading, and the Victorian Popular Theatre* (Cambridge, 1998), 3.

p. 61 'The theatrical developments... narratively': Ibid, 9.

'Hear Dickens, and die...': *The Scotsman*, 8 December 1868.

p. 62 Contemporary accounts and discussions of 'readings': see Philip Collins, 'Reading Aloud: A Victorian Metier', *Tennyson Society Monographs*, No 5, (Lincoln, 1972).

Readings by authors unprecedented: *The Times*, 2 January 1854.

'All our literati...': *Illustrated London News*, 15 May 1858.

p. 63 'It is also true...': Theresa Murphy, 'Interpretation in the Dickens Period', *Quarterly Journal of Speech*, 41 (1955), 246.

'On the stage... speaks all the words': Philip Collins, 'The Rev. John Chippendale Montesquieu Bellew', *The Listener*, 25 November 1971, 716.

'Poetry on Wheels': Edmund Yates, *Fifty Years of London Life* (New York, 1885), 267.

Bellew's Reading of *Drood*: *Brighton Gazette*, 8 September 1870.

p. 64 'Mr. Bellew for instance...': *Bath Chronicle*, 14 February 1867.

'The intrinsic repulsiveness... British classics': *Saturday Review*, 4 October 1862.

p. 65 'In my youth...': George R. Sims, *My Life* (1917), 310.

'Moralists know well...': *Athenaeum*, 12 February 1870.

'A sort of compromise...': *Belfast News-Letter*, 9 January 1869.

p. 66 'It was not a reading...': *Preston Pilot*, 14 December 1861.

'The stage was fitted up...': Bayle Bernard, *The Life of Samuel Lover* (1874), vol. I, 245.

p. 67 'I have always thought...': *Illustrated Times*, 16 February 1869.

P. B. Phillips and gestures: See *Athenaeum*, 17 April 1869.

'I have never... possess': Quoted in Kenneth Robinson, *Wilkie Collins: A Biography* (1951), 267–8.

'I don't flourish...': Quoted in N. Pharr Davis, *The Life of Wilkie Collins* (Urbana, Ill., 1956), 279.

p. 68 'The difference between... personal interview': *Preston Guardian*, 14 December 1861.

p. 69 'It was just as if we received...': *Illustrated London News*, 18 June 1870.

'To accompany you . . .': *Speeches*, 166.

'Nothing can be so delightful . . .': Ibid., 169.

p. 70 'That his audience would speedily . . .': *Brighton Gazette*, 18 November 1858.

'If you feel disposed . . .': *Speeches*, 169.

'[The Readings] continued . . .': Susan L. Ferguson, 'Dickens's Public Readings and the Victorian Author', *Studies in English Literature 1500–1900*, 41 (2001), 729–45: 744.

p. 71 'I cannot desire anything . . .': *Speeches*, 169.

'They would laugh . . .': *Brighton Gazette*, 18 November 1858.

'The absence of which . . .': Cuthbert Bede, 'Charles Dickens: A Reminiscence', *Dickensian*, 12 (1916), 208–9.

'In rather a condescending . . . easy laughing': *The Chester Chronicle*, 21 August 1858.

'We do not think his rendition . . .': *Syracuse Daily Standard*, 3 October 1868.

p. 72 'A mixed audience . . .': *Peterborough Advertiser*, 22 October 1859.

Coughing during 'Dr. Marigold': *The Ipswich Journal*, 20 March 1869.

'They very sensibly . . .': *The Worcester Herald*, 14 August 1858.

'Like the quiet narration . . .': *Torquay Directory & South Devon Journal*, 15 January 1862.

'He reads as if . . .': *Belfast News-Letter*, 28 August 1858.

'And—I—believe . . .': To Hon Mrs R. Watson, 13 January 1854: *Letters* VII, 244.

'I must go to Bradford . . .': To Hon Mrs R. Watson, 1 November 1854: Ibid, 454.

p. 73 'Every one seemed drawn . . .': J. T. Fields, *Biographical Notes and Personal Sketches* (1881), 153.

'Mr. Dickens carefully avoids . . .': *Northern Whig*, 21 March 1867.

'A dramatic monologue . . .': *Preston Guardian*, 14 December 1861.

p. 75 'Some hold that it should . . .': 'Mr. Dickens's Last Readings', *The Graphic*, 12 February 1870.

p. 76 'That it is the player's . . .': *Torquay Directory*, 20 January 1869.

'What would be pleasing . . . exaggeration': *Sheffield and Rotherham Independent*, 30 October 1858.

'Most people, we dare say . . .': Anon, *The Nation* (New York), 12 December 1867, 482.

p. 77 'Worthy of a minute study . . .': *The Times*, 17 January 1867.

p. 78 'Mr. Dickens is not a reader . . .': *Springfield Republican*, 21 March 1868.

Dickens's eyes on his audience: *Halifax Courier*, 18 September 1858.

'No mechanical drawback...': To Forster, [14 May 1867]: *Letters* XI, 366–7.

p. 79 'Not through the dead pages...': *Illustrated London News*, 31 July 1858.

'Surely Mr. Dickens...': *Manchester Guardian*, 4 February 1867.

Paperknife 'divided the leaves': *The Sheffield Times*, 29 December 1855: quoted in *Letters* VII, 771, n. 3.

p. 80 Philip Collins and 'Carol' Readings: See Collins, *Readings*, 1–4; and his edition of the facsimile of the *Carol* prompt-copy, *A Christmas Carol: The Public Reading Version* (New York, 1971): hereafter abbreviated to Collins, *Carol*.

'David Copperfield differs...pathetic': *Carlisle Journal*, 13 December 1861.

p. 81 'A sort of improved...': *Aberdeen Journal*, 6 October 1858.

'The great fires roar...': *New York Tribune*, 10 December 1867.

'It is a work of high finish...': *Bury and Norwich Post and Suffolk Herald*, 18 October 1859.

'On the whole...deserve to be read': *The Liverpool Daily Post*, 21 August 1858.

First London 'Carol' Reading took two and half hours: Kent, 52.

Two hours twenty minutes: *Bury and Norwich Post and Suffolk Herald*, 20 September 1859.

'Judicious curtailment...powerful': *The Times*, 2 January 1854.

p. 82 Pages 'cobwebbed': Kent, 23.

Ink blottings: Collins, *Carol*, p. xxvi.

'The only episode...': Collins, *Readings*, 2.

p. 83 'There are no printed abridgements...': To F. D. Finlay, 6 May 1861: *Letters* IX, 408.

Ordered copies with 22 lines per page: To Fred Chapman, 30 July 1861: *Letters* IX, 442–3.

'On making his appearance...': *Clifton Chronicle*, 4 August 1858.

p. 84 'The first gospel...culture-text': Paul Davis, *The Lives and Times of Ebenezer Scrooge* (Yale, 1990), 62.

'The *Carol*, we may remark...': *Bath Chronicle*, 4 February 1869.

'[The clerk...': Collins, *Carol*, 17.

p. 85 'Dramatic monologue': *The Courant* (Edinburgh), 30 September 1858.

'For they were a musical family...': Collins, *Carol*, 110–11.

'Once upon a time...Narrative': Ibid., 5.

p. 86 'I used to take...': 'Notes by Rowland Hill on Charles Dickens' "Christmas Carol"': Typescript at Charles Dickens Museum, 1.

'Suddenly to a rich...': Ibid., 2.

'Constantly omitted phrases...': Ibid., 3.

p. 87 'Why, LOR!...': Ibid., 10.

'POSITIVELY HISSED': Ibid., 11.

'I have been poring...': To Arthur Ryland, 29 January 1855: *Letters* VII, 515.

p. 88 **Collins's calculation of word-lengths:** Collins, *Readings*, 214.

Dickens's 6-chapter summary: E. W. F. Tomlin, 'Newly Discovered Dickens Letters,' *Times Literary Supplement*, 22 February 1974, 183–6. The summary is reproduced in Collins, *Readings*, 215.

p. 89 **'A series of tableaux':** *Carlisle Journal*, 13 December 1861.

'You know my mother...': Collins, *Readings*, 224.

'Visibly wrestling...': *Manchester Examiner*, 19 October 1868.

p. 90 '(last night) I read Copperfield...': To Miss Georgina Hogarth, 8 January 1862: *Letters* X, 7–8.

'The humour was delightful...': quoted in *Letters* X, 8 n 1.

p. 91 'Nickleby' compared with 'Marigold': *The Scotsman*, 19 April 1866.

'Barbox' compared with 'Boy at Mugby': *Yorkshire Post*, 1 February 1867.

p. 92 **Collins on Dickens and competitors:** Philip Collins, ' "Sikes and Nancy": Dickens's Last Reading', *TLS* 11 June 1971.

'The recollection...': To John Forster, [?15 November 1868]: *Letters* XII, 220.

Sensation fiction and drama, especially in 1860s: See, e.g., Winifred Hughes, 'The Sensation Novel', *A Companion to the Victorian Novel*, ed. P. Brantlinger and W. B. Thesing (Oxford, 2002), 260–78; and Michael Diamond, *Victorian Sensation: Or, the Spectacular, the Shocking and the Scandalous in Nineteenth-Century Britain* (2003), Chs 6 and 7.

'We are thrilled...': H. L. Mansel, 'Sensation Novels', *Quarterly Review*, 113 (April 1863), 489: quoted in Winifred Hughes, op. cit., 261.

'It is on our domestic hearths...': Anon, 'Our Novels. The Sensational School', *Temple Bar*, 29 July 1870, 422: quoted in Winifred Hughes, op. cit.

p. 93 'The public have been wanting...': To W. C. Macready, 19 November 1868: *Letters* XII, 224.

'...wild, and yet domestic': To W. Collins, 30 June 1867: *Letters* XI, 385.

p. 94 'I said to him...or the storm': To Messrs Fields, Osgood & Co., 14 May 1870: *Letters* XII, 526.

p. 95 'Every day for two...': Forster, 687.

'I have got the Copperfield Reading...': To Wilkie Collins, 28 August 1861: *Letters* IX, 447.

'Three months hard labour . . . ': J. T. Fields, *Yesterdays with Authors* (Boston, Mass., 1872), 241.

'Gone through it two-hundred-times': Kent, 244.

p. 96 'Gradually warming with excitement . . . ': Edmund Yates, 'Mr. Charles Dickens's New Reading,' *Tinsley's Magazine* IV (Feb. 1869), 62.

CHAPTER 3: IMPERSONATION

p. 97 'Mr Dickens has invented . . . ': *Illustrated London News*, 33, July–Dec. 1858, 100.

Douglas Thompson notice: Ibid., 56.

The Howards: Ibid., 129.

Mr Dolman's *Macbeth:* Ibid., 261.

Adolphus Francis and Seymour Carleton: Ibid., 429.

p. 98 'He had the power . . . ': Forster, 381.

'Every writer of fiction . . . ': *Speeches*, 202.

p. 99 Hollingshead article: John Hollingshead, 'Mr. Charles Dickens as a Reader', *The Critic*, 4 September 1858.

'Great gratification': To John Hollingshead, 6 September 1858: *Letters* VIII, 652.

'Every character in Mr Dickens's novels . . . ': Hollingshead, *Miscellanies* II, 278.

He took to a higher calling . . . assumptions of the theatre . . . ': Forster, 381.

p. 100 'I was a great writer . . . ': To Mrs Howitt, 7 September 1859: *Letters* IX, 119.

'The little boy . . . ': Robert Langton, *The Childhood and Youth of Charles Dickens* (1891), 26.

'It is curious . . . at a stretch': *David Copperfield,* ed. Malcolm Andrews, (Everyman Dickens, 1993), Ch. 4, 53.

'Every word of this . . . ': Forster, 6.

p. 101 'Always a leader . . . ': Ibid, 44.

'He could imitate . . . ': Collins, *I&R*, I, 11–12.

'I went to some theatre . . . ': To Forster, ?30–1 Dec 1844 and 1 Jan 1845: *Letters* IV, 245.

p. 102 'Every word said . . . ': G. H. Lewes, 'Dickens in Relation to Criticism', *Fortnightly Review*, 17(1872), 141–54: reprt. in Collins, *I&R*, II, 25.

'Suddenly the little character . . . ': To John Forster, ?early Nov 1865: *Letters* XI, 105.

'When I am describing . . . ': Henry F. Dickens, 'The Social Influence of Dickens', *Dickensian* 1 (1905), 63.

p. 103 'But may I not be forgiven...': To John Forster, ?October 1841: *Letters* II, 411.

'I was lying on the sofa...': Mamie Dickens, *My Father As I Recall Him* (1897), 48–9.

'Opposite the house...': Collins, *I&R*, II, 272.

p. 104 Luke Fildes and *Drood* illustrations: Margaret Cardwell (ed.), *The Mystery of Edwin Drood* (Oxford, 1972), 239.

James Fields at Gad's Hill: Annie Fields's diary entry: in George Curry, *Charles Dickens and Annie Fields* (Huntingdon Library, 1988), 47.

'It is difficult...': Percy Fitzgerald, *The Life of Charles Dickens* (1905) II, 313 n.

p. 105 '...convulsed with laughter': Annie Fields's diary entry: in George Curry, op. cit., 10.

'Assumption has charms...': To Edward Bulwer Lytton, 5 January 1851: *Letters* VI, 257.

'Parvenu civilisation': See Robin Gilmour, *The Victorian Period: The Intellectual and Cultural Context of English Literature 1830–1890* (1993), 1–8.

p. 106 Popularity of orphan fiction: See Robert A. Colby, *Fiction with a Purpose* (Indiana, 1967), Ch. 4, esp pp. 119–37.

'Wrapped in the blanket...': *Oliver Twist,* ed. Steven Connor (Everyman Dickens, 1994), Ch. 1, p. 5.

'Clothes gave us individuality...': Thomas Carlyle, *Sartor Resartus* (1896–9), Book I, Ch. 5, p. 31.

'Society...founded upon Cloth': Ibid., Ch. 9, 48.

p. 107 'Anxiety about pronunciation...': R. Chapman, *Forms of Speech in Victorian Fiction* (1994), 12.

Standard dialect and erased origins: B. H. Smart, *Walker Remodelled: A New Critical Pronouncing Dictionary of the English Language. Adapted to the Present State of Literature and Science* (1836), xl. See also Tony Crowley, *Standard English and the Politics of Language* (Houndmills, 1989), Ch. 4.

'Improvement has peered...': *Journalism,* I, 150.

'120,000 strangers' and other figures: James Grant, *The Great Metropolis* (London 1836): reprt. in J. Marriott and M. Matsumura (eds.), *The Metropolitan Poor: Semi-Factual Accounts, 1795–1910* (1999), I, 320.

p. 108 'Most people...': Oscar Wilde, 'De Profundis' (1905): Oscar Wilde, *Poems and Essays* (1956), 200.

'Becoming a self...': John Jervis, *Exploring the Modern* (Oxford, 1998), 21.

p. 109 'Connotes not only lies...': Nina Auerbach, op. cit., 4.

'See how near...business-like way...began to write...suspect me!': To Forster, ?30–1 December 1844 and 1 January 1845: *Letters* IV, 245.

p. 110 'A sort of mixture...': *Montreal Gazette*, 30 May 1842: See *Dickensian* 38 (1942), 74.

'As *Mr. Gabblewig*...': Laurence Hutton, *Plays and Players* (New York, 1875), 43.

'We certainly have rarely...': *New York Times*, 10 December 1867.

p. 111 Schlicke on Mathews and Dickens: Paul Schlicke, *Dickens and Popular Entertainment* (1985), Ch. 9.

Mathews's early career: See Richard L. Klepac, *Mr Mathews at Home* (Society for Theatre Research, 1979), 13. I am indebted throughout this discussion of Mathews's life and professional career to Klepac's study.

'Occasional assistance', with songs: Anne Mathews, *Memoirs of Charles Mathews, Comedian* 4 vols. (1839), II, 50.

p. 112 'It is idle and invidious...': Cited in Anne Mathews, op. cit., II, 114.

p. 113 Byron on Mathews: *Lady Blessington's Conversations of Lord Byron*, ed. E. J. Lovell Jr (Princeton, 1969), 140–1.

'His faculty is so decidedly...': 'Mathews in America', *Blackwood's Magazine* 15 (April 1824), 424: in Klepac, 51.

'Imitator of manner...': Anne Mathews, op. cit., III, 60–1.

'Before I enter ...': Ibid., 109.

p. 114 'This is also the reason...': Henri Bergson, *Laughter: An Essay on the Meaning of the Comic*, tran. C. Brereton and F. Rothwell (1911), 32–3.

p. 115 'As an actor, Mr. Mathews...': Anon., *History of the Private and Public Life of Mr. C. Mathews, Comedian* (1835?), 10.

'There never was a greater mistake...': Anne Mathews, *Memoirs* IV, 436.

'Mr. Dickens never...': *Bury and Norwich Post and Suffolk Herald*, 18 October 1859.

p. 116 'I believed I had...': To Forster, ?30–1 December 1844 and 1 January 1845: *Letters* IV, 244.

p. 117 *Trip to Paris* & 'Galomania': Klepac, op. cit., 37.

'Good morning, sir...': John Poole, *Sketches of Mr. Mathews's celebrated Trip to Paris* (1827), 8.

p. 118 Earle Davis on Mathews and Dickens: Earle Davis, *The Flint and the Flame: The Artistry of Charles Dickens* (1964), Ch. 3.

Zambrano on Mathews and Dickens: Ana Laura Zambrano, 'Dickens and Charles Mathews', *Moderna Sprak*, 66 (1972), 235–42.

'That melancholy region...': *The Atlas*, 3 April 1836.

Cockney sportsmen shooting crows: J. Poole [?compiler and part-author], *Mr. Mathews' At Home! An Excellent Collection of Recitations, Anecdotes, Songs* etc (1827), 13–15.

p. 119 'In theatrical art...': Robert Garis, *The Dickens Theatre* (Oxford, 1965), 54: the italics are Garis's.

'Mr Pickwick's Stage-Manager': 'Address' at the conclusion of No. 10 (January 1837) of *Pickwick Papers*.

'Not an entertainment of the stage': Record of the Select Committee of the House of Commons on Dramatic Literature, 2 July 1832: in Klepac, op. cit., 25.

'It is true the room...': G. Wightwick, 'My Acquaintance with the Late Charles Mathews', *Fraser's Magazine for Town and Country*, 13 (March 1836), 344.

p. 121 'His face relaxes...': *New York Times*, 10 December 1867.

'Putting himself *en rapport*...': *New York Post*, 10 December 1867.

'Great advantage... conversational web...': Anne Mathews, op. cit., II, 467.

p. 122 'Our laughter is always...': Henri Bergson, op. cit., 6.

p. 123 'All of the typically Dickensian...': Garis, op. cit., 63.

'Generate "behaviour"...': Ibid., 67.

'Dickens's presence in his prose...': Ibid., 9.

p. 124 'Figures impress one...': Anon., 'Charles Dickens', *Fraser's Magazine*, July 1870: in Philip Collins (ed.), *Charles Dickens: The Critical Heritage* (1971), 526.

'Another feature...': Percy Fitzgerald, 'Principles of Comedy and Dramatic Effect': quoted in T. E. Pemberton, *Dickens and the Stage* (1888), 184.

CHAPTER 4: CELEBRITY ON TOUR

p. 126 'To hear him roar...': *Saunders' News-Letter, Daily Advertiser*, 26 August 1858.

p. 128 Dickens reading at Genoa: F. Yeats-Brown, 'Dickens in Genoa', *The Spectator*, 22 September 1928.

Reading lamp and raisins: To T. Yeats Brown, 3 June 1845: *Letters* IV, 318, n.

p. 129 'Because our illustrious countryman...': To Macready, 1 November 1854: *Letters* VII, 452.

Fussy about desk size: *Bristol Times and Felix Farley's Bristol Journal*, 23 January 1858.

p. 130 '**Dickens himself came down . . .** ': *Peterborough Advertiser*, 26 October 1867. This was eve of departure for Dickens's Reading tour of America, and the *Advertiser* reprinted part of a report from their 18 December 1855 edition.

p. 131 '**Represents Dickens giving . . . May 6th [1858]**': Walter Dexter, 'Dickens as a Reader: Two Hitherto Unpublished Portraits', *Dickensian* 37 (1941), 134–5.

A singularly-shaped table . . . ': *Halifax Courier*, 18 September 1858.

'**A small table . . . chocolate-coloured screen**': Jack Shaw, 'Dickens in Ireland', *Dickensian* 5 (1909), 34.

'**The back-ground . . . green**': *Derby Mercury*, 27 October 1858.

Crimson cloth: *Sheffield Times*, 29 December 1855: in *Letters* VII, 771 n 3.

p. 132 **Early 1860s London Readings**: In 1911 W. Ridley Kent recalled attending a Reading of 'Nickleby' followed by 'Bardell and Pickwick' at St James's Hall, 'just half a century ago'. The only time Dickens performed that particular combination of Readings at St James's Hall was 24 April 1862. Kent's vivid recollection was of a 'little green reading desk studded with brass-headed nails': W. Ridley Kent, 'A Dickens Reading', *Dickensian* 7 (1911), 318.

p. 133 '**Neither Charles Dickens . . .** ': Gladys Storey, *Dickens and Daughter* (1939), 192. The details on the brass plate attached to the desk differ from Gladys Storey's account. The plate records that Dickens 'gave it to his daughter Kate the night of his last reading, the 16th March, 1870 [15th March was actual date of last Reading]': W. B. Matz, 'Charles Dickens's Reading Table', *Dickensian* 16 (1920), 87.

'**We believe it was first used . . .** ': Storey, op.cit., 88.

p. 135 '**The desk does not hide . . .** ': *Providence Daily Journal*, 21 February 1868.

'**It is plain . . .** ': Field, 12.

p. 136 **1855 flourishing of paperknife**: *Sheffield Times*, 29 December 1855.

p. 137 '**Mrs. Gamp' and the paperknife**: W. Ridley Kent, op. cit., 319.

'**Mr. DICKENS leaned . . .** ': *New York Times*, 11 December 1867.

p. 138 **Bonnets discouraged**: *The Nottingham Review*, 15 October 1858.

'**Everything was wrong . . .** ': To Mary Dickens, 12 August 1858: *Letters* VII, 625.

Back-screen measurements: E. F. Payne, *Dickens Days in Boston* (Boston, 1927), 190.

Four feet behind desk: *Syracuse Daily Standard*, 3 October 1868.

Replacement of back-screen: To Dolby, 19 December 1866: *Letters* XI, 284.

Construction and covering of back-screen: Dolby, 13.

'**Brown-crimson color**': *The Nation* (New York), 12 December 1867.

'**Very red face**': Letter in *New York Tribune*, 20 December 1867.

p. 139 '**As I have had much experience . . .**': To R. M. Morrell, 9 November 1865: *Letters* XI, 107.

p. 140 '**Your public close . . .**': To George Dolby, 29–30 August 1867: *Letters* XI, 415.

'**The scene at Manchester . . .**': To W. H. Wills, 15 December 1861: *Letters* IX, 540.

'**With a sounding board . . .**': F. G. Kitton, *Dickensiana: A Bibliography of the Literature relating to Charles Dickens and his Writings* (1886), 4.

Hanging up banners at Liverpool: To Georgina Hogarth, 8 April 1869: *Letters* XII, 327.

'**The whole unfortunate staff . . .**': To Mary Dickens, 27 January 1869: *Letters* XII, 283.

'**Very imperfectly**' **heard**: George W. Curtis, *From the Easy Chair* (1892), 51.

'**An instance of that part . . .**': To Georgina Hogarth, 17 August 1866: *Letters* XI, 186.

p. 141 '**The secret of which . . .**': Dolby, 82.

p. 142 '**MR. DICKENS: Is it all right? . . .**': Ibid. 173.

'**Over 200 . . .**': *Dundee Courier*, 6 October 1858.

'**Quite wonderful for sound . . .**': To Macready, 31 March 1863: *Letters* X, 227.

p. 143 '**To close in . . . more important**': To Mr and Mrs J. T. Fields, 16 July 1868: *Letters* XII, 247.

'**Like a Methodist chapel . . .**': To Mary Dickens, 22 January 1867: *Letters* XI, 302.

p. 144 '**A powerful light . . .**': *Sheffield Times*, 29 December 1855.

Developed own lighting rig: See To H. G. Adams, 30 November 1858: *Letters* VIII, 712.

'**My servant has a screen . . .**': To R. M. Morrell, 9 November 1865: *Letters* XI, 107.

Gas-fittings described: See Dolby, 13.

Positioning of gas-jets: See *Bolton Evening News*, 21 April 1869.

p. 145 **Dickens routinely scrutinized the gas**: *Boston Post*, 28 February 1868; in E. F. Payne. op. cit., 224.

Gas-lamps shielded: See *Derby Mercury,*27 October 1858.

'**The whole is artistically . . .**': *Hartford Daily Courant*, 19 February 1868.

Belfast lights failure: See *Belfast News-Letter*, 28 August 1858.

p. 146 **Damage to gas-lamps reflector:** See To Mary Dickens, 24 January 1867: *Letters* XI, 303.

'**I began with a small speech . . .**': To Mary Dickens, 4 February 1868: *Letters* XII, 35.

Poultry Club episode: Recalled in *The Evening Gazette* (Worcester, Mass.), 6 May 1965.

'**. . . antipathy to daylight reading**': To Hon Mrs Watson, 13 October 1861: *Letters* IX, 477.

'**It is a tough job . . .**': To Macready, 6 December 1854: *Letters* VII, 477.

'**It will be impossible . . .**': *The Graphic*, 12 February 1870: Giovanni Moroni, the sixteenth-century Italian artist, produced several portraits of imposing dark-robed, bearded gentlemen set against light backgrounds.

'**. . . circle of stage fire**': John Ruskin, *Unto this Last*, ed. P. M. Yarker (1970), 33.

p. 147 '**Best man of business . . .**': To Forster, 10 June 1857: *Letters* VIII, 345.

'**Exact fitness . . .**': Forster, 647.

'**Arthur is something . . .**': To Edmund Yates, 4 August [1858]: *Letters* VIII, 617.

Doubling seating in St Martin's Hall: To Miss Burdett Coutts, 28 April 1858: *Letters* VIII, 551.

Smith's remuneration: See To Forster, [28 April 1861]: *Letters* IX, 406.

'**Arthur bathed in checks . . .**': To Edmund Yates, 21 August 1858: *Letters* VIII, 631.

p. 148 **Time difference and Plymouth Reading:** *Plymouth, Devonport, and Stonehouse Herald*, 7 August 1858.

'**The subject matter' of the Readings . . .**': To Town Clerk of Blackburn, [Early March 1867]: *Letters* XI, 329.

'**It is the simple fact . . .**': To Georgina Hogarth, 22 November 1861: *Letters*, IX, 515.

'**Damned aggravating**': To Georgina Hogarth, 8 January 1862: *Letters* X, 8.

p. 149 '**Messrs. Chappell proposed . . .**': Dolby, 2.

p. 150 '**None the worse . . .**': To Georgina Hogarth, 6 March 1867: *Letters* XI, 328.

Dolby's commission: To John Forster, [?Late April 1868]: *Letters* XII, 101.

Dolby 'certainly earned more . . .': Edwin Percy Whipple, *Charles Dickens: The Man and His Work* (Boston, 1912), 307.

'**Dolby is as tender . . .**': To Mary Dickens, 7 April 1868: *Letters* XII, 92.

'**As a dresser . . .**': To Georgina Hogarth, 21 January 1867: *Letters* XI, 301.

p. 151 **Scott weeping:** See To Georgina Hogarth, 22 December 1867: *Letters* XI, 519.

'**We immediately telegraphed . . .**': To Mary Dickens, 5 March 1869: *Letters* XII, 303.

'**Steadiest . . . ever employed**': To Mary Dickens, 7 April 1868: *Letters* XII, 92.

'**We have a regular clerk . . .**': To Georgina Hogarth, 3 January 1868: *Letters* XII, 3.

p. 152 **Dickens sits for Gurney:** See Noel C. Peyrouten, 'The Gurney Photographs', *Dickensian* 54 (1958), 152.

'**Mr. Dickens's character . . .**': *New York Daily Times*, 13 December 1867.

p. 154 '**I will guarantee . . .**': Quoted in Sidney Moss, 'A New-Found Mathew Brady Photograph of Dickens', *Dickensian* 79 (1983), 105.

'**We beg to assert . . .**': Ibid. 106.

'**Alas for those artists . . .**': *New York Herald*, 13 December 1867.

p. 155 '**. . . portrait of the Ancient Mariner**': To John Watkins, 28 September 1861: *Letters* IX, 466.

1861 portrait: see Malcolm Andrews, 'Mathew Brady's Portrait of Dickens: "a fraud and imposition on the public"?', *History of Photography* Vol 28, No 4 (Winter 2004), 375–79.

p. 156 '**Looking at this portrait . . . countenance**': *New York Tribune*, 13 December 1867.

'**Dickens looks as if . . .**': Field, 13.

'**Some consulted Mr. Dickens's portraits . . .**': *Berkshire Chronicle*, 23 December 1854.

p. 157 '**The vague expression . . .**': *Halifax Courier*, 18 September 1858.

Beard conceals the mouth: *Derby Mercury*, 27 October 1858.

'**As yet we have failed . . .**': *Wolverhampton Chronicle*, 18 August 1858.

'**At every turn . . .**': Charles H. Taylor in *Boston Tribune*, 2 December 1867: quoted in Edward F. Payne, op. cit., 188.

'**Further cemented . . .**': Gerald Curtis, *Visual Words: Art and the Material Book in Victorian England* (Hampshire, 2002), 144.

p. 158 '**We had ceased . . .**': Cited in *Walt Whitman: A Critical Anthology*, ed Francis Murphy (Harmondsworth, 1969), 58.

p. 159 '**A photograph likeness . . . your social existence**': *Saunders' News-Letter, Daily Advertiser*, 26 August 1858.

'Mr. Charles Dickens is "starring it" . . . ': *Exeter Flying Post*, 15 January 1861.

p. 160 Requests for autographs: Dolby, 170.

Gurney portraits marketed: Peyrouten, op. cit., 152.

'We think the generality . . . ': *Syracuse Daily Standard*, 10 March 1868.

'His photographs give . . . ': *Portland Transcript*, 4 April 1868.

'When it is remembered . . . ': Field, p. xix.

'We don't know . . . ': Ibid.

'small and slim-legged . . . ': *New York Tribune*, 20 December 1867.

p. 161 'I hope you may have seen . . . ': To Hon. Mrs. Richard Watson, 8 July 1861: *Letters* IX, 438.

p. 162 'I declined . . . ': To Lovell Reeve, 16 April 1864: *Letters* X, 384.

'Somehow I never . . . ': To R. H. Horne, [31] December 1865: *Letters* XI, 129.

Dickens's Will: Forster, 859.

'But I have no faith . . . ': To W. Hepworth Dixon, 31 January 1861: *Letters* IX, 379.

p. 163 'I have a particular objection . . . ': To Frank Smedley, 8 May 1855: *Letters* XII, 661.

'Then they look at you . . . ': Dickens reported in conversation: W. P. Frith, *My Autobiography and Reminiscences* (New York, 1888), 217.

p. 164 '[The head] of DICKENS . . . ': *The Nation* (Dublin), 28 August 1858.

p. 165 'His face, latterly . . . ': G. D. Leslie, 'Recollections', in F. G. Kitton, *Charles Dickens: By Pen and Pencil*, (1890): reprt. in Corinna Russell (ed.), *Charles Dickens*, Vol. 2 in *Lives of Victorian Literary Figures* (2003), 266.

'Mr. Dickens appears to be . . . ': Letter from Richard Stratford, ?early Feb 1859: E. V. Lucas, 'Charles Dickens as a Public Reader', *Dickensian* 21 (1925), 85.

p. 166 'Dressed in a suit . . . awake and honest': E. F. Payne, op. cit., 191.

'If young ladies expect . . . ': *Saunders' News-Letter, Daily Advertiser* (Dublin), 26 August 1858.

'There is a self-dependence . . . ': T. C. DeLeon, 'Mr. Dickens' Readings,' *The Land We Love* (North Carolina, March 1868), 429.

p. 167 'But that queer old head . . . ': Mark Twain, *Alta California* (San Francisco), 5 February 1868.

' . . . in the same breath': *Harper's Weekly*, 28 December 1867.

'If the truth were told . . . ': *Springfield Republican*, 21 March 1868.

p. 168 'The newspapers are constantly . . . ': To Forster, [14 January 1868]: *Letters* XII, 13.

'Nothing can be less prepossessing...': Letter of 14 March 1862: Quoted in *Dickensian* 19 (1923), 235.

p. 169 'A convict in golden fetters': G. A. Sala, *Charles Dickens*, (1870): reprt. in Corinna Russell (ed), *Charles Dickens*, Vol. 2 in *Lives of Victorian Literary Figures* (2003), 153.

'The advent of Mr Dickens...': *Syracuse Daily Standard*, 10 March 1868.

p. 170 'Will you then try...there an end': To Forster [30 March 1858]: *Letters* VIII, 539.

'His lifelong love-affair...': John Butt and Kathleen Tillotson, *Dickens at Work* (1957: reprt. 1968), 75.

'The manner in which...': To Miss Burdett Coutts, 27 October 1858: *Letters* VIII, 689.

p. 171 'Go where I will...': To D. M. Moir, 17 June 1848: *Letters* V, 341.

'I never beheld...': To Georgina Hogarth, 5 August 1858: *Letters* VIII, 67.

'The greatest personal affection...': To Forster, [?29 August 1858]: *Letters* VIII, 642.

'I was brought very near...': To Forster [11 September 1858]: *Letters* VIII, 657.

'As to the truth...': To Forster, 10 October 1858: *Letters* VIII, 676–7.

p. 172 'How the densest...': Ibid.

'Success attends me...personal friend': To Mrs Henry Austin, 4 January 1862: *Letters* X, 4.

'The audience...moving to see': To Mamie Dickens, 20 April 1866: *Letters* XI, 190.

Office boy sent for ices: Arthur Humphreys, 'Links with Charles Dickens', *Dickensian* 14 (1918), 66.

'I am in lavender...': To Richard Monckton Milnes, 1 April 1862: *Letters* X, 63.

p. 173 'Knowing that I am...': To Mrs Thomas Fitzgerald, 7 March 1867: *Letters* XI, 330.

'Silence, a darkened room...': To Horatio Woodman, 4 December 1867: *Letters* XI, 503.

'I miss the quiet...': To Miss Burdett Coutts, 9 August 1858: *Letters* VIII, 621.

p. 174 'Flexible alter-ego': *Journalism* IV, xvii.

'Sauntering among the ropemaking...': Ibid. 295.

'The platform absorbs my individuality': To W. H. Wills, 10 and 11 December 1867: *Letters* XI, 507.

p. 175 'Watching him...': Kent, 32.

'I am as restless...': To Dolby, 15 February 1869: *Letters* XII, 290.

'Like a comet...': R. Shelton Mackenzie, *Life of Charles Dickens* (Philadelphia, 1870), 298.

'One of the largest lions of the day': *Saunders' News-Letter, Daily Advertiser,* 26 August 1858.

CHAPTER 5: PERFORMANCE

p. 176 Scott's role and discretion: To Georgina Hogarth, 21 January 1867: *Letters* XI, 301.

p. 177 'He has chosen ... exaggeration': *Sheffield and Rotherham Independent,* 30 October 1858.

'An artist who produces...': *Hartford Daily Courant,* 19 February 1868.

p. 178 'The greater the room...': To Henry Chorley, 12 January 1866: *Letters* XI, 137.

'Is she sure...': To J. R. Osgood, 11 March 1868: *Letters* XII, 72.

'Hiding the art...': *The Nation* (Dublin), 28 March 1858.

p. 179 'I set myself to carrying out...': To W. H. Wills, 23 January 1870: *Letters* XII, 470.

p. 180 'Open your mouth...': To Henry Dickens, 17 February 1870: *Letters* XII, 480.

Testing acoustics: See Dolby, 171.

'Without much greater expenditure...': To Georgina Hogarth, 7 March 1869: *Letters* XII, 306.

p. 181 'Mrs. Cay ... always heard': To Rev Christopher Cay, 7 November 1864: *Letters* X, 449.

p. 182 'If you could be a little louder...': To Henry Chorley, 1 March 1862: *Letters* X, 42.

'Runs up at the end...': *Providence Daily Journal,* 21 February 1868.

'He closed each sentence...': R. Shelton MacKenzie, *Life of Charles Dickens* (Philadelphia, 1870), 80.

p. 183 'Naturally monotonous voice': Field, 23.

'Sing-song tone...': *Cork Herald,* 4 September 1858.

Hint of a lisp: *New York Times,* 10 December 1867.

Hissed sibilants: *Town Talk,* 5 January 1858: in *Dickensian,* 37 (1941), 223.

'Counthory' and rolled 'r's: *Limerick Reporter and Tipperary Vindicator,* 3 September 1858.

'Slight but pleasant ... exaggerate': *New York Times,* 16 December 1867.

Lozenges: Letter from W. H. Wills to his wife, in Lady Priestley, *The Story of a Lifetime* (2nd edn., 1908), 217.

Beaten egg and bottled stout: See J. E. Carpenter (ed.), *The Popular Elocutionist and Reciter* (London and New York, 1887), 30–1.

p. 184 **Deterioration in vocal clarity**: Kent, 96–7.

'His voice . . . feminine tone': *Limerick Reporter and Tipperary Vindicator*, 3 September 1858.

'He reads slightly too fast . . .': *Liverpool Daily Post*, 17 August 1858.

The 'level' portions . . . 'vocal modulations': *The Nation* (Dublin), 28 August 1858.

p. 185 **'Almost invariable monotone . . .'**: *Manchester Guardian*, 18 October 1858.

Dramatic pause and 'furious speed': C. J. Hamilton, 'How I Heard Charles Dickens Read', *Chambers's Journal*, October 1926, 683.

'I have tested . . .': To Forster, [14 May 1867]: *Letters* XI, 367.

'Neither straining . . .': *Dover Express*, 9 November 1861.

'The great fault . . . monotonous': Report in *Evening Standard* (New Bedford), 28 March 1868: quoted in Ian Crawford, 'Dickens in the Whaling City', *Dickens Quarterly* 18 (2001), 182.

p. 186 **'Drum and trumpet declaration'**: *Aberdeen Journal*, 6 October 1858.

'He laughs the "*Rules*" . . .': New York *Tribune*, 13 December 1867.

'As a speaker . . .': Dowager Duchess of Argyll (ed.), *George Douglas, Eighth Duke of Argyll, 1823–1900: Autobiography and Memoirs* (1906), I, 417.

p. 187 **'The Englishman . . .'**: John Hullah, *The Cultivation of the Speaking Voice* (Oxford, 1870), 60.

'He had most expressive hands . . .': Sir Arthur Helps, 'In Memoriam [Charles Dickens]', *Macmillan's Magazine*, 22 (July 1870): reprt. in Corinna Russell (ed.), *Lives of Victorian Literary Figures*, Vol. 2: *Charles Dickens*, 510.

'We might object . . .': *Liverpool Daily Post*, 17 August 1858.

'Unless we are mistaken . . .': *Manchester Guardian* [?A. W. Ward], 12 October 1868.

p. 188 **Colloquial radius, etc**: See J. H. Hindmarsh, *The Rhetorical Reader* (4th edn., 1845), esp. pp. xix–xx., and H. Campbell, R. F. Brewer et al. *Voice, Speech and Gesture: A Practical Handbook to the Elocutionary Art* (1897), 110 et seq.

'He hardly ever gesticulates . . .': *New York Tribune*, 20 December 1867.

p. 189 **'His right hand . . .'**: *Weekly* (New York), 28 December 1867: *Dickensian* 6 (1910), 208–9.

p. 190 **'Frequently a mere motion . . .'**: *Belfast News-Letter*, 9 January 1869.

'Makes pictures . . .': *The Times*, 7 October 1868.

'How Mr. Dickens twirled . . .': *Speeches*, 166 n.

p. 191 'Hear me speak...curtain of the bed...Murder coming': Collins, *Readings*, 481–82 & notes.

'"Fagin raised..."': Kent, 261.

p. 192 **Dented cuff-links**: The cuff-links were exhibited at the 1970 exhibition *Charles Dickens*, at the Victoria and Albert Museum: G. Reynolds et al. *Charles Dickens: An Exhibition to Commemorate the Centenary of his Death* (1970), 105.

'What Dickens *does*...': Field, 20.

Stirred gravy...dusted hot plates: *New York Times*, 10 December 1867.

'Sniffing and smelling...chucked': Field, 20, 24.

Jonas biting thumbnail: *Belfast News-Letter*, 30 August 1858.

p. 193 'He never seemed to forget...': *Bath Chronicle*, 14 February 1867.

'...gestures with his legs': *New York Times*, 13 December 1867.

'Whose words he speaks...': *The Times*, 1 July 1857.

'Personated...the various characters...': *Aris's Birmingham Gazette*, 2 January 1854.

p. 194 'Looking at the Author...hungry wickedness': Kent, 256–7.

'You read...attitudes': Edmund Yates, 'Mr. Charles Dickens's New Reading', *Tinsley's Magazine*, 4 (February 1869), 62.

'As splendid a piece...': Charles Kent, *The Sun*, 17 November 1868.

p. 195 **No caricature stage Jew**: Edmund Yates, op. cit., 62.

'He seems to try...': T. C. De Leon, 'Mr. Dickens Readings', *The Land We Love* (North Carolina, March 1868), IV, 430.

'I shall never forget...pig': R. C. Lehmann, *Memories of Half a Century: A Record of Friendships* (1908), 82.

p. 196 'I see him "swelling"': Field, 26–7.

p. 197 'The true theory...': Anon., *The Nation* (New York), 12 December 1867, 482.

p. 198 'Now the art...': A. W. Ward, *Charles Dickens* (1882), 153–4.

p. 199 'Unless we are mistaken...': *Manchester Guardian* [?A. W. Ward], 12 October 1868.

'He has always trembled...': *The Times*, 17 November 1868.

'Gradually warming...': Edmund Yates, op. cit., 62.

p. 200 'In the first pages...': *New York Times*, 10 November 1867.

'He can in a minute command...': *The Scotsman*, 19 April 1866.

p. 201 'There was noticeable...': A. W. Ward, *Charles Dickens* (1882), 153–4.

p. 202 'It is not reading...': *Providence Daily Journal*, 21 February 1868.

'Hard charmless readings': Henry James, *Notebooks*, ed. F. E. Matthiessen and K. Murdock (New York, 1947), 319.

'Each character that is introduced...': *The Courant* (Edinburgh), 28 November 1861.

'Scrooge was himself...': *Springfield Republican*, 21 March 1868.

p. 203 'Had the faculty...wholly different voice': Dowager Duchess of Argyll, op. cit., 417.

'The excellent taste...': *Manchester Guardian*, 4 February 1867.

'With a characteristic voice...': *Nottingham Review*, 28 October 1859.

p. 204 'That it is the player's...': *Torquay Directory*, 20 January 1869.

'As I have to make...': To J. R. Osgood, 11 March 1868: *Letters* XII, 72.

p. 205 'Take a comb...': Field, 81.

p. 206 '*Court.* "Have—you—any—..." is remarkable': Ibid., 68–9.

'Constantly omitted phrases...': Rowland Hill, 'Notes... on Charles Dickens' "Christmas Carol"': typescript, The Charles Dickens Museum, 3.

p. 207 'He throws himself...': *The Times*, 1 July 1857.

'His power of reproducing...': Sir Frederick Pollock, quoted in 'Dickens as a Reader', Anon., *Dickensian* 23 (1927), 272.

'...those childish footsteps': *Brighton Gazette*, 18 November 1858.

p. 208 '...pathos feeding upon itself': R. H. Hutton, 'The Genius of Dickens', *Spectator*, 18 June 1870, 751.

'Stated in simple language...': *The Saturday Review*, 19 June 1858.

p. 209 'The appearance of Mr. Dickens...personal observation': *The Times*, 2 January 1854.

p. 210 'The multiplication of books...': Ibid.

'He does not...to his audience': *Cambridge Independent Press*, 17 October 1859.

'He reads...circle of friends': *Belfast News-Letter*, 28 August 1858.

'He spoke,...anything else': *The Scotsman*, 28 November 1861.

'Addressing his hearers...': *Saunders' News-Letter*, 24 August 1858.

p. 211 'We soon perceive...': *Hartford Daily Courant*, 19 February 1868.

'His stories, dramatic...roles': Alison Byerly, 'From Schoolroom to Stage: Reading Aloud and the Domestication of Victorian Theater', in P. Scott and P. Fletcher (eds.), *Culture and Education in Victorian England* (Lewisburg, 1990), 135–6.

p. 212 'Anti-authorial...the characters': Susan L. Ferguson, 'Dickens's Public Readings and the Victorian Author', *Studies in English Literature 1500–1900*, 41 (2001), 738.

'Quite without mannerism...': *The Ipswich Journal*, 9 November 1861.

'Nor in the actor...': *The Times*, 2 January 1854.

'Referring to his own works...': Dolby, 19.

p. 213 'He comes in . . .': *Portland Transcript*, 4 April 1868.

'The whole tone . . .': *Edmund Yates: His Recollections and Experiences* (4th edn., 1885), 165.

'Rendered additionally pleasing . . .': *Saunders' News-Letter*, 24 August 1858.

'He at once repays . . .': *New York Evening Post*, 10 December 1867.

'The opening sentences . . .': Kent, 96.

'Infuses life and warmth . . .': *The Times*, 24 May 1866.

p. 214 'Magnetic': To Georgina Hogarth, 29 October 1861: *Letters* IX, 486.

' "Genteel" frigidity': Cuthbert Bede, 'Charles Dickens: A Reminiscence', *Dickensian* 12 (1916), 208.

'His tragedy needed force . . .': Field, 23.

'Dickens's audience . . . dispensed with me': Herman Merivale, 'About Two Great Novelists,' *Temple Bar*, 83 (June 1888), 203–4.

p. 215 'He could so identify . . .': Dolby, 26.

'They really laughed . . .': To Georgina Hogarth, 7 November 1861: *Letters* IX, 500.

'So carried away . . .': *Boston Journal*, quoted in E. F. Payne, *Dickens Days in Boston* (1927), 193.

p. 216 'The author laughs . . .': *Syracuse Daily Standard*, 3 October 1868.

'A consummate actor . . .': *Sheffield and Rotherham Independent*, 30 October 1858.

'Lifted out of myself': To Georgina Hogarth, 1 February 1863: *Letters* X, 205.

p. 217 'So real are my fictions . . .': To Hon. Robert Lytton, 17 April 1867: *Letters* XI, 354.

'Mr. DICKENS seems to enjoy . . .': *New York Times*, 10 December 1867.

'A most fascinating air . . . these emotions': *Belfast News-Letter*, 21 March 1867.

'There was little variety . . .': *New York Times*, 17 December 1867.

'We had the opportunity . . .': *New York Tribune*, 14 December 1867.

p. 218 'Our senses respond . . .': Robert Patten, 'Dickens Time and Again', *Dickens Studies Annual*, 2 (1972), 170.

'SIKES AND NANCY': A READING

p. 219 *Description of Boots:* John Hollingshead, 'Mr. Charles Dickens as a Reader', *The Critic*, 4 September 1858.

'I shall tear . . .': Kent, 87.

p. 220 *'I have been trying . . .'* To Revd. W. Brookfield, 24 May 1863: *Letters* X, 250.

'*The recollection of something* ... ': To Forster, [?15 November 1868]: *Letters* XII, 220.

'*Fagin the receiver of stolen goods* ... ': All quotations from 'Sikes and Nancy' are taken from Collins, *Readings*, 472–86.

Bolter half-stupid: The Times, 8 January 1869.

Hunched shoulders, claw-hands, vulpine aspect: The Sun, 17 November 1868.

p. 221 *No stage Jew:* Edmund Yates, 'Mr. Charles Dickens's New Reading', *Tinsley's Magazine*, IV (Feb. 1869).

Realism of London Bridge setting: Sir Frederick Pollock, *Personal Remembrances* (1887), ii, 199: Quoted in Collins, *Readings*, 475.

p. 222 *Door-opening and curtain-drawing:* The prompt-copy has 'Action' written in the margin beside this passage, as for the striking down of Nancy: Ibid., 482–3.

p. 223 *Hands covering faces: The Times*, 8 January 1869.

Stillness in the hall: Frank Marzials, *Life of Charles Dickens* (1887), 125.

'... *fixed expression of horror* ... ': To Mr. and Mrs. J. T. Fields, 9 March 1869: *Letters* XII, 329.

p. 224 *Iced brandy and water:* To Georgina Hogarth, 26 February 1869: *Letters* XII, 299.

CHAPTER 6: A 'NEW EXPRESSION OF THE MEANING OF MY BOOKS'

p. 227 '**Plays [his works]** ... ': *Nottingham Review*, 28 October 1859.

'... *performs his novels*': Turgenev quoted in Patrick Waddington, 'Dickens, Pauline Viardot, Turgenev: A Study in Mutual Admiration', *New Zealand Slavonic Journal*, I (1974), 66.

'**Mr. Dickens is a delightful interpreter** ... ': *Exeter Flying Post*, ?4 August 1858.

'**It is not everyday** ... ': *Manchester Guardian*, 4 February 1867.

'**Wished not merely to verify** ... ': *Chester Chronicle*, 26 January 1867.

p. 228 '**Creations** ... **so real** ... ': *Manchester Guardian,* 4 February 1867.

'**As the author intended** ... ': *Hampshire Telegraph and Sussex Chronicle*, 26 May 1866.

'**If I choose to conceive my Sam Weller** ... ': T. C. De Leon, 'Mr Dickens' Readings', *The Land We Love* (Charlotte, N. C., March 1868), 427.

'**It is an inestimable privilege** ... ': *Daily Telegraph*, 24 November 1868.

'**That they fixed** ... **Dickens's work**': G. K. Chesterton, *Charles Dickens* (1913), 169–70.

'Having once heard his Little Dombey...': Field, 41.

'Whine there in simple monotony...': *New York Times*, 16 December 1867.

p. 229 'I had devoured...been recovered': *Talks in a Library with Laurence Hutton*, Recorded by Isabel Moore (New York, 1909), 32–3.

p. 230 'Now he is scattered...': W. H. Auden, 'In Memory of W. B. Yeats': *W. H. Auden: A Selection by the Poet* (Harmondsworth, 1958), 66.

p. 231 'The author gives additional colouring...': *The Times*, 16 April 1858.

'Everybody has read...': *Leamington Spa Courier*, 6 November 1858.

'...pre-Raphaelistic distinctness': *Berkshire Chronicle*, 22 December 1854.

p. 232 Jack Hopkins description: See Field, 60–1, and Kent, 158.

'There are little jets of illumination...': *Providence Daily Journal*, 22 February 1868.

'If we were asked...': New York *Tribune*, 13 December 1867.

p. 233 'There is so little...': David Christie Murray, *Recollections* (1907), 50.

'Sly touches of humour...': *Belfast News-Letter*, 26 August 1856.

'By a judicious management...': *Aris's Birmingham Gazette*, 2 January 1854.

'We use the term "practical commentator"...': *The Times*, 22 March 1862.

p. 234 'The *viva voce*... ': [J. Friswell], *Dickens: A Critical Biography* (1858), 80.

'Poetry is what attaches...': Yves Bonnefoy, 'Lifting our Eyes from the Page', *Critical Inquiry* 16 (1990): reprt. in Andrew Bennett (ed.), *Readers and Reading* (1995), 223–34.

p. 235 'Wept, and laughed...': To C. C. Felton, 2 January 1844: *Letters* IV, 2.

'Wonderful verbal...margin of the text': J. Hillis Miller, 'The Genres of *A Christmas Carol*', *Dickensian*, 89 (1993), 193–206.

p. 236 'The town was drunk...': To W. H. Wills, 24 September 1858: *Letters* VIII, 669.

'The energy of the novels...': See Chapter 4 generally in Susan Horton, *The Reader in the Dickens World* (Houndmills, 1981).

p. 237 '...producer of the text...language': Roland Barthes, *S/Z* (New York, 1974), 4, 10–11.

'Many if not most...': Reuben Brower, 'Reading in Slow Motion', R. A. Brower and Richard Poirier (eds.), *In Defense of Reading: A Reader's Approach to Literary Criticism* (New York, 1962), 6.

'Texts are only realized . . . ': David Cole, *Acting as Reading: The Place of the Reading Process in the Actor's Work* (Ann Arbor, Mich., 1992), 27.

p. 238 **Anne Ritchie, 'my sister and I . . . ':** Collins, *I&R*, I, 177.

'The air about him . . . ': Blanchard Jerrold, *A Day with Charles Dickens* (1871): reprt. in *Lives of Victorian Literary Figures I*, Vol 2, ed. Corinna Russell (2003), 483.

'As he entered . . . ': Percy Fitzgerald, *Life of Charles Dickens* (1905), II, 247–8.

p. 239 'He would insist . . . ': Mamie Dickens, *My Father as I Recall Him* (1897), 31.

p. 240 'What is exaggeration . . . ': Preface to the Charles Dickens edn. (1867) of *Martin Chuzzlewit*.

'Are Dickens's descriptions . . . ': Geoffrey Tillotson, *A View of Victorian Literature* (Oxford, 1978), 124–5.

'The writers were compelled . . . ': Percy Fitzgerald quoted in Harry Stone (ed.), *The Uncollected Writings of Charles Dickens* (Harmondsworth, 1969) I, 34.

'Brighten it, . . . ': To W. H. Wills, 5 August 1853: *Letters* VII, 126.

p. 241 'If to read a story . . . ': *The Scotsman*, 19 April 1866.

'Eminently sombre . . . foliage brown': John Ruskin, 'Of Modern Landscape', *Modern Painters* (1901), III, 267.

'Color these people always want . . . ': To Miss Burdett Coutts, 15 November 1856: *Letters* VIII, 223.

p. 242 'Fusion of the graces . . . ': 'A Last Household Word', *Household Words*, 28 May 1859.

'Many expressed their surprise . . . ': *Preston Guardian*, 14 December 1861.

' "I never knew how to read . . . " ': *Hampshire Independent*, 13 November 1858.

'He imparts to his works . . . ': *Newcastle Daily Chronicle*, 5 March 1867.

p. 243 'His writings have been . . . ': *Yorkshire Post*, 1 February 1867.

'His characters were real . . . ': Edwin Coggleshall, 'Some Evenings with Dickens in New York': *Dickensian* 16 (1920), 201.

'So real are my fictions . . . ': To the Hon. Robert Lytton, 17 April 1867: *Letters* XI, 354.

'Expands traits into people . . . ': Walter Bagehot, 'Charles Dickens', *National Review* VII (October 1858): reprt. in Michael Hollington (ed.), *Charles Dickens: Critical Assessments* (Mountfield, 1991), I, 179–80.

'Where the temptation to caricature...': *Bath Chronicle*, 4 February 1869.

p. 244 'The great value of Dickens's readings...': Edwin P. Whipple, *Charles Dickens: The Man and His Work* (Boston, 1912), II, 328–9.

'Sergeant Buzfuz himself...': *Chester Chronicle*, 26 January 1867.

p. 245 'Had intended that [Sam]...': *Bury and Norwich Post and Suffolk Herald*, 18 October 1859.

'While losing none of the oddity...': *The Courant* (Edinburgh), 30 September 1858.

On Robertson and the new naturalism: See Lynton Hudson, *The English Stage, 1850-1950* (1951).

On Fechter: See George Taylor, *Players and Performances in the Victorian Theatre*, (Manchester, 1989), 93–4.

'"Bow wow" school': Clement Scott, *The Drama of Yesterday and Today* (1899) I, 458.

p. 246 'The younger generation wanted...': Ibid., 459.

'Dickens's delight...': John Ruskin, letter to Charles Eliot Norton, 8 July 1870: *The Works of John Ruskin*, ed. E. T. Cook and A. Wedderburn (1903–12), vol. 37, p. 10.

'Mr Dickens as a writer... outrageous caricature... excess of caricature': *Bath Chronicle*, 14 February 1867.

p. 247 'Drum and trumpet...': *The Aberdeen Journal*, 6 October 1858.

'His manner was undeniably "stagey"...': R. A. Hammond, *The Life and Writings of Charles Dickens* (Toronto, 1871), 365.

'Utterly void of mannerism...': *Western Times*, 11/13 January 1862.

'Simply a good reader...': *Bury and Norwich Post and Suffolk Herald*, 18 October 1859.

'Coat-and-waistcoat realism... become photographers': G. H. Lewes, *The Principles of Success in Literature* (1865; Farnborough, 1969), 14.

Melodramatic actor 'is required...': G. H. Lewes, *On Actors and the Art of Acting* (1895), 15.

p. 248 Sol Eytinge's illustrations 'remarkable': To J. T. Fields, 2 April 1867: *Letters* XI, 349.

'Charles Dickens has to contend...': *Saunders' News-Letter, Daily Advertiser* (Dublin), 26 August 1858.

'I have been trying...': To John Forster, [?end of May–Early June 65]: *Letters* XI, 48.

p. 249 Collins on Dombey's relative unpopularity: Collins, *Readings*, 125.

'People dislike...': Field, 39.

'You will not have to complain...': To John Forster, [early October, 1860]: *Letters* IX, 325.

p. 250 'As if to take in the character...': R. A. Hammond, *The Life and Writings of Charles Dickens* (Toronto, 1871), 364.

'Ready homage...' *The Times*, 2 January 1854: the quotation is from *Troilus and Cressida*— 'One touch of nature makes the whole world kin'.

p. 251 'You play with the heart...': quoted in *Letters* XI, 354 n.

'There are some far better readers...': T. C. De Leon, 'Mr Dickens' Readings', *The Land We Love* (Charlotte, N. C., March 1868), 431.

Magnetic Sympathy: Arthur J. Cox, 'Magnetic Sympathy in *The Mystery of Edwin Drood*', *Dickensian*, 96 (2000), 127–50, 209–42: on Dickens and the 'Doctrine of Sympathy,' see esp 129–35. The Brontë quotation is from *Villette*, Ch. 15.

p. 252 'They were not magnetic...': To Georgina Hogarth, 29 October 1861: *Letters* IX, 486.

'Every eye was bent...': *New York Times*, 11 December 1867.

p. 253 '...special Dickensian *energy*...unscripted, and deceptive': Carol Hanbery Mackay, *Dramatic Dickens* (Houndmills, 1989), 2–3.

'You are not so tolerant...': To John Forster, 5 September 1857: *Letters* VIII, 434.

'Canon records...': Mackay, op. cit., 6.

'The earnest performers...': James Kincaid, in Mackay, op. cit., 12.

p. 254 'Having stuffed the novels...': John Carey, *The Violent Effigy: A Study of Dickens' Imagination* (1973), 62.

Quilp 'symbolises...': Terry Eagleton, *Criticism and Ideology: A Study in Marxist Literary Theory* (1976): extract reprt. in S. Connor (ed.), *Charles Dickens* (Harlow, 1996), 156.

p. 255 'Impresses us with the belief...': Field, 34.

'There were two people...': Stephanie Harvey, 'Dickens's Villains: A Confession and a Suggestion', *Dickensian*, 98 (2002), 233.

p. 256 'Man is not truly one...independent denizens': R. L. Stevenson, *Dr Jekyll and Mr Hyde and Other Stories* (Ware, Hertfordshire, 1993), 42.

'His [Childers's] legs...': *Hard Times*, ed. Graham Law (Peterborough, Ontario, 1996), 67–8.

p. 258 'Assumption has charms...wild reasons': To Sir Edward Bulwer Lytton, 5 January 1851: *Letters* VI, 257.

'I feel like a Wild Beast...': To Wilkie Collins, 6 June 1856: *Letters* VIII, 130.

Dickens and 'flânerie': Michael Hollington, 'Dickens the Flâneur', *The Dickensian*, 77(1981), 71–87.

p. 259 'A strange figure . . . ': *A Christmas Carol*, ed. Richard Kelly (Peterborough, Ontario, 2003), 61–2.

'When he reached the end . . . ': *Leamington Spa Courier*, 6 November 1858.

p. 260 'He looked at all things . . . ': Sir Arthur Helps, 'In Memoriam', *Macmillan's Magazine*, XXII (July 1870): reprt. in *Lives of Victorian Literary Figures I*, 2, ed. Corinna Russell, 508.

'The power of self-annihilation . . . ': *Comic Annual* 4 (April 1833): quoted in Anne Mathews, *Memoirs of Charles Mathews*, IV, 178.

'I have just come back . . . people': To Mrs Brown, 28 August 1857: *Letters* VIII, 421.

'I shall tear . . . ': Kent, 87.

'The modern embodiment . . . ': To the Hon. Mrs. Richard Watson, 7 December 1857: *Letters* VIII, 488.

'My large miscellaneous following . . . ': To W. H. Wills, 28 January 1866: *Letters* XI, 146.

'The fusion of different classes . . . ': *Aris's Birmingham Gazette*, 2 January 1854.

p. 261 'The very aspect . . . ': *The Times*, 1 July 1857

'Open a story . . . ': Fred Kaplan (ed.), *Charles Dickens' Book of Memoranda, A Photographic and Typographic Facsimile of the Notebook Begun in January 1855* (New York, 1982), 19.

'I had a transitory satisfaction . . . ': To Hon. Mrs. Richard Watson, 7 December 1857: *Letters* VIII, 488.

p. 262 'I never saw a crowd . . . ': To [Daniel Maclise] [?11 June 1858]: *Letters* VIII, 584.

FINALE: LONDON, MARCH 1870

p. 263 'He looked desperately aged . . . ': Edmund Yates, *Fifty Years of London Life: Memoirs of a Man of the World* (New York, 1885), 300.

'As Mr. Dickens . . . ': Flora Sampson, reported in E. F. Payne, *Dickens Days in Boston* (New York, 1927), 252.

p. 264 Impossible to say 'Pickwick': Charles Dickens Jnr, 'Reminiscences of my Father', *The Windsor Magazine* Christmas Supplement 1934, 30.

'A certain sense of deadness . . . ': Dolby, 406.

p. 265 'You must be there . . . ': Charles Dickens Jnr, op. cit., 30.

'Trial' characters cheered: Dolby, 447–8.

'Ladies and gentlemen . . . ': *Speeches*, 413.

p. 266 **A kind of sigh:** Henry Fielding Dickens, *Memories of My Father* (1928),
      21.

   One brief tremor: Noted by both Dolby (445) and Kent (270).

   Funeral Card inscription: Kent, 270.

Index

The Index covers names and titles only (but excludes names of fictional characters). Principal themes and topics are indicated on the Contents page